O9-BTL-680

APR 2011

THE
CULTURE
OF
CHINA

UNDERSTANDING CHINA

THE CULTURE OF CHINA

EDITED BY KATHLEEN KUIPER, MANAGER, ARTS AND CULTURE

Prospect Heights Public Library
12 N Elm Street
Prospect Heights, IL 60070
www.phpl.info

Britannica
Educational Publishing

IN ASSOCIATION WITH

ROSEN
EDUCATIONAL SERVICES

Published in 2011 by Britannica Educational Publishing
(a trademark of Encyclopædia Britannica, Inc.)
in association with Rosen Educational Services, LLC
29 East 21st Street, New York, NY 10010.

Copyright © 2011 Encyclopædia Britannica, Inc. Britannica, Encyclopædia Britannica,
and the Thistle logo are registered trademarks of Encyclopædia Britannica, Inc. All
rights reserved.

Rosen Educational Services materials copyright © 2011 Rosen Educational Services, LLC.
All rights reserved.

Distributed exclusively by Rosen Educational Services.
For a listing of additional Britannica Educational Publishing titles, call toll free (800) 237-9932.

First Edition

Britannica Educational Publishing
Michael I. Levy: Executive Editor
J.E. Luebering: Senior Manager
Marilyn L. Barton: Senior Coordinator, Production Control
Steven Bosco: Director, Editorial Technologies
Lisa S. Braucher: Senior Producer and Data Editor
Yvette Charboneau: Senior Copy Editor
Kathy Nakamura: Manager, Media Acquisition
Kathleen Kuiper: Manager and Senior Editor, Arts and Culture

Rosen Educational Services
Alexandra Hanson-Harding: Editor
Nelson Sá: Art Director
Cindy Reiman: Photography Manager
Matthew Cauli: Designer, Cover Design
Introduction by Amy Miller

Library of Congress Cataloging-in-Publication Data

The culture of China / edited by Kathleen Kuiper.—1st ed.
    p. cm.—(Understanding China)
"In association with Britannica Educational Publishing, Rosen Educational Services."
Includes bibliographical references and index.
ISBN 978-1-61530-140-9 (library binding)
1. China. 2. China—Civilization. I. Kuiper, Kathleen.
DS706.C84 2010
951—dc22

                                                    2010008759

Manufactured in the United States of America

On the cover: The Summer Palace in Beijing, China, is a UNESCO World Heritage site. ©
www.istockphoto.com/Robert Churchill

Back cover Andrea Pistolesi/The Image Bank/Getty Images

On page 12: The entrance to a pavilion in the Forbidden City in Beijing, China, in 1973.
Keystone/Hulton Archive/Getty Images

On page 18: A man communes with Daoist gods by spitting rice wine into the air while
using a large snake whip during the Full Moon Festival in Sanshia, China. Eightfish/The
Image Bank/Getty Images

CONTENTS

26

38

44

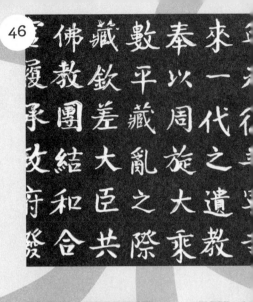

46

59

66

98

109

114

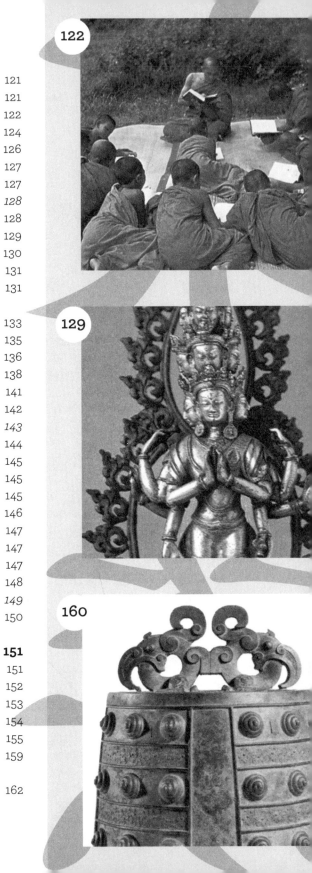

122

129

160

229

251

255

267

283

285

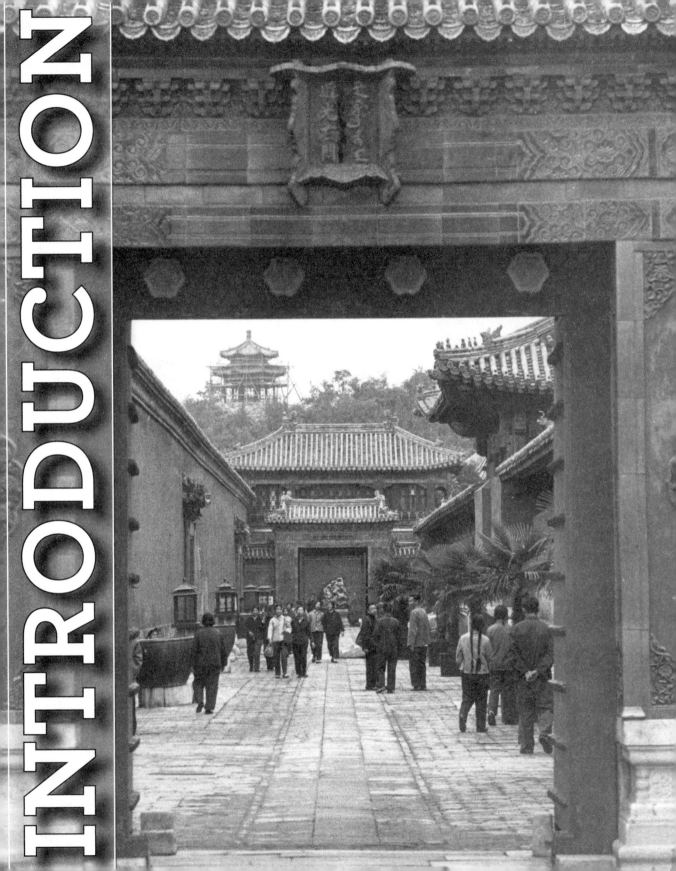

INTRODUCTION

China spared no expense celebrating its arts and culture during the opening ceremony of the 2008 Beijing Summer Olympics. Viewers at National Stadium (the "Bird's Nest") in China and in front of television screens across the world witnessed dancers, acrobats, pianists, drummers, and opera singers in spectacular performance. Yet no matter how cutting-edge or extravagant they were, the performances remained steeped in China's ancient traditions. The events as a whole were a reminder that China is home to one of the world's oldest continuous civilizations, one that stretches back millennia.

After the communist government took over in 1949, the leaders undertook extensive reforms. But pragmatic policies alternated with periods of revolutionary upheaval, most notably in the Great Leap Forward and the Cultural Revolution. During this period, the government prohibited the practice of many traditional arts. But by the end of the 1970s, China's leaders had started to renew economic and political ties with the West and had begun to once again invest in the arts.

Today, China's cultural contributions are once again being overshadowed, this time by the country's economic success. Images of its billowing factories and booming cities are the focus of the world's news media. Goods of all sorts bear the label "Made in China." This book reorients readers to China's powerful influence in the arts and reveals how the country's rich cultural history has shaped the lives of the more than 1 billion people who live within its boundaries.

The book introduces readers to the diversity of China's people. About 92 percent of Chinese are Han. They speak different dialects in different parts of the country, but they are united by a common writing system. The remainder of the population includes some 55 minority groups, many of whom speak languages unrelated to Sino-Tibetan.

Of the Chinese dialects (or languages), the most important is Mandarin, the country's official language. The Beijing-based dialect is also known as *putonghua*, or "common language." But it's hardly the only Han dialect spoken. In and around the city of Guangzhou in southern China, people speak Cantonese. The non-Chinese languages include Uighur, a Turkic language spoken in the Northwest, and Lahu, a Tibeto-Burman language that is closer to Burmese than to Chinese.

China's cuisine is just as diverse as its people. Beijing is famed for its pork buns, fried tofu, and multicourse Peking duck. Spicy hot peppers, peanuts, and garlic dominate dishes prepared in central China's Sichuan province. Adventurous diners in the Guangdong region savour exotic ingredients such as snakes, eels, and frogs—foods that do not appeal to many other Chinese people. The special preparation of food has deep and ancient roots. By the 10th or 11th century, China's distinctive culinary style began to emerge. It is a cuisine based on principles of balance—hot and cold, grains and vegetables with meat—that reached its height in the Qing dynasty (1644–1911/12).

China is also one of the great centres of world religious thought, as this book demonstrates. Confucianism, Daoism, and Buddhism have formed the basis of Chinese society and governance for centuries.

The ideas of Confucius and his followers have guided the lives of China's people and leaders for about two millennia. Confucius was born in 551 BCE, and though he received little recognition during his lifetime, he may be said to have become China's most famous philosopher and teacher. His teachings, compiled mainly in a text known as the *Lunyu*, or *Analects*, inspired a rich tradition—known in the West as "Confucianism"—of philosophers, scholars, political leaders, and occasional religious figures that helped to shape not only Chinese culture but that of Korea, Japan, and Vietnam as well.

Confucius lived at a time in which society was highly fragmented into competing principalities. He believed that in order to stem the tide of social decay and to promote a flourishing and humane society as had existed in antiquity, the *dao*, or the way, of the ancient sage-kings needed to be revived. To accomplish this, Confucius advocated the institution of a meritocracy of cultured, virtuous scholar-officials who would advise kings to rule justly. Yet his social vision did not apply only to the ruling class; Confucius's stress on moral character influenced every level of Chinese society. While it is

not technically a religion, its emphases on personal virtue and on ethical action within human society continue to influence Chinese spiritual life.

The other great Chinese tradition that has its roots in pre-Han dynasty China is Daoism. Like Confucianism, Daoism emerged as a vision for stopping social decline and promoting good government. It took a different track. Instead of a particular *dao* of a group of historical leaders or group of political leaders, pre-Han Daoist thinkers stressed the *Dao* that generated the cosmos as the appropriate model for human action. The *Daodejing*, a philosophical and spiritual text attributed to the mythical sage Laozi, emphasized *wuwei*, or nonaction; however, this meant that people, and particularly the rulers, should take no action that is contrary to nature but should instead cultivate attunement with the natural fluctuation of the cosmos. In later centuries, this more naturalistic spiritual sense of attunement with the universe became increasingly religious, and Laozi became revered as a deity, especially after Buddhism, which was founded in India, transformed Chinese culture.

Buddhism arrived in China probably by way of Central Asian trade routes in about the 1st century CE. The most common form of Buddhism practiced there is Mahayana Buddhism in China and Vajrayana in Tibet. According to legend, Buddhism came to China after the Han emperor Mingdi (reigned 57–75) had a dream about a flying golden god that was interpreted as a vision of the Buddha.

While Confucianism remained the philosophical and ethical system of the bureaucracy and the imperial court, Daoism and Buddhism became the main sources of philosophical and religious ingenuity in China between the end of the Han and the late Tang dynasty (618-907). Each tradition influenced the other: Buddhist concepts were explained to the Chinese through a process of "matching the meanings" to Daoist concepts, and the Buddhist *sangha* (community of monks and nuns) sparked the emergence of Daoist monasticism. Early on, many people believed that after Laozi left China for the West (according to legend), he traveled to India, where he was honored for his wisdom and became the Buddha. By the time of the Sui dynasty (581–618), Buddhism received state support. In the 7th century, Chan (later known in Japan as Zen), which stressed the sudden experience of enlightenment, demonstrated a purely Chinese variety of Buddhism.

During a brief period of persecution starting in 845, Emperor Wuzong destroyed Buddhist temples and shrines and forced monks and nuns to marry and return to lay life. During the Song dynasty (960–1279), a group of thinkers reinvigorated Confucian thinking and helped it to reclaim its past glory in Chinese thought. The "Neo-Confucians" called their movement *daoxue* ("Learning of the Way"), and claimed to be reviving the original *dao* of Confucius that had been lost for centuries. In reclaiming lost ground from Daoism and Buddhism, it borrowed or adapted certain concepts that augmented the spiritual dimension of the tradition while emphasizing the moral character of government officials. Buddhism and Daoism remained widely popular in Chinese spiritual life, but they never again matched Confucianism's prominence in Chinese intellectual life.

The book also details the history of Chinese art, especially its pottery, bronzes, and sculpture. In China, art has played a social and moral role. Noble themes were favoured in traditional Chinese art. Artists' reputations could be damaged or rejuvenated by their work, depending on the rightness of their practice or their character.

The world has reaped the rewards of their efforts. Perhaps nowhere in the world has pottery assumed such an importance as it has in China. The influence of Chinese porcelain on later European pottery has been profound.

The Chinese have been casting remarkable bronzes from approximately 1700 BCE. From 1500–300 BCE, bronzes were vessels for making sacrifices of food to clan spirits, from the round-bodied *li* in which food was cooked to the *gui*, a bowl in which the food was presented. In the field of painting, landscapes predominate, usually done with black ink on fine paper or silk, often with colour washes. The landscape paintings from the Song dynasty (960–1279) to the Ming (1368–1644) dynasty are especially noteworthy.

Calligraphy is another notable fine art. Calligraphy masters spend years learning the craft of letting the complex characters that form China's written language flow directly and naturally from their brushstrokes. Connoisseurs prize the personality and rhythmic elegance shown by the artists of different schools, from the controlled "seal" school to the free, loose "grass" schools of calligraphy, using words like balance, vitality, energy, wind, and strength to describe the beauties of different styles. According to legend, Cangjie, the inventor of Chinese writing, got his ideas from observing animal footprints in the sand.

China's musical tradition is at least 5,000 years old, one of the oldest and most highly developed of all known musical systems. Not only do written records confirm China's long musical history, but archaeologists uncovered a number of ancient instruments, including such objects as bronze bells and stone chimes. These and other instruments were classified in early times according to the material used in their construction: stone, earth (pottery), bamboo, metal, skin, silk, wood, and gourd.

Today the musical instruments most associated with China include stringed instruments such as the four-string *pipa* lute and the 25-string *se* zither as well as drums such as the *dagu*, used in China to accompany a narrative. Other noteworthy instruments include the *sheng*, a mouth organ with 17 pipes attached in a basin, and the *fangxiang*, made up of 16 iron slabs suspended in a wooden frame.

Chinese scholars have devoted much attention to musical principles as well. The *Shijing* ("Classic of Poetry"), compiled by Confucius, contains the texts of 305 songs that are dated from the 10th to the 7th centuries BCE. In 1345 scholars created the *Songshi* ("Song History"), a book of 496 chapters, 17 of which are devoted solely to music.

China also has distinct theatrical traditions, including Chinese opera. Over the centuries, two main schools have developed—quiet, refined *kunqu*, which started as a folk art, but which later became famed for being sophisticated and refined, and energetic *jingxi* (Peking) opera, so called because it is closely associated with China's capital city of Beijing (formerly spelled Peking). Unlike *kunqu*, which is poetic and accompanied by flutes and stringed instruments, *jingxi* is lively, less refined, and popular. It features clappers and cymbals to make emotional points and energetic acrobatics during battle scenes. Yet, both styles are highly stylized and rely on the audience to understand a full range of symbols. A black flag carried across the stage, for example, signifies to knowledgeable operagoers that a storm has blown in. As in China's visual arts, conventional morality is a strong theme, and the importance of doing good and avoiding evil is strongly emphasized.

But *jingxi* and *kunqu* are not the only forms of Chinese opera. Today more than 300 kinds of opera are found around the nation, each type performed according to local musical styles and in regional languages.

The ideals that have defined China's artwork and performing artists have inspired its finest architectural achievements as well. Today the skylines of many Chinese cities reflect contemporary trends elsewhere in the world. Skyscrapers and bold designs, however, give no hint of China's long tradition of achievement in the field of architecture. Although many of China's oldest buildings have disappeared—some falling victim to modernization efforts, others to the enemies of wood construction—the timeless principles of traditional Chinese architecture are still evident. One of the most distinctive features of Chinese architecture is the use of beautiful sloping and gabled roofs, such as those seen in the country's Buddhist pagodas with their several storied towers. The first curved roof appeared in China around 500 CE. Great care is also given to where buildings are placed and what they are facing, according to the geomantic principles of feng shui. The system of feng shui (meaning literally "wind water") was developed during the Five Dynasties (907–960) or Ten Kingdoms period, and its purpose was to harmonize a site or structure with cosmic principles or spiritual forces) and thus to ensure good fortune.

Architecture had become highly stylized by the time of the Song dynasty, so that certain elements showed which buildings had greater and lesser importance. All those elements can be easily identified in one of China's greatest architectural achievements: the Forbidden City. Located within the inner city of Beijing, this palace compound—the world's largest—was used by 24 emperors during the Ming (1368–1644) and Qing (1644–1911/12) dynasties. The Forbidden City has 800 buildings that have a total of about 9,000 rooms. Today it has been listed by UNESCO as the largest collection of preserved ancient wooden structures in the world. It was declared a World Heritage Site in 1987 and is now a public museum.

For the 2008 Beijing Summer Olympics, China invited acclaimed international architects to design many of the games' signature structures, including the Bird's Nest. These structures connect China to the contemporary world culture, to be sure, but they give little hint of the complexity and richness of China's vast contribution to the world. We hope this volume serves to unveil China's cultural wealth.

CHAPTER 1

PEOPLE

China is a multinational country, with a population composed of a large number of ethnic and linguistic groups. So thoroughly did the Han dynasty (206 BCE–220 CE) establish what was thereafter considered Chinese culture that "Han" became the Chinese word denoting someone who is Chinese. The Han is the largest ethnic group, and it outnumbers the minority groups or minority nationalities in every province or autonomous region except Tibet and Xinjiang. The Han, therefore, form the great homogeneous mass of the Chinese people, sharing the same culture, the same traditions, and the same written language. For this reason, the general basis for classifying the country's population is largely linguistic rather than ethnic.

SELECTED ETHNIC GROUPS

Some 55 minority groups are spread over approximately three-fifths of the country's total area. Where these minority groups are found in large numbers, they have been given some semblance of autonomy and self-government; autonomous regions of several types have been established on the basis of the geographic distribution of nationalities. The government takes great credit for its treatment of these minorities; it has advanced their economic well-being, raised their living standards, provided educational facilities,

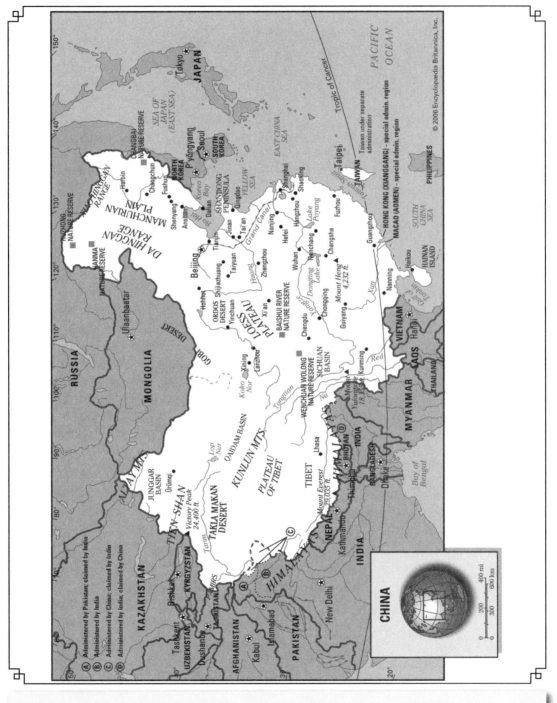

This map shows China and its special administrative regions.

promoted their national languages and cultures, and raised their literacy levels, as well as introduced a written language where none existed previously. It must be noted, however, that some minorities (e.g., Tibetans) have been subject to varying degrees of repression. Still, of the 50-odd minority languages, only 20 had written forms before the coming of the communist regime in 1949; and only relatively few written languages—e.g., Mongolian, Tibetan, Uighur, Kazakh (Hasake), Dai, and Korean (Chaoxian)—were in everyday use. Other written languages were used chiefly for religious purposes and by a limited number of people. Educational institutions for national minorities are a feature of many large cities, notably Beijing, Wuhan, Chengdu, and Lanzhou. This chapter includes a sampling of minority groups.

BAI

The Bai (Bo) people live in northwestern Yunnan province, southwest China. Minjia is the Chinese (Pinyin) name for them; they call themselves Bai or Bo in their own language, which has been classified as a Tibeto-Burman language. Until recently their language was not written. It contains many words borrowed from Chinese but is itself a non-Chinese, tonal, polysyllabic language with a markedly different grammatical structure.

Occupying a triangular area from Shigu on the upper Yangtze River down to Dali (Xiaguan) at the foot of Lake Er, the Bai in the early 21st century were estimated to number nearly two million, about half of whom lived on the fertile plain between the Cang Mountains and the lake.

Since the establishment of the People's Republic of China, the Bai, in accordance with the Communist Party's policy toward non-Chinese peoples, have been given status as a national minority. Their principal city, Dali, was from the 6th to the 9th century the capital of the kingdom of Nanzhao. The Bai probably already formed the bulk of the population of the locality at that time.

Most of the Bai are cultivators of wet rice, along with various vegetables and fruits. Those in the hills grow barley, buckwheat, oats, and beans. The lake is heavily fished.

They have their own social and kinship organization, based on the village and the extended family (parents, married sons and their families). Their religion differs little from that of the Chinese; they venerate local deities and ancestral spirits as well as Buddhist and Daoist gods.

DAUR

Another ethnic minority of China, the Daur (Daghor, Daghur, or Dagur) people are of Mongol descent. They live mainly in the eastern portion of Inner Mongolia autonomous region and western Heilongjiang province of China and were estimated in the early 21st century to number more than 132,000. Their language, which varies widely enough from other Mongolian languages to once have been thought to be Tungusic or a mixture of Mongolian and Tungus, is now known to be an archaic Mongolian dialect that preserves features found in 13th-century documents.

Russian settlers in the 17th century found the Daur well established in eastern Transbaikalia and the Amur region, and the Orthodox church sent missionaries to them in 1682. The Chinese government, not wishing the Daur to fall under Russian sway, resettled them. By the early 20th century many Daur lived in Heilongjiang, around the city of Hailar, and in the Nen River valley near the city of Qiqihar. Their chief occupations are agriculture, logging, hunting, stock raising, and horse breeding. The clan system prevails. Their religion is shamanistic, although some are adherents of Tibetan Buddhism.

DONG

The Dong (Dongjia, Dongren) are found in southeastern Guizhou province and in neighbouring Zhuang Autonomous Region of Guangxi and Hunan province. According to most linguists the Dong speak a Kam-Sui language that is closely related to the Tai languages, and they call themselves Kam.

The Dong first appeared in China during the Song dynasty (960–1279 CE), moving southwest in a series of migrations, possibly forced by the advancing Mongols. Concentrated today in sparsely populated Guizhou, they share the area with the Buyei, another official ethnic minority.

Most Dong are lowland farmers with glutinous rice as their primary crop. They have also long produced cotton and cotton cloth for sale. The Dong are known as fish breeders, raising fish in specially constructed ponds as well as in some flooded paddy fields. Before 1949 they were integrated into the periodic market system of southern China and since the opening of China have increasingly shifted to production for the market.

Like related minority peoples, but, unlike the Han Chinese, they live in large houses built on pilings. They are known for pagoda-like wooden drum towers that can be as tall as 30 metres (100 feet). These towers and distinctive covered bridges, together with revived festivals, particularly those involving water-buffalo fights—once associated with animal sacrifices in traditional Dong religion—have made some Dong villages attractive for tourists.

According to data from the 1982 and 1990 censuses, the Dong had the highest birth rate of any ethnic group in China. In the early 21st century they numbered nearly three million.

HANI

The Hani (Woni, Houni) live mainly on the high southwestern plateau of Yunnan province, China, specifically concentrated in the southwestern corner. There are also several thousands of Hani or related peoples in northern Thailand, Laos, and Vietnam and in eastern Myanmar (Burma). Altogether they numbered some two million in the early 21st century.

Thirteen subgroups of this official classification call themselves by other names, but they speak mutually intelligible Tibeto-Burman languages of the Sino-Tibetan language family. Classified as tribes of the larger Yi ethnic group, the Hani are believed to be a branch of the ancient Qiang from the north, appearing in the Dadu River region in Han times. They were slightly infiltrated by Thai who were fleeing the Mongols. Contemporary Hani are mostly farmers who produce two excellent types of tea and are also known for their remarkable terraced rice paddies.

A distinct subgroup of the Hani known as the Akha live in China, as well as parts of Myanmar, Thailand, Vietnam, Laos, and Cambodia. They are believed to be of Chinese origin, though, for a variety of reasons, they have lived a wandering life. A notable feature of female dress is an elaborate headdress made with silver or white beads and silver coins. This and other features of the Akha culture are dissipating under pressure of both missionary work and other outside forces.

HUI

The nearly 10 million Hui (Hwei, Huihui) are Chinese Muslims (i.e., neither Turkic nor Mongolian) who have intermingled with the Han Chinese throughout China but are relatively concentrated in western China—in the provinces or autonomous regions of Xinjiang, Ningxia, Gansu, Qinghai, Henan, Hebei, Shandong, and Yunnan. Considerable numbers also live in Anhui, Liaoning, and Beijing. The Hui are also found on the frontier between China and Myanmar (Burma) and in Kazakhstan, Uzbekistan, and Kyrgyzstan, in Central Asia. They speak Mandarin as a first language.

The Hui are distinguished as Hui only in the area of their heaviest concentration, the Hui Autonomous Region of Ningxia. Other Hui communities are organized as autonomous prefectures (*zizhizhou*) in Xinjiang and as autonomous counties (*zizhixian*) in Qinghai, Hebei, Guizhou, and Yunnan. Increasingly, the Hui have been moving from their scattered settlements into the area of major concentration, possibly in order to facilitate intermarriage with other Muslims.

The ancestors of the Hui were merchants, soldiers, handicraftsmen, and scholars who came to China from Islamic Persia and Central Asia from the 7th to the 13th century. After these ancestors settled in China, they intermarried with the Han Chinese, Uighur, and Mongolian nationalities and came to speak Chinese languages, or dialects (while often retaining Arabic, too). Eventually their appearance and other cultural characteristics became thoroughly Chinese. They now engage mostly in agriculture, and most of them live in rural areas, although urban dwellers are significantly increasing. There have been a number of famous Hui thinkers, navigators, scientists, and artists. The "Hui Brigade" was active in World War II, in the resistance against Japan (1937–45).

Lahu

The peoples known as Lahu, or Muhso (Musso, Mussuh), live in upland areas of Yunnan, China, eastern Myanmar (Burma), northern Thailand, northern Laos, and Vietnam. They speak related dialects of Tibeto-Burman languages. Although there is no indigenous Lahu system of writing, three different romanized Lahu orthographies exist; two of these were developed by Christian missionaries and the other by Chinese linguists. Literacy in Lahu is primarily for religious purposes; educated individuals also know the national language of the country in which they live.

The Lahu have historically lived in relatively autonomous villages. From time to time, however, a Lahu leader would be able to attract a following from many villages for a temporary period of time. Since the mid-20th century, the Lahu have been increasingly integrated into the countries in which they reside, albeit often as a marginalized minority.

Most Lahu traditionally engaged in slash-and-burn agriculture. Like other traditional peoples, they have been increasingly compelled by external political and economic influences to adopt settled agriculture. Some Lahu have been involved in the production of opium, although they have never been as involved in this work as have such other upland groups in the region as the Hmong and the Mien. Many Lahu have combined religious practices adopted from neighbouring Tai-speaking peoples with their own form of animism.

From the late 20th century onward, a growing number of Lahu converted to Christianity. At the beginning of the 21st century, estimates of the Lahu population indicated approximately 450,000 individuals in China, with smaller numbers elsewhere.

Lisu

The Lisu people numbered more than 630,000 in China in the early 21st century. They have spread southward from Yunnan province as far as Myanmar (Burma) and northern Thailand. The Chinese distinguish between Black Lisu, White Lisu, and Flowery Lisu, terms that seem to relate to their degree of assimilation of Chinese culture. In the 1960s the Black Lisu, living highest up in the Salween River valley, were least assimilated; they wore coarse clothes of homespun hemp, while the others dressed in colourful and elaborate garments. In their migrations the Lisu have kept to the highest parts of hill ranges, where they cultivate hill rice, corn (maize), and buckwheat on frequently shifted fields worked mainly with hoes. Their houses are of wood and bamboo. Crossbows, poisoned arrows, and dogs are used for hunting. They have a clan organization, and marriage is always between members of two different clans. Their religion combines ancestor veneration with animism and includes gods of earth and sky, wind, lightning, and forest.

MANCHU

The Manchu (Man) people have lived for many centuries mainly in Manchuria (now the Northeast) and adjacent areas of China. In the 17th century they conquered China and ruled for more than 250 years. The term Manchu dates from the 16th century, but it is certain that the Manchu are descended from a group of peoples collectively called the Tungus (the Even and Evenk are also descended from that group). The Manchu, under other names, had lived in northeastern Manchuria in prehistoric times. In early Chinese records they were known as the Donghui, or "Eastern Barbarians"; in the 3rd century BCE they were given the name Sushen, or Yilou; in the 4th to 7th centuries CE Chinese historians spoke of them as Wuji, or Momo; and in the 10th century CE as Juchen (Nüzhen in Pinyin). These Juchen established a kingdom of some extent and importance in Manchuria, and by 1115 CE their dynasty (called Jin in Chinese records) had secured control over northeastern

China. The kingdom was annihilated by the Mongols in 1234, and the surviving Juchen were driven back into northeastern Manchuria. Three centuries later the descendants of these Juchen again came into prominence, but before long they dropped the name Juchen for Manchu. They regained control of Manchuria, moved south, and conquered Beijing (1644); and by 1680 the Manchu had established complete control over all sections of China under the name of the Qing dynasty. The Manchu managed to maintain a brilliant and powerful government until about 1800, after which they rapidly lost energy and ability. It was not, however, until 1911/12 that the Qing dynasty was overthrown.

Modern research shows that the Juchen-Manchu speak a language belonging to the sparse but geographically widespread Manchu-Tungus subfamily of the Altaic languages. At an early date, probably about the 1st century CE, various Manchu-Tungus-speaking tribes moved from their homeland in or near northeastern Manchuria to the north and west and eventually occupied most of Siberia between the Yenisey River and the Pacific Ocean. The Manchu became established in the south, while the Even, Evenk, and other peoples predominated in the north and west.

From the Chinese records it is evident that the Yilou, the Tungus ancestors of the Manchu, were essentially hunters, fishers, and food gatherers, though in later times they and their descendants,

the Juchen and Manchu, developed a primitive form of agriculture and animal husbandry. The Juchen-Manchu were accustomed to braid their hair into a queue, or pigtail. When the Manchu conquered China they forced the Chinese to adopt this custom as a sign of loyalty to the new dynasty. Apart from this, the Manchu made no attempt to impose their manners and customs upon the Chinese. After the conquest of China, the greater part of the Manchu migrated there and kept their ancestral estates only as hunting lodges. Eventually these estates were broken up and sold to or occupied by Chinese (Han) immigrant farmers. By 1900 even in Manchuria the new Chinese settlers greatly outnumbered the Manchu.

The Manchu emperors—despite their splendid patronage of Chinese art, scholarship, and culture over the centuries—made strenuous efforts to prevent the Manchu from being absorbed by the Chinese. The Manchu were urged to retain the Manchu language and to give their children a Manchu education. Attempts were made to prevent the intermarriage of Manchu and Chinese, so as to keep the Manchu strain ethnically "pure." Social intercourse between the two peoples was frowned upon. All these efforts proved fruitless. During the 19th century, as the dynasty decayed, efforts to preserve cultural and ethnic segregation gradually broke down. The Manchu began to adopt the Chinese customs and language and to intermarry with the Chinese. Few, if any, spoke the Manchu language in the early 21st century.

China's government, however, continues to identify the Manchu as a separate ethnic group (numbering more than 10.5 million in the early 21st century). The Manchu live mainly in Liaoning, Jilin, Heilongjiang, and Hebei provinces, in Beijing, and in the Inner Mongolia Autonomous Region.

MIAO

The Miao are mountain-dwelling peoples of China, Vietnam, Laos, Burma, and Thailand, who speak languages of the Hmong-Mien (Miao-Yao) family.

Miao is the official Chinese term for four distinct groups of people who are only distantly related through language or culture: the Hmu people of southeast Guizhou, the Qo Xiong people of west Hunan, the A-Hmao people of Yunnan, and the Hmong people of Guizhou, Sichuan, Guangxi, and Yunnan. There are some nine million Miao in China, of whom the Hmong constitute probably one-third, according to the French scholar Jacques Lemoine, writing in the *Hmong Studies Journal* in 2005. The Miao are

This photo from 1920 shows two Manchu women in their national dress. J. Thompson/Hulton Archive/Getty Images

related in language and some other cultural features to the Yao; among these peoples the two groups with the closest degree of relatedness are the Hmong (Miao) and the Iu Mien (Yao).

The customs and histories of the four Miao groups are quite different, and they speak mutually unintelligible languages. Closest linguistically to the Hmong are the A-Hmao, but the two groups still cannot understand each others' languages. Of all the Miao peoples, only the Hmong have migrated out of China.

Agriculture is the chief means of subsistence for all the groups, who in the past practiced the shifting cultivation of rice and corn (maize), together with the opium poppy. Opium was sold in lowland markets and brought in silver, which was used as bridewealth payments. Shifting cultivation and opium production have now largely ceased, and in Thailand the Hmong have turned to the permanent field cultivation of market garden vegetables, fruit, corn, and flowers.

Traditionally, the Miao had little political organization above the village level, and the highest position was that of village leader. In China the Miao have come under the political organization common to the whole of China; where minority populations are dense, they live in autonomous counties, townships, or prefectures, where a certain amount of self-representation is allowed.

In religion, most Miao practice ancestor worship and believe in a wide variety of spirits. They have shamans who may exorcise malevolent spirits or recall the soul of a sick patient, and animal sacrifice is widespread. However, a complete lack of religious faith is common among educated Miao in China, while significant proportions of the A-Hmao in China and the Hmong in Southeast Asia have become Christian.

Young people are permitted to select their own mates and premarital sex is tolerated, although sexual regimes are stricter in China, as are controls on reproduction. One form of institutionalized courtship involves antiphonal singing; another is the throwing back and forth of a ball between groups of boys and girls from different villages, at the New Year. Polygyny is traditional but in practice has been limited to the well-to-do. The household is usually made up of several generations, including married sons and their families. The youngest son usually stays with the parents and inherits the house, while elder sons may move out with their own families to form new households.

MONGOL

The Mongol people are a Central Asian ethnographic group of closely related tribal peoples who live on the Mongolian Plateau and share a common language and nomadic tradition. Their homeland is now divided into the independent country of Mongolia (Outer Mongolia) and the Inner Mongolia Autonomous Region of China. Owing to wars and migrations, Mongols are found throughout Central Asia.

POPULATION DISTRIBUTION

Mongols form the bulk of the population of independent Mongolia, and they constitute about one-sixth of the population in China's Inner Mongolia Autonomous Region. Elsewhere in China there are enclaves of Mongols in Qinghai province and the autonomous regions of Xinjiang and Tibet and in the Northeast (Manchuria; Liaoning, Jilin, and Heilongjiang provinces), and there are groups in Russia's Siberia. All of these populations speak dialects of the Mongol languages.

Present-day Mongol peoples include the Khalkha, who constitute almost four-fifths of the population of independent Mongolia; the descendants of the Oyrat, or western Mongols, who include the Dorbet (or Derbet), Olöt, Torgut, and Buzawa and live in southwestern Russia, western China, and independent Mongolia; the Chahar, Urat, Karchin, and Ordos Mongols of the Inner Mongolian region of China; the Bargut and Daur Mongols of Manchuria; the Monguors of the Chinese province of Gansu; and the Buryat of Russia, who are concentrated in Buryatia and in an autonomous district in the vicinity of Lake Baikal.

LIFESTYLE AND LIVELIHOOD

With a few exceptions, Mongol social structure, economy, culture, and language showed very little change over many centuries. They were basically nomadic pastoralists who were superb horsemen and traveled with their flocks of sheep, goats, cattle, and horses over the immense grasslands of the steppes of Central Asia.

Traditional Mongol society was based on the family, the clan, and the tribe, with clan names derived from those of common male ancestors. As clans merged, the tribal name was taken from that of the strongest clan. In the tribe, weaker clans retained their own headmen and livestock but were subordinate to the strongest clan. In periods of tribal unity, khans (Mongol monarchs) assigned commanders to territories from which troops and revenues were gathered. Mongol history alternated between periods of tribal conflict and tribal consolidation.

RISE OF THE MONGOL EMPIRE

Among the tribes that held power in Mongolia were the Xiongnu, a confederated empire that warred with the young Chinese state for centuries before dissolving in 48 CE. The Khitan ruled in Manchuria and North China, where they established the Liao dynasty (907–1125) and formed an alliance with a little-known tribal confederacy known as All the Mongols. After the fall of the Liao, the Tatars—a Mongol people but not members of the league—appeared as allies of the Juchen, the Khitan's successors.

During this time Genghis (Chinggis) Khan (1162–1227) came to power within the All the Mongols league and was proclaimed khan in 1206. He skillfully gained control over the Mongols outside the league. Between 1207 and 1227 he undertook military campaigns that extended Mongol domains as far west as European Russia and as far east as northern China, taking Beijing in 1215. He died on campaign against the Xi Xia in northwest China. By this time the Mongol empire stretched over an immense swath of Asia between the Caspian Sea (west) and the China Sea (east), and Siberia (north) and the Pamirs, Tibet, and central China (south). The amazing military achievements of the Mongols under Genghis Khan and his successors were largely due to their armies of mounted archers, who possessed great speed and mobility.

After Genghis Khan's death the Mongol empire passed to his four sons, with overall leadership going to Ögödei. Jochi received the west extending to Russia; Chagatai obtained northern Iran and southern Xinjiang; Ögödei inherited northern Xinjiang and western Mongolia; and Tolui was awarded eastern Mongolia. Ögödei dominated his brothers and undertook further conquests. In the west the Golden Horde under Jochi's successor, Batu, controlled Russia and terrorized eastern Europe; in the east advances were made into China. With Ögödei's death in 1241 the branches fell into war and intrigue among one another for leadership. Tolui's son Möngke became great khan in 1248 and continued an expansionist policy. Möngke's brother Kublai

(1215–94) became great khan in 1260, and Mongol power reached its zenith during his rule. The Mongols destroyed the Southern Song dynasty and reunified China under the Yuan, or Mongol, dynasty (1206–1368).

DISSOLUTION OF THE MONGOL EMPIRE

Mongol khans relied on their subjects and on foreigners to administer their empire. Over time, power shifted from the Mongols to their bureaucrats, and this, added to the continual feuding among the different khanates, led to the empire's decline. In 1368 the Mongols lost China to the native Ming dynasty. In the same period, the Il-Khanid dynasty of Persia disintegrated, and the western Golden Horde was defeated by a Muscovy-led alliance in 1380. Soon the empire was reduced to the Mongol homeland and scattered khanates. Eventually Ming incursions into Mongolia effectively ended Mongol unity.

In the 15th and 16th centuries supremacy passed from tribe to tribe. Military gains were made but never held, and politically all that was achieved was a loose confederation. First were the western Mongolian Oyrat, who penetrated into Tibet and Xinjiang, where the Ming were weak. Next the Ordos in the Huang He (Yellow River) region challenged the Oyrat and warred successfully against the Ming. Finally power came to the Chahar in the north, but tribal defections and the rise of the Manchu led to the end of the confederation under Ligdan Khan (1603–34). This period also saw the widespread introduction of Tibetan Buddhism into Mongolia as a means of unifying the people.

FORMATION OF INNER AND OUTER MONGOLIA

The Manchu finally conquered Mongolia in two stages that led to its division into Inner Mongolia and Outer Mongolia. In invading China, the Manchu employed the eastern Mongolian Khalkha, and by 1691 the Manchu officially occupied southern and eastern Mongolia, which became Inner Mongolia. Though the western Mongolian Oyrat attempted to unite the Mongols under their leadership against the Manchu, the Khalkha joined the Manchu in a savage campaign that resulted in the conquest of Outer Mongolia in 1759 and in the near extermination of the Oyrat. The Manchu victory ended Mongol tribal warfare. It also caused the dispersal of many tribes into neighbouring regions and the division of Mongolia into two political units.

Under Manchu rule there was stagnation. Chinese colonists controlled the trade and barter systems, cultivated the pastures of Inner Mongolia, and in Inner Mongolia outnumbered the Mongolian natives. Cultural differences developed between the two regions, with Inner Mongolia becoming more nearly Chinese in character and population.

By the 20th century there was widespread dissatisfaction in both Mongolias, compounded by Russian and Japanese intrigue in the region. After the 1911 Chinese Revolution, Outer Mongolia declared its independence, but the situation was unsettled until 1921, when a Mongol-Russian force captured Ulaanbaatar and formed the Mongolian People's Republic from Outer Mongolia. Efforts to unite Inner and Outer Mongolia failed, and Inner Mongolia remained a part of China while Outer Mongolia (now Mongolia) maintained its independence, though it was a client state of the Soviet Union until the early 1990s.

NAXI

The Naxi (Nakhi, Nasi) of China live mainly in Yunnan and Sichuan provinces; some live in Tibet. They speak a Tibeto-Burman language that is closely related to that of the Yi and were estimated in the early 21st century to number more than 300,000. The Naxi have two indigenous writing systems: Dongba, an early script created with components of Chinese characters, and Geba, a syllabic script. A third, alphabetic script based on the Latin alphabet was created in 1957.

Most of the Naxi engage in agriculture and grow rice, corn (maize), wheat, potatoes, beans, hemp, and cotton. Their indigenous religion, called Dongba, is a form of shamanism influenced by Tibetan Buddhism. Matriarchal family structure predominated among the Naxi until the mid-20th century, and remnants of it can still be observed.

SHE

The She people live in the mountainous areas of Fujian, Zhejiang, Jiangxi, Anhui, and Guangdong provinces of South China. Their language (which is classified as either Hmong-Mien [Miao-Yao] or Sino-Tibetan) appears to be related to that of the Yao, though most She are now thoroughly Sinicized and speak Chinese even among themselves. Most She are farmers engaged in wet-rice cultivation, and they are also well known as tea producers. Their bamboo handicrafts are highly esteemed in the region. Their religion contains elements of both animism and ancestor worship. In the early 21st century the She numbered more than 700,000.

TIBETAN

The Tibetan people inhabit Tibet or nearby regions and speak Tibetan. All Tibetans share the same language. It is highly stylized, with an honorific and an ordinary word for most terms of reference. The honorific expression is used when speaking to equals or superiors and the ordinary word when addressing inferiors or referring to oneself. There is an additional set of higher honorifics to be used when addressing the highest lamas and nobles.

In the late 21st century the number of Tibetans in Tibet proper (and other areas in western China) was estimated to be about 4.6 million, with perhaps an additional 2 million in the Tibetan ethnic areas of Bhutan, India, northern Nepal, and the Ladakh region of Jammu and Kashmir.

Prior to the Chinese annexation of Tibet in 1959, social classes among the Tibetans could be defined in terms of opposition: cleric versus lay, noble versus peasant, merchant versus labourer, agriculturalist versus nomad, and trader versus townsman. The agriculturalists traditionally formed the peasantry of Tibet, most of them working as tenants or hired labourers on land owned by the monasteries or the nobility. The herdsmen and shepherds pastured their flocks on the high steppes; some of them remained in the lowlands during the winter and migrated upward in summer. Before 1959 it was estimated that about one-quarter of the population belonged to the clerical order. The monasteries were the main seats of learning. Tibetan Buddhism is an admixture of Buddhist teachings and the pre-Buddhist religion, Bon.

Most marriages are monogamous, although both polygyny and polyandry have been practiced under certain circumstances, usually in order to keep an estate intact and within the paternal line of descent. Thus, the eldest son of a noble family would take a bride; and, if any of his younger brothers so desired, they were included in the marriage contract as junior husbands.

Dwellings are commonly one- or two-story buildings with walls of stone or brick and flat clay roofs. The nomadic pastoralists live in tents of yak hair, rectangular in shape and ranging from 3.5 to 15 metres (12 to 50 feet) in length. Most of the noble families traditionally maintained town houses in the capital city, Lhasa. These were built of stone around a rectangular courtyard, on three sides of which were stables and storehouses. On the fourth side, opposite the gate, was the mansion itself, usually three stories high.

The staple diet of most Tibetans is barley flour, yak meat, mutton, cheese, and tea. These basic items may be supplemented by rice, fruit, vegetables, chicken, and sometimes fish. The main beverage is a tangy tea mixed with yak butter and salt.

Tujia

The Tujia people, who refer to themselves as Bizika, are distributed throughout western Hunan and southwestern Hubei provinces in China. They numbered more than eight million in the early 21st century. Their language, which remains unwritten and is spoken by only a few hundred thousand of the total population, belongs to the Tibeto-Burman group of Sino-Tibetan languages, and, two dialects, northern and southern, are often distinguished. Most Tujia, however, speak and write Chinese, and, many also understand the language of the neighbouring Miao people, to whom they are related. Like the Miao, the Tujia grow corn (maize) on small terraced fields in the foothills and narrow valleys of their homeland. They also cultivate beets, ramie, cotton, tea oil, tea, and tung oil,

and sell tung oil and medicinal herbs. They are noted for their handicrafts, particularly weaving and embroidery, and for several traditional dances, especially a hand dance in which some 70 hand gestures are used to describe daily life. The Tujia are known to have been a distinct group as early as the 10th century CE.

Uighur

The Uighur (Uygur, Uyghur, Weiwu'er) people are a Turkic-speaking people of interior Asia. They live for the most part in northwestern China, in the Uygur Autonomous Region of Xinjiang; a small number live in the Central Asian republics. There were nearly 9,000,000 Uighurs in China and about 300,000 in Uzbekistan, Kazakhstan, and Kyrgyzstan in the early 21st century.

The Uighur language is part of the Turkic group of Altaic languages, and the Uighurs are among the oldest Turkic-speaking peoples of Central Asia. They are mentioned in Chinese records from the 3rd century CE. They first rose to prominence in the 8th century, when they established a kingdom along the Orhon River in what is now north-central Mongolia. In 840 this state was overrun by the Kyrgyz, however, and the Uighurs migrated southwestward to the area around the Tien Shan ("Celestial Mountains"). There the Uighurs formed another independent kingdom in the Turfan region, but this was overthrown by the expanding Mongols in the 13th century.

The Uighurs are, in the main, a sedentary, village-dwelling people who live in the network of oases formed in the valleys and lower slopes of the Tien Shan, Pamirs, and related mountain systems. The region is one of the most arid in the world; hence, for centuries they have practiced irrigation to conserve their water supply for agriculture. Their principal food crops are wheat, corn (maize), *kaoliang* (a form of sorghum), and melons. The chief industrial crop is cotton, which has long been grown in the area. Many Uighurs are employed in petroleum extraction, mining, and manufacturing in urban centres.

The chief Uighur cities are Ürümqi, the capital of Xinjiang, and Kashgar (Kashi), an ancient centre of trade near the Russian-Chinese border. The Uighurs have lacked political unity in recent centuries, except for a brief period during the 19th century when they were in revolt against Beijing. Their social organization is centred on the village. The Uighurs of Xinjiang are Sunni Muslims.

Large numbers of Han Chinese have moved into Xinjiang, especially since the 1990s. This circumstance has produced economic disparities and ethnic tensions between the Uighur and Han populations that sometimes resulted in protests and other disturbances. A particularly violent outbreak occurred in July 2009, mainly in Ürümqi, in which scores of people were killed and hundreds more were injured.

WA

The Wa (Va, Lawa, Hkawa, Kawa, or Kala) peoples live in the upland areas of eastern Myanmar (Burma) and southwestern Yunnan province of China. They speak a variety of Austroasiatic languages related to those spoken by upland-dwelling groups in northern Thailand and Laos. At the beginning of the 21st century, they numbered approximately 600,000 in Myanmar and 350,000 in China.

Until the middle of the 20th century, most Wa practiced slash-and-burn agriculture. They lived in relatively autonomous villages; like other upland peoples in the area, they sometimes organized themselves into temporary confederations under a chief called a *ramang*. Their traditional religion centred on the propitiation of ancestors and local spirits and on securing the soul to ensure good health and well-being. Most Wa communities have had extensive historical contact with Tai-speaking Buddhists, and over the 20th century an increasing number adopted Buddhism. Some also have adopted Christianity.

The Wa living in the remote upland areas of the China-Myanmar border once had a reputation for violence. Until after World War II, many of the Wa in this area were known to colonial officials as the "wild" Wa because of their practice of headhunting, which was associated with magical rites performed to ensure the fertility of the land. During the colonial period, the area inhabited by Wa became a major source of opium; production of the narcotic markedly increased after Myanmar gained independence in 1949. Many Wa joined military groups, which for years were organized by the Communist Party of Burma. From the 1980s on, many of these militia were organized into the United Wa State Army, an organization ostensibly seeking Wa autonomy; in fact, however, this group has been primarily involved in protecting the narcotics trade.

YI

The Yi people were formerly called Lolo or Wuman. They are of Austroasiatic origin and live chiefly in the mountains of southwest China. Their language, classified as Tibeto-Burman, is spoken in six relatively distinct dialects. Other minorities within the Yi language group are the Lisu, Naxi, Hani, Lahu, and Bai. The Yi numbered more than 7.5 million in the early 21st century. Their principal concentrations were in Yunnan and Sichuan provinces, with smaller numbers in northwestern Guizhou province and in the northern part of Guangxi Zhuang Autonomous Region. Almost two-thirds live in Yunnan province.

The traditional Yi culture includes a hoe-based agriculture, livestock herding, and hunting. A caste system formerly

Yi ethnic vendors sell pork at a market to celebrate the Yi New Year in 2009, in Zhaojue county of Liangshan Yi Autonomous Prefecture, Sichuan province. Nearly two million Yi people live in Liangshan prefecture. China Photos/Getty Images

divided the Yi into three groups. The Black Bone Yi, the ruling group, were apparently descended from a people that originated in northwest China. The far more numerous White Bone Yi and the Jianu ("Family Slaves") were formerly subjugated or enslaved by the Black

Bones. The subjugation of the White Bones and the Jianu was ended by the Chinese government in the 1950s. The White Bones have spread over the highlands of Yunnan and Guizhou, while the heartland of the Black Bones lies in the great and lesser Liang Mountains southwest of the Sichuan Basin.

ZHUANG

The Zhuang people form the largest ethnic minority of South China, chiefly occupying the Zhuang Autonomous Region of Guangxi (created 1958) and Wenshan in Yunnan province. They numbered some 16 million in the early 21st century. The Zhuang speak two closely related Tai dialects, one classified as Northern and the other as Central Tai, with Chinese as their second language.

The culture ancestral to that of modern Tai speakers, including the Zhuang, appears to have developed in the regions of Sichuan and the lower Yangtze River valley; its maximum geographic distribution occurred about 2,500 years ago, during the period of its earliest contact with Han Chinese culture. The advance of the empire controlled by the Han dynasty pushed the Tai-speaking peoples southward. Other cultural heirs of these early peoples include the Thai of Thailand, the Lao of Laos, the Shan of Myanmar (Burma), the Tai of Yunnan, and the Buyei of Guizhou. Of these, the Zhuang and Buyei have become the most assimilated into contemporary China's predominantly Han culture.

The Zhuang have nevertheless retained several cultural characteristics that distinguish them from the Han. Most Zhuang prefer to settle on valley lands adjacent to streams, to cultivate wet rice with the use of buffalo or oxen, and to build their houses on pilings rather than on the ground. Most also allow young people to contract marriages without the intervention of middlemen; brides remain with their natal family from marriage until the birth of their first child, as that birth is regarded as the consummation of the marriage. Magical rites, sorcery with human figurines, and ancestor veneration are additional elements that distinguish Zhuang culture. In the late 20th century and continuing into the 21st, customs associated with the use of bronze drums were revived as tourist attractions.

CULTURAL INSTITUTIONS, FESTIVALS, AND SPORTS IN DAILY LIFE

Beijing remains China's cultural centre, home to the Chinese Academy of Sciences and numerous major research institutes. Notable repositories there include the National Library of China (housed in the Beijing Library), the Central Archives of China, and the libraries of the academy and of the city's three major universities; libraries in Nanjing, Shanghai, and Changsha in Hunan province also have important collections. Paramount among China's museums is the Palace Museum, which occupies the former imperial palaces of the Forbidden City in central Beijing.

LUNAR NEW YEAR

Also known as the Spring Festival, the Lunar New Year is celebrated in China (where it is called Chunjie) and other Asian countries. It begins with the first new moon of the lunar calendar and ends on the first full moon of the lunar calendar, 15 days later. Because the lunar calendar is based on the cycles of the moon, the dates of the holiday vary slightly from year to year, beginning some time between January 21 and February 20 according to Western calendars.

Approximately 10 days before the beginning of the new lunar year, houses are thoroughly cleaned to remove any bad luck that might be lingering inside, a custom called "sweeping of the grounds." Traditionally, New Year's eve and New Year's day are reserved for family celebrations, including religious ceremonies honouring ancestors. Also on New Year's day, family members receive red envelopes (lai see) containing small amounts of money. Dances and fireworks are prevalent throughout the holidays, culminating in the Lantern Festival, which is celebrated on the last day of the New Year's celebrations. On this night colourful lanterns light up the houses, and traditional foods such as yuanxiao (sticky rice balls that symbolize family unity), fagao (prosperity cake), and yusheng (raw fish and vegetable salad) are served.

The origins of the Lunar New Year festival are thousands of years old and are steeped in legends. One legend is that of Nian, a hideous beast believed to feast on human flesh on New Year's day. Because Nian feared the colour red, loud noises, and fire, red paper decorations were pasted to doors, lanterns were burned all night, and firecrackers were lit to frighten the beast away.

Chinese art and artifacts have found their way into various collections around the world. The most important collection of fine arts is in the National Palace Museum in Taipei, Taiwan, the bulk of the superb traditional palace collection having been ferried across the Taiwan Strait when the Nationalists abandoned the mainland in 1948–49. (Excellent collections of Chinese painting, calligraphy, and bronzes are also found in such museums as the Freer Gallery of Art of the Smithsonian Institution in Washington, D.C., and the Museum of Fine Arts, Boston.) Significant collections remain in major museums in Beijing, Shanghai, Nanjing, and Wuhan.

Since the 1950s, new archaeological discoveries have filled China's provincial and local museums with fabulous treasures, and new facilities have been constructed to study and display these artifacts. Especially notable is the renowned Qin tomb near Xi'an, in Shaanxi province, which preserves the life-size terra-cotta army of the first Qin emperor, Shihuangdi. The army, complete with soldiers, horses, and chariots, was discovered in 1974. Since then much of the site has been excavated, and many of its figures have been painstakingly removed and placed on public display.

China observes a number of national holidays, including New Year's Day, the

TAI CHI CHUAN

Also called tai chi or Chinese boxing, tai chi chuan (taijiquan) is an ancient and distinctive Chinese form of exercise or attack and defense that is popular throughout the world. The name means "supreme ultimate fist." As exercise, tai chi chuan is designed to provide relaxation in the process of body-conditioning exercise and is drawn from the principles of taiji, notably including the harmonizing of the yin and yang, respectively the passive and active principles. It employs flowing, rhythmic, deliberate movements, with carefully prescribed stances and positions, but in practice no two masters teach the

Beijing residents exercise by practicing the traditional Chinese martial art of tai chi chuan in a park. Andrew Wong/Getty Images

system exactly alike. As a mode of attack and defense, tai chi chuan resembles kung fu and is properly considered a martial art. It may be used with or without weapons.

Freehand exercise to promote health was practiced in China as early as the 3rd century, and, by the 5th century, monks at the Buddhist monastery of Shao Lin were performing exercises emulating the five creatures: bear, bird, deer, monkey, and tiger. The snake was added later, and, by the early Ming dynasty (1368), the yin and yang principles had been added to harmonize the whole. An assimilation of these developments, the art of tai chi chuan was codified and named in the early Qing dynasty (1644–1911/12).

There have been many schools of tai chi chuan, and five are popular and distinctive. Depending on school and master, the number of prescribed exercise forms varies from 24 to 108 or more. The forms are named for the image created by their execution, such as "White stork displays its wings" and "Fall back and twist like monkey." All start from one of three stances, weight forward, weight on rear foot, and horse riding, or oblique.

Spring Festival (Lunar New Year), Youth Day (May 4), and National Day (October 1). Notable festivals are the Lantern Festival (late winter), Tomb Sweep Day (April 4 or 5), and the Mid-Autumn Festival (October). Scores of local festivals are also held at various times throughout the country.

Physical exercise is a staple of Chinese culture. Millions gather daily at dawn to practice martial arts (notably tai chi chuan [*taijiquan*]), wield swords in a graceful ballet, or perform a synchronized dance of pliés and turns. Acrobatics are especially popular and have enjoyed a new surge of interest since 1950, when the China Acrobatic Troupe was organized in Beijing; from it have grown satellite companies in Shanghai, Chongqing, Shenyang, Wuhan, and Dalien (Lüda). Imported sports such as basketball, baseball, and football (soccer) have become hugely popular, drawing millions of participants and spectators. Of China's indigenous forms of sport, the martial arts have the longest history by far. Their origin dates to at least two thousand years ago, to a period in which contending warlords, bandits, and foreign invaders controlled large portions of China and forbade the populace to own weapons.

China has become one of the dominant countries in international sports competitions since it began participating regularly in the Olympic Games, at the 1980 Winter Games. Since then the country's finest Olympic moment came at the 2004 Summer Games. Chinese athletes took a total of 63 medals, dominating the badminton, diving, table tennis, and weightlifting events and making strong showings in a variety of others, including shooting and women's judo. Beijing was hosted the 2008 Summer Games.

CHAPTER 2

CHINESE CUISINE

Chinese culture can also be understood through the vehicle of food. Chinese cuisine, like Chinese philosophy, is organized along Daoist principles of opposition and change: hot is balanced by cold, spicy by mild, fresh by cured. The cooking of Sichuan province in central China is distinguished by the use of hot peppers. The lush southern interior of the country prizes fresh ingredients; Cantonese cuisine in particular is a symphony of subtle flavours from just-picked vegetables and lightly cooked meats. No matter what the region, foods of all kinds are viewed as an accompaniment to grains, the staple of the Chinese diet.

Apart from French cuisine, the highest expression of the gastronomic art is generally regarded to be that of the Chinese. In ancient China the preparation and service of food played an important part in court rituals. The first act of many emperors was to appoint a court chef, and once they were on the job these chefs strove mightily to outdo each other.

Hunting and foraging supplied much of the food in ancient China. Wild game, such as deer, elk, boar, muntjac (a small deer), wolf, quail, and pheasant, was eaten, along with beef, mutton, and pork. Vegetables such as royal fern, smartweed, and the leafy thistle (*Sonchus*) were gathered from the land. Meats were preserved by salt-curing, pounding with spices, or fermenting in wine. To provide a contrast in flavours the meat was fried in the fat of a different animal.

As Chinese agriculture developed, styles of food were determined to a great degree by the natural resources available in certain parts of the country, thus the vastly different manners of cooking and the development of distinctive regional cuisines of China. As a more varied fare began to emerge, tastes grew more refined. By the time of Confucius (551–479 BCE), gastronomes of considerable sophistication had appeared on the scene. Confucius wrote of one of these fastidious eaters,

For him the rice could never be white enough. When it was not cooked right, he would not eat. When the food was not in season, he would not eat. When the meat was not cut correctly, he would not eat. When the food was not served with the proper sauce, he would not eat.

EMERGENCE OF A CUISINE

Like all other forms of haute cuisine, classic Chinese cooking is the product of an affluent society. By the 2nd century CE the Chinese court had achieved great splendour, and the complaint was heard that idle noblemen were lounging about all day, feasting on smoked meats and roasts.

By the 10th or 11th century a distinctive cuisine had begun to emerge, one that was developed with great attention to detail. It was to reach its zenith in the Qing dynasty (1644–1911/12). This cuisine was a unique blend of simplicity and elegance.

The object of cooking and the preparation of food was to extract from each ingredient its unique and most enjoyable quality.

As in the case of the French cuisine, the hors d'oeuvre set the tone of the meal. "The hors d'oeuvre must look neat," say the Chinese gastronomic authorities Lin Zuifeng and her daughter Lin Xiangru.

They are best served in matched dishes, each containing one item. Many people like to garnish the dishes with parsley and vegetables cut in the shape of birds, fish, bats, etc., or even to make baskets of flowers from food. These are all acceptable if kept under control, and if the rest of the meal is served in the same florid style. The worst offense would be to start with a florid display of food and then suddenly change style midway...

COMMON FOODS AND TRADITIONS

The theory of balancing *fan* (grains and rice) with *cai* (vegetables and meat) is one of the factors that distinguishes Chinese gastronomy from that of all other nations. This refined proportion of harmony and symmetry of ingredients was practiced whenever possible in households throughout the ages and is not limited to formal or high cuisine or to meals served on special occasions.

In addition to taste that pleases (a most elemental requirement in China), astrological, geographical, and personal characteristics had to satisfy the complex system of the yin-yang balance of hot and cold, the Daoist perception of the cosmic equilibrium. According to this theory, every foodstuff possesses an inherent humour; thus, consuming foods and beverages at proper and complementary temperatures can adjust the possible deviation of the normal state of the two intertwining forces.

Certain foods and culinary traditions are prevalent throughout most of the country. Rice is the staple except in the north, where wheat flour takes its place. Fish is extremely important in all regions. Pork, chicken, and duck are widely consumed, as well as large quantities of such vegetables as mushrooms, bamboo shoots, water chestnuts, and bean sprouts. The Chinese traditionally seasoned their dishes with monosodium glutamate and soybean sauce, rather than salt. Another distinctive feature of Chinese cooking is the varied and highly imaginative use of fat, which is prepared in many different ways and achieves the quality of a true delicacy in the hands of a talented Chinese cook. The Chinese take tea with their meals, whether green or fermented. Jasmine tea is served with flowers and leaves in small-handled cups.

GREAT CHINESE SCHOOLS

Traditionally, China is divided into five gastronomic regions, three of which are characterized by the great schools of Chinese cooking, Beijing, Sichuan, and

Zhejiang-Jiangsu. The two other regions are Fujian and Guangdong, whose cuisine is less known outside of China.

BEIJING

Beijing is the land of fried bean curd and water chestnuts. Among foods traditionally sold by street vendors are steamed bread and watermelon seeds. Vendors also dispensed buns called *baoze* that were stuffed with pork and pork fat, and *jiaoze*, or crescents, cylindrical rolls filled with garlic, cabbage, pork, and scallions. Wheat cakes wrapped around a filling of scallions and garlic, and noodles with minced pork sauce are also traditional Beijing specialties. But the greatest of all delicacies of this region is of course the Peking duck.

Peking duck, so named because the classic dish called for a specific breed of duck (the Imperial Peking), is an elaborate, world-renowned dish that requires lengthy preparation and is served in three separate courses. In its preparation, the skin is first puffed out from the duck by introducing air between the skin and the flesh. The duck is then hung out to dry for at least 24 hours, preferably in a stiff, cold breeze. This pulls the skin away from the meat. Then the duck is roasted until the skin is crisp and brown. The skin is removed, painted with hoisin sauce (a sweet, spicy sauce made of soybeans), and served inside the folds of a bun as the first course. The duck meat is carved from the bones and carefully cut into slivers.

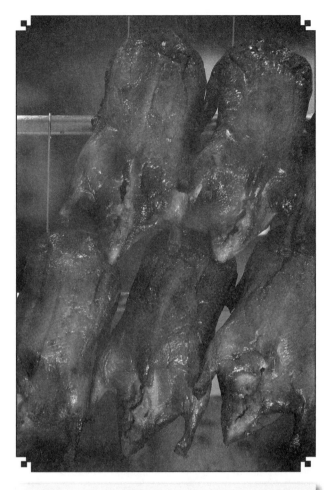

A whole crispy-skinned duck is the prelude to Peking duck, a popular dish in Beijing. Cate Gillon/Getty Images

cooked with cabbage and sugar until the cabbage is tender. Because of the complicated preparation, Peking duck is primarily restaurant fare.

SICHUAN

The cooking of Sichuan in central China is distinguished by the use of hot peppers, which are indigenous to the region. The peppers lend an immediate sensation of fiery hotness to the food, but, once this initial reaction passes, a mingled flavour of sweet, sour, salty, fragrant, and bitter asserts itself. Fried pork slices, for example, are cooked with onions, ginger, red pepper, and soy sauce to achieve this aromatic hotness. Peanuts are another common ingredient, as in kung pao (*gongbao*) chicken, a highly popular dish throughout the world.

ZHEJIANG AND JIANGSU

Sautéed onions, ginger, and peppers are added to the duck meat and cooked with bean sprouts or bamboo slivers. This forms the second course. The third course is a soup. The duck bones are crushed and then water, ginger, and onion are added to make a broth. The mixture is boiled, then drained, and the residue is

The provinces of Zhejiang and Jiangsu feature a broad variety of fish—shad, mullet, perch, and prawns. Minced chicken and bean-curd slivers are also specialties of these provinces. Foods are often arranged in attractive floral patterns before serving.

FUJIAN

Fujian, which lies farther south, features shredded fish, shredded pork, and

Food is part of many holidays in China. Here, survivors of the 2008 Sichuan earthquake feast in celebration of the Lunar New Year, hoping for better times ahead. China Photos/ Getty Images

popia, or thin bean-curd crepes filled with pork, scallions, bamboo shoots, prawns, and snow peas. The use of seafood of all sorts is characteristic of the Fujian style, as are such ingredients as bamboo shoots and mushrooms that are gathered from mountainous areas. Soups and broths are also common. Seasonings are used lightly to emphasize the freshness of ingredients. Another characteristic is the technique of slicing ingredients thinly.

GUANGDONG

Many foreigners are most familiar with the cooking typical of Guangdong, for Canton lies within this coastal province. Mushrooms, sparrows, wild ducks, snails, snakes, eels, oysters, frogs, turtles, and winkles are among the many exotic ingredients of the province. More familiar to Westerners are such Cantonese specialties as egg roll, egg foo yung (*furong*), and roast pork.

CHAPTER 3

CHINESE LANGUAGES AND WRITING SYSTEM

S everal major language families are represented in China. By far the largest groups are speakers of Sino-Tibetan and Altaic languages, with considerably smaller numbers speaking Indo-European, Austroasiatic, and Tai languages.

SINO-TIBETAN

The Sino-Tibetan family, both numerically and in the extent of its distribution, is by far the most prominent; within this family, Han Chinese is the most widely spoken language. Although unified by their tradition—the written ideographic characters of their language as well as many other cultural traits—the Han speak several mutually unintelligible dialects and display marked regional differences. By far the most important Chinese tongue is Mandarin, or *putonghua*, meaning "ordinary language" or "common language." There are three variants of Mandarin. The first of these is the northern variant, of which the Beijing dialect, or Beijing *hua*, is typical and which is spoken to the north of the Qin Mountains–Huai River line; as the most widespread Chinese tongue, it has officially been adopted as the basis for a national language. The second is the western variant, also known as the Chengdu or Upper Yangtze variant; this

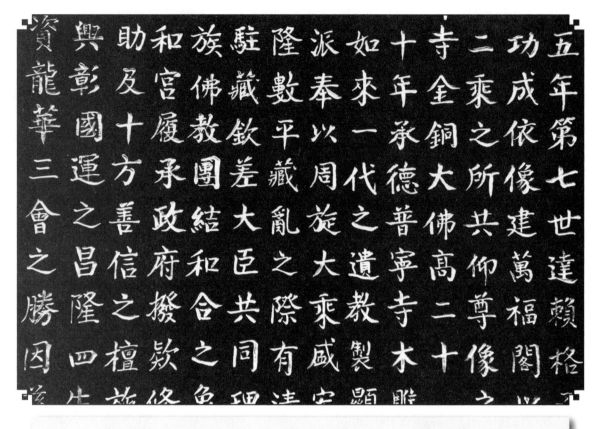

This Buddhist temple wall in Beijing shows traditional Chinese characters. Bambu Productions/Iconica/Getty Images

is spoken in the Sichuan Basin and in adjoining parts of southwestern China. The third is the southern variant, also known as the Nanjing or Lower Yangtze variant, which is spoken in northern Jiangsu and in southern and central Anhui. Some authorities also recognize a fourth variant, northwestern, which is used in most of northwestern China. Related to Mandarin are the Hunan, or Xiang, language, spoken by people in central and southern Hunan, and the Gan dialect. The Huizhou language, spoken in southern Anhui, forms an enclave within the southern Mandarin area.

Less intelligible to Mandarin speakers are the dialects of the southeast coastal region, stretching from Shanghai to Guangzhou (Canton). The most important of these is the Wu language, spoken in southern Jiangsu and in Zhejiang. This is followed, to the south, by the Fuzhou, or Northern Min, language of northern and central Fujian and by the Xiamen-Shantou (Amoy-Swatow), or Southern Min, language of southern Fujian and easternmost

Guangdong. The Hakka language of southernmost Jiangxi and northeastern Guangdong has a rather scattered pattern of distribution. Probably the best known of these southern dialects is Yue, particularly Cantonese, which is spoken in central and western Guangdong, Hong Kong, and in southern Guangxi—a dialect area in which a large proportion of overseas Chinese originated.

The Hua dialect of Mandarin spoken in Beijing, pictured here, has been adopted as the basis for a national language. Liu Jin/AFP/Getty Images

In addition to the Han, the Manchu and the Hui also speak Mandarin and use the Chinese writing system. Manchu is virtually a dead language—though it is closely related to Sibo (or Xibe), which is still vital.

ALTAIC

While the minorities of the Sino-Tibetan language family are concentrated in the south and southwest, the second major language family—the Altaic—is represented entirely by minorities in northwestern and northern China. The Altaic family falls into three branches: Turkic, Mongolian, and Manchu-Tungus. The Turkic language branch is by far the most numerous of the three Altaic branches. The Uighur, who are Muslims, form the largest Turkic-speaking minority. They are distributed over chains of oases in the Tarim and Junggar basins of Xinjiang and mainly depend on irrigated agriculture for a livelihood. Other Turkic minorities in Xinjiang are splinter groups of nationalities living in neighbouring countries of Central Asia, including the Kazakhs and the Kyrgyz, all being adherents of Islam. The Kazakhs and Kyrgyz are pastoral nomadic peoples who still show traces of tribal organization. The Kazakhs live mainly as herders in northwestern and northern Xinjiang (notably in the Ili River region), tending flocks in summer pastures and retiring to camps in the valleys during the winter. The Kyrgyz are high-mountain pastoralists and are concentrated mainly in the westernmost part of Xinjiang.

The Mongolians, who are by nature a nomadic people, are the most widely dispersed of the minority nationalities of China. Most of them are inhabitants of the Inner Mongolia Autonomous Region. Small Mongolian and Mongolian-related groups of people are scattered throughout the vast area from Xinjiang through Qinghai and Gansu and into the provinces of the Northeast (Jilin, Heilongjiang, and Liaoning). In addition to the Inner Mongolia Autonomous Region, Mongolians are established in two autonomous prefectures in Xinjiang, a joint autonomous prefecture with Tibetans and Kazakhs in Qinhai, and several autonomous counties in the western area of the Northeast. Some Mongolians retain their tribal divisions and are pastoralists, but large numbers practice sedentary agriculture, and others combine crop growing with herding. Those who depend on animal husbandry travel each year around the pastureland—grazing sheep, goats, horses, cattle, and camels—and then return to their point of departure. A few engage in hunting and fur trapping to supplement their income. Mongolian languages are sometimes divided into a western group (including Oyrat and Kalmyk) and an eastern group (including Buryat and Mongol), but their subclassification is controversial. Religion is the main unifying force, and most Mongolians profess Tibetan Buddhism.

OTHER LANGUAGES

A few linguistic minorities in China belong to neither the Sino-Tibetan nor the Altaic language family. The Tajiks of westernmost Xinjiang are related to the people of Tajikistan, and their language belongs to the Iranian branch of the Indo-European family. The Kawa people of the border area adjacent to Myanmar (Burma) speak a tongue of the Mon-Khmer branch of the Austroasiatic family. Speakers of languages in the Tai family are concentrated in southern Yunnan, notably in two autonomous prefectures—one whose population is related most closely to the Thai of northern Thailand and another whose Tai speakers are related to the Shan people of Myanmar. The Li of Hainan Island form a separate group whose dialects are related to the Tai and Austronesian languages. They share with the Miao people a district in the southern part of the island. A significant number of Koreans are concentrated in an autonomous prefecture in eastern Jilin along the North Korean border.

LINGUISTIC CHARACTERISTICS OF SINITIC (CHINESE) LANGUAGES

All modern Sinitic languages—i.e., the "Chinese dialects"—share a number of important typological features. They have a maximum syllabic structure of the type consonant–semivowel–vowel–semivowel–consonant. Some languages lack one set of semivowels, and, in some, gemination (doubling) or clustering of vowels occurs. The languages also employ a system of tones (pitch and contour), with or without concomitant glottal features, and occasionally stress. For the most part, tones are lexical (i.e., they distinguish otherwise similar words); in some languages tones also carry grammatical meaning. Nontonal grammatical units (i.e., affixes) may be smaller than syllables, but usually the meaningful units consist of one or more syllables. Words can consist of one syllable, of two or more syllables each carrying an element of meaning, or of two or more syllables that individually carry no meaning. For example, Modern Standard Chinese *tian* "sky, heaven, day" is a one-syllable word; *ritou* "sun" is composed of *ri* "sun, day," a word element that cannot occur alone as a word, and the noun suffix *tou*; and *hudie* "butterfly" consists of two syllables, each having no meaning in itself (this is a rare type of word formation). The southern languages have more monosyllabic words and word elements than the northern ones.

The Sinitic languages distinguish nouns and verbs with some overlapping, as do Sino-Tibetan languages in general. There are noun suffixes that form different kinds of nouns (concrete nouns, diminutives, abstract nouns, and so on), particles placed after nouns indicating relationships in time and space, and verb particles for modes and aspects. Adjectives act as one of several kinds of verbs. Verbs can occur in a series (concatenation) with irreversible order (e.g., the verbs "take" and "come" placed next to one another denote the concept "bring"). Nouns are collective in nature, and only classifiers can be counted and referred to singly. Specific particles are used to indicate the relationship of nominals (e.g., nouns and noun phrases) to verbs, such as transitive verb–object, agent–passive verb; in some of the languages this system forms a sentence construction called ergative, in which all nominals are marked for their function and the verb stays unchanged. Final sentence particles convey a variety of meanings (defining either the whole sentence or the predicate) that indicate "question, command, surprise, or new situation." The general word order of subject–verb–object and complement and modifier–modified is the same in all the languages, but the use of the preposed particles and verbs in a series varies considerably. Grammatical elements of equal or closely related values in various languages are very often not related in sounds.

The Sinitic languages fall into a northern and a southern group. The northern languages (Mandarin dialects) are more similar to each other than are the southern (Wu, Xiang, Gan, Hakka, Yue, Min).

MODERN STANDARD CHINESE (MANDARIN)

The pronunciation of Modern Standard Chinese is based on the Beijing dialect, which is of the northern, or Mandarin, type. It employs about 1,300 different syllables. There are 22 initial consonants, including stops (made with momentary, complete closure in the vocal tract), affricates (beginning as stops but ending with incomplete closure), aspirated consonants, nasals, fricatives, liquid sounds (*l*, *r*), and a glottal stop. The medial semivowels are *y* (*i*), *ɥ* (*ü*), and *w* (*u*). In final position, the following occur: nasal consonants, *ɹ* (retroflex r), the semivowels *y* and *w*, and the combinations *ŋr* (nasalization plus *r*) and *wr* (rounding plus *r*). There are nine vowel sounds, including three varieties of *i* (retroflex, apical, and palatal). Several vowels combine into clusters.

There are four tones: (1) high level, (2) high rising crescendo, (3) low falling diminuendo with glottal friction (with an extra rise from low to high when final), and (4) falling diminuendo. Unstressed syllables have a neutral tone, which depends on its surroundings for pitch. Tones in sequences of syllables that belong together lexically and syntactically ("sandhi groups") may undergo changes known as tonal sandhi, the most important of which causes a third tone before another third tone to be pronounced as a second tone. The tones influence some vowels (notably *e* and *o*), which are pronounced more open in third and fourth tones than in first and second tones.

A surprisingly low number of the possible combinations of all the consonantal, vocalic, and tonal sounds are utilized. The vowels *i* and *ü* and the semivowels *y* and *ɥ* never occur after velar sounds (e.g., *k*) and occur only after the palatalized affricate and sibilant sounds (e.g., *tś*), which in turn occur with no other vowels and semivowels.

Many alternative interpretations of the distinctive sounds of Chinese have been proposed; the interaction of consonants, vowels, semivowels, and tones sets Modern Standard Chinese apart from many other Sinitic languages and dialects and gives it a unique character among the major languages of the world. The most widely used transcription system (romanization) is the official Chinese transcription system, known as the *pinyin zimu* ("phonetic spelling") or simply Pinyin (adopted in 1958). The former system, Wade-Giles (first propounded by Sir Thomas Francis Wade in 1859 and later modified by Herbert A. Giles), marks aspiration by ' (*p'*, *t'*, and so on). The semivowels are *y*, *yü*, and *w* in initial position; *i*, *ü*, and *u* in medial; and *i* and *u* (but *o* after *a*) in final position. Final retroflex *r* is written *rh*. Wade-Giles indicated the tones by raised figures after the syllables (1, 2, 3, 4).

The Pinyin system, on the other hand, indicates unaspirated stops and affricates by means of traditionally voiced consonants (e.g., *b*, *d*) and aspirated consonants by voiceless sounds (e.g., *p*, *t*). The semivowels are *y*, *yu*, and *w* initially; *i*, *ü*, and *u* medially; and *i* and *u* (*o* after *a*) finally. Final retroflex *r* is written *r*. The tones are indicated by accent markers, 1 = ¯, 2 = ´, 3 = ˇ, 4 = ` (e.g., *mā, má, mǎ, mà* = Wade-Giles *ma1, ma2, ma3, ma4*).

Pinyin is used in the following discussion of Modern Standard Chinese grammar.

The most common suffixes that indicate nouns are -*zi* (as in *fangzi* "house"), and -*tou* (as in *mutou* "wood"). A set of postposed noun particles express space and time relationships (-*li* "inside," -*hou* "after"). An example of a verbal affix is -*jian* in *kanjian* "see" and *tingjian* "hear." Important verb particles are -*le* (completed action), -*guo* (past action), and -*zhe* (action in progress). The directional verbal particles -*lai* "toward speaker" and -*qu* "away from speaker" and some verbal suffixes can be combined with the potential particles *de* "can" and *bu* "cannot"—e.g., *na chulai* "take out," *na bu chulai* "cannot take out"; *tingjian* "hear," *ting de jian* "can hear." The particle *de* indicates subordination and also gives nominal value to forms for other parts of speech (e.g., *wo* "I," *wode* "mine," *wo de shu* "my book," *lai* "to come," *lai de ren* "a person who comes"). The most important sentence particle is *le*, indicating "new situation" (e.g., *xiayu le* "now it is raining," *bu lai le* "now there is no longer any chance that he will be coming"). *Ge* is the most common noun classifier (*i* "one," *yi ge ren* "one person"); others are *suo* (*yi suo fangzi* "one house") and *ben* (*liang ben shu* "two books").

Adjectives can be defined as qualitative verbs (*hao* "to be good") or stative verbs (*bing* "to be sick"). There are equational sentences with the word order subject–predicate—e.g., *wo shi Beijing ren* "I am a Beijing-person (i.e., a native of Beijing)"—and narrative sentences with the word order subject (or topic)–verb–object (or complement)—e.g., *wo chifan* "I eat rice," *wo zhu zai Beijing* "I live in Beijing." The preposed object takes the particle *ba* (*wo da ta* "I beat him," *wo ba ta dale yidun* "I gave him a beating"), and the agent of a passive construction takes *bei* (*wo bei ta dale yidun* "I was given a beating by him").

STANDARD CANTONESE

The most important representative of the Yue languages is Standard Cantonese of Canton, Hong Kong, and Macau. It has fewer initial consonants than Modern Standard Chinese (*p, t, ts, k* and the corresponding aspirated sounds *ph, th, tsh, kh; m, n, ŋ; f, s, h; l, y*), only one medial semivowel (*w*), more vowels than Modern Standard Chinese, six final consonants (*p, t, k, m, n, ŋ*), and two final semivowels (*y* and *w*). The nasals *m* and *ŋ* occur as syllables without a vowel.

There are three tones (high, mid, low) in syllables ending in -*p*, -*t*, and -*k*; six tones occur in other types of syllables (mid level, low level, high falling, low falling, high rising, low rising). Two tones are used to modify the meaning of words (high level °, and low-to-high rising *), as in *yin°* "tobacco" from *yin* "smoke," and *nöy** "daughter" from *nöy* "woman." Some special grammatical words also have the tone °. There is no neutral tone and little tonal sandhi (modification).

There are more than 2,200 different syllables in Standard Cantonese, or almost twice as many as in Modern

Standard Chinese. The word classes are the same as in Modern Standard Chinese. The grammatical words, although phonetically unrelated, generally have the same semantic value (e.g., the subordinating and nominalizing particle *kɛ*, Modern Standard Chinese *de; mo* "not," Modern Standard Chinese *bu*; the verbal particle for "completed action" and the sentence particle for "new situation," both *le* in Modern Standard Chinese, are Standard Cantonese *tsɔ* and *lɔ*, respectively). A classifier preceding a noun in subject position (before the verb) functions as a definite article (e.g., *tsek sün* "the boat").

MIN LANGUAGES

The most important Min language is Amoy (Xiamen) from the Southern branch of Min. The initial consonants are the same as in Standard Cantonese with the addition of two voiced stops (*b* and *d*) and one voiced affricate (*dz*), developed from original nasals. There are two semivowels (*y, w*), six vowels and several vowel clusters, plus the syllabic nasal sounds *m* and *ŋ* functioning as vowels, the same finals as in Standard Cantonese, and, in addition, a glottal stop (*ʔ*) and a meaning-bearing feature of nasalization, as well as a combination of the last two features. There are two tones in syllables ending in a stop, five in other syllables. Tonal sandhi operates in many combinations.

Fuzhou is the most important language of the Northern branch of Min. The very extensive sandhi affects not only tones but also consonants and vowels,

so that the phonetic manifestation of a syllable depends entirely on interaction with the surroundings. There are three initial labial sounds (*p, ph, m*), five dental sounds (*t, th, s, l, n*), three palatal sounds (*tś, tśh, ń*), and five velars (*k, kh, h, ʔ,* and *ŋ*). Syllables can end in -*k*, -*ŋ*, *ʔ* (glottal stop), a semivowel, or a vowel. The tones fall into two classes: a comparatively high class comprising high, mid, high falling, and high rising (only in sandhi forms) and a rather low one, comprising low rising and low rising-falling (circumflex). Certain vowels and diphthongs occur only with the high class, others occur only with the low class, and the vowel *a* occurs with both classes. Sandhi rules can cause tone to change from low class to high class, in which case the vowel also changes.

OTHER SINITIC LANGUAGES OR DIALECTS: HAKKA, WU (SUZHOU AND SHANGHAI), AND XIANG

Of the different Hakka dialects, Hakka of Meizhou (formerly Meixian) in Guangdong is best known. It has the same initial consonants, final consonants, and syllabic nasals as Standard Cantonese; the vowels are similar to those of Modern Standard Chinese. Medial and final semivowels are *y* and *w*. There are two tones in syllables with final stops, four in the other syllabic types.

Wu consists of a variety of Chinese dialects spoken in Shanghai, in southeastern Jiangsu province, and in Zhejiang province by more than 8 percent of the population of China (some 85 million people) at the turn of the 21st century. Major cities in which Wu is spoken include Hangzhou, Shanghai, Suzhou, Ningpo, and Wenzhou.

The Wu language originally spread from Suzhou, a cultural centre since the 5th century BCE, and gained great importance at least as early as the period of the Ming dynasty (1368–1644), when Shanghai became an important metropolitan area. Wu differs from Modern Standard Chinese in preserving the initial voiced stops (sounds formed with complete closure in the vocal tract) and in using seven or eight tones to distinguish meanings between words or word elements that have the same series of consonants and vowels. (Modern Standard Chinese uses only four tones for such a purpose.) Like Modern Standard Chinese and the Mandarin language of northern China, the Wu language has lost most of the Ancient Chinese final consonants.

Suzhou vernacular is usually quoted as representative of the Wu languages. It is rich in initial consonants, with a contrast of voiced and voiceless stops as well as palatalized and nonpalatalized dental affricates, making 26 consonants in all. (Palatalized sounds are formed from nonpalatal sounds by simultaneous movement of the tongue toward the hard palate. Dental affricates are sounds produced with the tongue tip at first touching the teeth and then drawing slightly away to allow air to pass through, producing a hissing sound.) Medial semivowels are as in Modern Standard Chinese. In addition,

there are also 10 vowels and 4 syllabic consonants (l, m, n, η); -n and -η occur in final position, as do the glottal stop and nasalization.

The Shanghai dialect belongs to Wu. The use of only two tones or registers (high and low) is prevalent; these are related in an automatic way to the initial consonant type (voiceless and voiced).

The Xiang languages, spoken only in Hunan, are divided into New Xiang, which is under heavy influence from Mandarin and includes the language of the capital Changsha, and Old Xiang, more similar to the Wu languages, as spoken for instance in Shuangfeng. Old Xiang has 28 initial consonants, the highest number for any major Sinitic language, and 11 vowels, plus the syllabic consonants m and n. It also uses five tones, final -n and -η, and nasalization, but no final stops.

HISTORICAL SURVEY OF CHINESE

For reconstructing the pronunciation of older stages of Sinitic, the Chinese writing system offers much less help than the alphabetic systems of such languages as Latin, Greek, and Sanskrit within Indo-European or Tibetan and Burmese within Sino-Tibetan. Therefore, the starting point must be a comparison of the modern Sinitic languages, with the view of recovering for each major language group the original common form, such as Proto-Mandarin for the northern languages and Proto-Wu and others for the languages south of the Yangtze River.

Reconstruction of Chinese Protolanguages

Because data are still lacking from a great many places, the once-standard approach to understanding ancient pronunciations was to compare major representatives of each group for the purpose of reconstructing the language of the important dictionary *Qieyun* of 601 CE (Sui dynasty). This dictionary mainly represents a southern language type. One difficulty is that the language in a given area represents a mixture of at least two layers: an older one of the original local type, antedating the language of the *Qieyun*, and a younger one that is descended from the *Qieyun* language or a slightly younger but closely related tongue—the so-called Tang koine, the standard spoken language of the Tang dynasty. The relationship of the protolanguages is further complicated by the different substrata of non-Chinese stock that underlie many if not most of the major languages.

The degree to which the Sinitic languages have been influenced by the Tang (or Middle Chinese) layer varies. In the North the Old Chinese layer still dominates in phonology; in Min the two layers are kept clearly apart from each other, and the Middle Chinese layer is most important in the reading pronunciation of the characters; Yue has two Chinese layers of the Southern type and is typologically similar to a Tai substratum.

The Old Chinese layer is characterized by early decay of final consonants, late development of tones from sounds or suprasegmental features located toward the end of the syllable, change of final articulation type because of similar initial type (as in syllables with more than one voiced activity, which may change or lose one of these; phenomena later manifested as a tonal change), and influence of sounds and tones in a syllable on those of surrounding ones (sandhi).

The New Southern stratum in Sinitic languages is characterized by early change of final articulation types into tones, extensive development of registers according to type of initial consonant, and late or no loss of final stops. The Old layer cannot be the direct ancestor of the New layer. The division into northern and southern dialects must be very old. It might be better to speak of a Tang and a pre-Tang layer, or a Tang and a Han layer (the Han dynasty was characterized by extensive settlement in most parts of what is now China proper).

Qieyun Dictionary

For a long time the *Qieyun* dictionary was assumed to represent the language of the capital of the Sui dynasty, Chang'an (in the present province of Shaanxi), but research has demonstrated that its major component was the language of the present-day Nanjing area with a certain attempt at compromise with other speech habits. As its first criterion for classifying syllables, the *Qieyun* takes the tones, of which it has four: *ping*, *shang* (here transcribed with a colon, as in *pa:*), *qu* (here transcribed with a hyphen, as in *pa-*), and *ru*, or even, rising, falling, and entering ("checked") tones. The entering tone comprised those syllables that ended in a stop (*-p, -t, -k*). The rising and falling tones may have retained traces of the phonetic conditioning factor of their origin, voiced and voiceless glottal or laryngeal features, respectively. The even tone probably was negatively defined as possessing no final stop and no tonal contour.

Next, the dictionary is divided according to rhymes, of which there are 61, and, finally, according to initial consonants. Inside each rhyme an interlocking spelling system known as *fanqie* was used to subdivide the rhymes. There were 32 initial consonants and 136 finals. The number of vowels is not certain, perhaps six plus *i* and *u*, which served also as medial semivowels. The dictionary contained probably more vowels than either Archaic Chinese or Modern Standard Chinese, another indication that the development of the Northern Chinese phonology did not pass the stage represented by *Qieyun*.

ADDITIONAL SOURCES

There are additional sources for reconstructing the *Qieyun* language: Chinese loanwords in Vietnamese, Korean, and Japanese (Japan has two different traditions—Go-on, slightly older than *Qieyun* but representing a southern language type like *Qieyun*, and Kan-on, contemporary with *Qieyun* but more similar to the northern tradition) and Chinese renderings of Indo-Aryan (Indic) words. Voiced stops are recovered through Wu, Xiang, and Go-on (e.g., Modern Standard Chinese *tian* "field," Wu and Xiang *di*, Go-on *den*, *Qieyun dhien*), final stops especially through Yue and Japanese (e.g., Modern Standard Chinese *mu* "wood," Yue *muk*, Go-on *mok* [*moku*], *Qieyun muk*), and retroflex initial sounds from Northern Chinese (e.g., Modern Standard Chinese *sheng* "to live," *Qieyun* ʂʌŋ [the ʂ is a retroflex]).

Early Archaic Chinese is the old stage for which the most information is known about the pronunciation of characters. The very system of borrowing characters to write phonetically related words gives important clues, and the rhymes and alliteration of the *Shijing* furnish a wealth of details. Even though scholars cannot always be sure that prefixes and infixes are correctly recovered, and though the order in which recoverable features were pronounced in the syllable is not always certain (*rk-* or *kr-*, *-wk* or *-kw*, and so on), enough details can be obtained to determine the typology of Old Chinese and to undertake comparative work with the Tibeto-Burman and Karenic languages. The method employed in this part of the reconstruction of Chinese has been predominantly internal reconstruction, the use of variation of word forms within a language to construct an older form. As knowledge of the old layer of modern languages and dialects increases, however, the comparative method, which draws on similarities in several related tongues, gains importance. Through further internal reconstruction, features of the Proto-Sinitic stage, antedating Archaic Chinese, can then be restored.

EARLY CONTACTS

Old Chinese vocabulary already contained many words not generally occurring in the other Sino-Tibetan languages. The words for "honey" and "lion," and probably also "horse," "dog," and "goose," are connected with Indo-European and were acquired through trade and early contacts. (The nearest known Indo-European languages were the Tocharian languages and Sogdian, a middle Iranian language.) A number of words have Austroasiatic cognates and point to early contacts with the ancestral language of Muong-Vietnamese and Mon-Khmer—e.g., the name of the Yangtze River, *kruŋ*, is still the word for "river"—Cantonese *kɔŋ*, Modern Standard Chinese *jiang*, pronounced *kroŋ* and *kloŋ* in some modern Mon-Khmer languages. Words for "tiger," "ivory," and "crossbow" are also Austroasiatic. The names of the key terms of the Chinese calendar ("the branches") have this same non-Chinese origin. It has been suggested that a great many cultural words that are shared by Chinese and Tai are Chinese loanwords from Tai. Clearly, the Chinese received many aspects of culture and many concepts from the Austroasiatic and Austro-Tai peoples whom they gradually conquered and absorbed or expelled.

From the 1st century CE, China's contacts with India, especially through the adoption of Buddhism, led to Chinese borrowing from Indo-Aryan (Indic) languages, but, very early, native Chinese equivalents were invented. Sinitic languages have been remarkably resistant to direct borrowing of foreign words. In modern times this has led to an enormous increase in Chinese vocabulary without a corresponding increase in basic meaningful syllables. For instance, *tielu* "railroad" is based on the same concept expressed in the French *chemin de fer*, using *tie* "iron" and *lu* "road"; likewise, *dianhua* "telephone" is a compound of *dian* "lightning, electricity" and *hua* "speech." A number of such words were coined first in Japanese by means of Chinese elements and then borrowed back into Chinese. The reason that China has avoided the incorporation of foreign words is first and foremost a phonetic one; such words fit very badly into the Chinese pattern of pronunciation. A contributing factor has been the Chinese script, which is ill-adapted to the process of phonetic loans. In creating new words for new ideas, the characters have sometimes been determined first and forms have arisen that cannot be spoken without ambiguity ("sulfur" and "lutecium" coalesced as *liu*, "nitrogen" and "tantalum" as *dan*). It is characteristic of Modern Standard Chinese that the language from which it most freely borrows is one from its own past: Classical Chinese. In recent years it has borrowed from Southern Sinitic languages under the influence of statesmen and revolutionaries (Chiang Kai-shek was originally a Wu speaker and Mao Zedong a Xiang speaker). Influence from English and Russian (in word formation and syntax) has been increasingly felt.

PRE-CLASSICAL CHINESE

The history of the Chinese language can be divided into three periods, pre-Classical (*c.* 1500 BCE–*c.* 200 CE), Classical (*c.* 200–*c.* 1920), and post-Classical Chinese (with important forerunners as far back as the Tang dynasty).

The pre-Classical period is further divided into Oracular Chinese (Shang dynasty [*c.* 1600–1046 BCE]), Archaic Chinese (Zhou and Qin dynasties [1046–207 BCE]), and Han Chinese (Han dynasty [206 BCE–220 CE]).

Oracular Chinese is known only from rather brief oracle inscriptions on bones and tortoise shells. Archaic Chinese falls into Early, Middle (*c.* 800–*c.* 400 BCE), and Late Archaic. Early Archaic is represented by bronze inscriptions, parts of the *Shujing* ("Classic of History"), and parts of the *Shijing* ("Classic of Poetry"). From this period on, many important features of the pronunciation of the Chinese characters have been reconstructed. The grammar depended to a certain extent on unwritten affixes. The writing system kept apart forms with or without medial consonants, which in some cases were meaningful infixes. Early Archaic Chinese possessed a third-person personal pronoun in three cases (nominative and genitive *gyəg*, accusative *tyəg*, and another special genitive *kywat*, used only

with concepts intimately connected with the owner). No other kind of written Chinese until the post-Classical period possessed a nominative of the third-person pronoun, but the old form survived in Cantonese (*khöy*) and is probably also found in Tai (Modern Thai *khǎw*).

Middle Archaic Chinese is the language of some of the earliest writings of the Confucian school. Important linguistic changes that had occurred between the Early and Middle phases became still more pronounced in Late Archaic, the language of the two major Confucian and Daoist writers, Mencius (Mengzi) and Zhuangzi, as well as of other important philosophers. The grammar by then had become more explicit in the writing system, with a number of well-defined grammatical particles, and it can also be assumed that the use of grammatical affixes had similarly declined. The process used in verb formation and verb inflection that later appeared as tonal differences may at this stage have been manifested as final consonants or as suprasegmental features, such as different types of laryngeal phonation. The word classes included nouns, verbs, and pronouns (each with several subclasses), and particles. The use of a consistent system of grammatical particles to form noun modifiers, verb modifiers, and several types of embedded sentences (i.e., sentences that are made to become parts of another independent sentence) became blurred in Han Chinese and was gone from written Chinese until the emergence of post-Classical

Chinese. In Modern Standard Chinese the subordinating particle *de* combines the functions of several Late Archaic Chinese particles, and the verb particle *le* and the homophonous sentence particle *le* have taken over for other Late Archaic forms.

HAN AND CLASSICAL CHINESE

Han Chinese developed more polysyllabic words and more specific verbal and nominal (noun) categories of words. Most traces of verb formation and verb conjugation began to disappear. An independent southern tradition (on the Yangtze River), simultaneous with Late Archaic Chinese, developed a special style, used in the poetry *Chuci* ("Elegies of Chu"), which was the main source for the refined *fu* (prose poetry). Late Han Chinese developed into Classical Chinese, which as a written idiom underwent few changes during the long span of time it was used. It was an artificial construct, which for different styles and occasions borrowed freely and heavily from any period of pre-Classical Chinese but in numerous cases without real understanding for the meaning and function of the words borrowed.

At the same time the spoken language changed continually, as did the conventions for pronouncing the written characters. Soon Classical Chinese made little sense when read aloud. It depended heavily on fixed word order and on rhythmical and parallel passages.

It has sometimes been denied the status of a real language, but it was certainly one of the most successful means of communication in human history. It was the medium in which the poets Li Bai (701–762) and Du Fu (712–770) and the prose writer Han Yu (768–824) created some of the greatest masterpieces of all times and was the language of Neo-Confucianist philosophy (especially of Zhu Xi [1130–1200]), which was to influence the West deeply. Classical Chinese was also the language in which the Italian Jesuit missionary Matteo Ricci (1552–1610) wrote in his attempt to convert the Chinese empire to Christianity.

POST-CLASSICAL CHINESE

Post-Classical Chinese, based on dialects very similar to the language now spoken in North China, probably owes its origin to the Buddhist storytelling tradition; the tales appeared in translations from Sanskrit during the Tang dynasty (618–907). During the Song dynasty (960–1279) this vernacular language was used by both Buddhists and Confucianists for polemic writings; it also appeared in indigenous Chinese novels based on popular storytelling. During and after the Yuan dynasty (1206–1368) the vernacular was used also in the theatre.

Modern Standard Chinese has a threefold origin: the written post-Classical language, the spoken standard of Imperial times (Mandarin), and the vernacular language of Beijing. These

Matteo Ricci (left), *Jesuit missionary to China, is shown with his first convert.* Hulton Archive/Getty Images

idioms were clearly related originally, and combining them for the purpose of creating a practical national language was a task that largely solved itself once the signal had been given. The term National Language (*guoyu*) had been borrowed from Japanese at the beginning of the 20th century, and, from 1915, various committees considered the practical implications of promoting it. The deciding event was the action of the May Fourth Movement of 1919; at the instigation of the liberal savant Hu Shi, Classical Chinese (also known as *wenyan*) was rejected as the standard written language. (Hu Shi also led the vernacular literature movement of 1917; his program for literary reform appeared on Jan. 1, 1917.) The new written idiom has gained ground faster in literature than in science, but there can be no doubt that the days of Classical Chinese as a living medium are numbered. After the establishment of the People's Republic of China, some government regulation was applied successfully, and the tremendous task of making Modern Standard Chinese understood throughout China was effectively undertaken. In what must have been the largest-scale linguistic plan in history, untold millions of Chinese, whose mother tongues were divergent Mandarin or non-Mandarin languages or non-Chinese languages, learned to speak and understand the National Language, or Putonghua, a name it is now commonly called; with this effort, literacy was imparted to great numbers of people in all age groups.

THE CHINESE WRITING SYSTEM

The Chinese writing system is non-alphabetic. It applies a specific character to write each meaningful syllable or each nonmeaningful syllabic that is part of a polysyllabic word.

PRE-CLASSICAL CHARACTERS

When the Chinese script first appeared, as used for writing Oracular Chinese (from c. 1500 BCE), it must already have undergone considerable development. Although many of the characters can be recognized as originally depicting some object, many are no longer recognizable. The characters did not indicate the object in a primitive nonlinguistic way but only represented a specific word of the Chinese language (e.g., a picture of the phallic altar to the earth is used only to write the word *earth*). It is therefore misleading to characterize the Chinese script as pictographic or ideographic; nor is it truly syllabic, for syllables that sound alike but have different meanings are written differently. Logographic (i.e., marked by a letter, symbol, or sign used to represent an entire word) is the term that best describes the nature of the Chinese writing system.

Verbs and nouns are written by what are or were formerly pictures, often consisting of several elements (e.g., the character for "to love" depicts a woman and a child; the character for "beautiful" is a picture of a man with a huge headdress with ram's horns on top). The exact meaning of the word is rarely deducible from even a clearly recognizable picture, because the connotations are either too broad or too narrow for the word's precise meaning. For example, the picture "relationship of mother to child" includes more facets than "love," a concept that, of course, is not restricted to the mother-child relation, and a man adorned with ram's horns undoubtedly had other functions than that of being handsome to look at, whereas the concept "beautiful" is applicable also to men in other situations, as well as to women. Abstract nouns are indicated by means of concrete associations. The character for "peace, tranquility" consists of a somewhat stylized form of the elements "roof," "heart," and "(wine) cup." Abstract symbols have been used to indicate numbers and local relationships.

Related words with similar pronunciations were usually written by one and the same character (the character for "to love, to consider someone good" is a derivative of a similarly written word "to be good"). This gave rise to the most important invention in the development of the Chinese script—that of writing a word by means of another one with the same or similar pronunciation. A picture of a carpenter's square was primarily used for writing "work, craftsman; to work" and was pronounced *kuŋ*; secondarily it was used to write *kuŋ-* (the hyphen stands for an element that was perhaps *s*) "to present," *guŋ* "red," *kuŋ* "rainbow," and *kruŋ* "river." During the Archaic period this practice was developed to such a degree that too

many words came to be written as one and the same character. In imitation of the characters that already consisted of several components an element was added for each meaning of a character to distinguish words from each other. Thus "red" was no longer written with a single component but acquired an additional component that added the element "silk" on the left; "river" acquired an additional component of "water." The original part of the character is referred to as its phonetic and the added element as its radical.

QIN DYNASTY STANDARDIZATION

During the Qin dynasty (221–207 BCE) the first government standardization of the characters took place, carried out by the statesman Li Si. A new, somewhat formalized style known as seals was introduced—a form that generally has survived until now, with only such minor modifications as were necessitated by the introduction of the writing brush about the beginning of the 1st century CE and printing about 600 CE. As times progressed, other styles of writing appeared, such as the regular handwritten form *kai* (as opposed to the formal or scribe style *li*), the running hand *xing*, and the cursive hand *cao*, all of which in their various degrees of blurredness are explicable only in terms of the seal characters.

The Qin dynasty standardization comprised more than 3,000 characters. In addition to archaeological finds, the most important source for the early history of Chinese characters is the huge dictionary *Shuowen jiezi*, compiled by Xu Shen about 100 CE. This work contains 9,353 characters, a number that certainly exceeds that which it was or ever became necessary to know offhand. Still, a great proliferation of characters took place at special times and for special purposes. The *Guangyun* dictionary of 1008 had 26,194 characters (representing 3,877 different syllables in pronunciation). The *Kangxi zidian*, a dictionary of 1716, contains 40,545 characters, of which, however, fewer than one-fourth were in actual use at the time. The number of absolutely necessary characters has probably never been much more than 4,000–5,000 and is today estimated at fewer than that.

TWENTIETH CENTURY

By the 20th century the feeling had become very strong that the script was too cumbersome and an impediment to progress. The desire to obtain a new writing system necessarily worked hand in hand with the growing wish to develop a written language that in grammar and vocabulary approached modern spoken Chinese. If a phonetic writing system were to be introduced, the classical language could not be used at all because it deviates so markedly from the modern language. None of the earlier attempts gained any following, but in 1919 a system of phonetic letters (inspired by the Japanese syllabaries called *kana*) was devised for writing Mandarin. (In 1937 it received formal backing from the government, but World War II stopped further progress.) In 1929 a National Romanization, worked out by the author and language scholar Lin Yutang, the linguist Zhao Yuanren, and others, was adopted. This attempt also was halted by war and revolution. A rival Communist effort known as *Latinxua*, or Latinization of 1930, fared no better. An attempt to simplify the language by reducing the number of characters to about 1,000 failed because it did not solve the problems of creating a corresponding "basic Chinese" that could profitably be written by the reduced number of symbols.

The government of China took several important steps toward solving the problems of the Chinese writing system. The first and basic step of making one language, Modern Standard Chinese, known throughout the country has been described on p. 60. In 1956 a simplification of the characters was introduced that made them easier to learn and faster to write. Most of the abridged characters were well-known unofficial variants, used in handwriting but previously not in printing; some were innovations. In 1958 the previously mentioned romanization known as *pinyin zimu* was introduced. This system is widely taught in the schools and is used for many transcription purposes and for teaching Modern Standard Chinese to non-Han Chinese peoples in China and to foreigners. Pinyin romanization, however, is not intended to replace the Chinese characters but to help teach pronunciation and popularize the Beijing-dialect-based Putonghua.

CHAPTER 4

CONFUCIANISM

The story of Confucianism does not begin with Confucius (Kongfuzi; 551–479 BCE). Nor was Confucius the founder of Confucianism in the sense that Buddha was the founder of Buddhism and Christ the founder of Christianity. Rather, Confucius considered himself a transmitter who consciously tried to reanimate the old in order to attain the new.

Confucius was China's most famous teacher, philosopher, and political theorist, whose ideas have influenced the civilization of East Asia.

Confucius's life, in contrast to his tremendous importance, seems starkly undramatic, or, as a Chinese expression has it, it seems "plain and real." The plainness and reality of Confucius's life, however, underlines that his humanity was not revealed truth but an expression of self-cultivation, of the ability of human effort to shape its own destiny. The faith in the possibility of ordinary human beings to become awe-inspiring sages and worthies is deeply rooted in the Confucian heritage, and the insistence that human beings are teachable, improvable, and perfectible through personal and communal endeavour is typically Confucian.

Although the facts about Confucius's life are scanty, they do establish a precise time frame and historical context. Confucius was born in the 22nd year of the reign of Duke Xiang of Lu (551 BCE). The traditional claim that he was born on the 27th day of the eighth lunar month has been questioned by historians, but September 28 is still widely observed in East

Asia as Confucius's birthday. It is an official holiday, "Teachers' Day," in Taiwan.

Confucius was born in Qufu in the small feudal state of Lu in what is now Shandong province, which was noted for its preservation of the traditions of ritual and music of the Zhou civilization. His family name was Kong and his personal name Qiu, but he is referred to as either Kongzi or Kongfuzi (Master Kong) throughout Chinese history. The adjectival "Confucian," derived from the Latinized Confucius, is not a meaningful term in Chinese, nor is the term Confucianism, which was coined in Europe as recently as the 18th century.

Confucius's ancestors were probably members of the aristocracy who had become virtual poverty-stricken commoners by the time of his birth. His father died when Confucius was only three years old. Instructed first by his mother, Confucius then distinguished himself as an indefatigable learner in his teens. He recalled toward the end of his life that at age 15 his heart was set upon learning. A historical account notes that, even though he was already known as an informed young scholar, he felt it appropriate to inquire about everything while visiting the Grand Temple.

Confucius had served in minor government posts managing stables and keeping books for granaries before he married a woman of similar background when he was 19. It is not known who Confucius's teachers were, but he made a conscientious effort to find the right masters to teach him, among

other things, ritual and music. His mastery of the six arts—ritual, music, archery, charioteering, calligraphy, and arithmetic—and his familiarity with the classical traditions, notably poetry and history, enabled him to start a brilliant teaching career in his 30s.

Confucius is known as the first teacher in China who wanted to make education broadly available and who was instrumental in establishing the art of teaching as a vocation, indeed as a way of life. Before Confucius, aristocratic families had hired tutors to educate their sons in specific arts, and government officials had instructed their subordinates in the necessary techniques, but he was the first person to devote his whole life to learning and teaching for the purpose of transforming and improving society. He believed that all human beings could benefit from self-cultivation. He inaugurated a humanities program for potential leaders, opened the doors of education to all, and defined learning not merely as the acquisition of knowledge but also as character building.

For Confucius the primary function of education was to provide the proper way of training exemplary persons (junzi), a process that involved constant self-improvement and continuous social interaction. Although he emphatically noted that learning was "for the sake of the self" (the end of which was self-knowledge and self-realization), he found public service integral to true education. Confucius confronted learned hermits who challenged the validity of his desire to serve the world; he resisted the temptation to "herd with birds and animals," to live apart from the human community, and opted to try to transform the world from within. For decades Confucius tried to be actively involved in politics, wishing to put his humanist ideas into practice through governmental channels.

In his late 40s and early 50s Confucius served first as a magistrate, then as an assistant minister of public works, and eventually as minister of justice in the state of Lu. It is likely that he accompanied King Lu as his chief minister on one of the diplomatic missions. Confucius's political career was, however, short-lived. His loyalty to the king alienated him from the power holders of the time, the large Ji families, and his moral rectitude did not sit well with the king's inner circle, who enraptured the king with sensuous delight. At 56, when he realized that his superiors were uninterested in his policies, Confucius left the country in an attempt to find another feudal state to which he could render his service. Despite his political frustration he was accompanied by an expanding circle of students during this self-imposed exile of almost 12 years. His reputation as a man of vision and mission spread. A guardian of a border post once characterized him as the "wooden tongue for a bell" of the age, sounding heaven's prophetic note to awaken the people (Analects, 3:24). Indeed, Confucius was perceived as the heroic conscience who knew realistically that he might not succeed but, fired by a righteous passion, continuously did the

best he could. At the age of 67 he returned home to teach and to preserve his cherished classical traditions by writing and editing. He died in 479 BCE, at the age of 73. According to the *Records of the Historian*, 72 of his students mastered the "six arts," and those who claimed to be his followers numbered 3,000.

THOUGHT OF CONFUCIUS

Confucius proposed revitalizing the meaning of the past by advocating a ritualized life. His love of antiquity was motivated by his strong desire to understand why certain life forms and institutions, such as reverence for ancestors, human-centred religious practices, and mourning ceremonies, had survived for centuries. His journey into the past was a search for roots, which he perceived as grounded in humanity's deepest needs for belonging and communicating. He had faith in the cumulative power of culture. The fact that traditional ways had lost vitality did not, for him, diminish their potential for regeneration in the future. In fact, Confucius's sense of history was so strong that he saw himself as a conservationist responsible for the continuity of the cultural values and the social norms that had worked so well for the idealized civilization of the Western Zhou dynasty.

HISTORICAL CONTEXT

The scholarly tradition envisioned by Confucius can be traced to the sage-kings of antiquity. Although the earliest dynasty confirmed by archaeology is the Shang dynasty (c. 1600–1046 BCE), the historical period that Confucius claimed as relevant was much earlier. Confucius may have initiated a cultural process known in the West as Confucianism, but he and those who followed him considered themselves part of a tradition, later identified by Chinese historians as the *rujia*, "scholarly tradition," that had its origins two millennia previously, when the legendary sages Yao and Shun created a civilized world through moral persuasion.

Confucius's hero was Zhougong, or the duke of Zhou (d. 1094 BCE), who was said to have helped consolidate, expand, and refine the "feudal" ritual system. This elaborate system of mutual dependence was based on blood ties, marriage alliances, and old covenants as well as on newly negotiated contracts. The appeal to cultural values and social norms for the maintenance of interstate as well as domestic order was predicated on a shared political vision, namely, that authority lies in universal kingship, heavily invested with ethical and religious power by the "mandate of heaven" (*tianming*), and that social solidarity is achieved not by legal constraint but by ritual observance. Its implementation enabled the Western Zhou dynasty to survive in relative peace and prosperity for more than five centuries.

Inspired by the statesmanship of Zhougong, Confucius harboured a lifelong dream to be in a position to emulate

This Qing dynasty statuette shows Confucius as a Mandarin, or public official. Musee Guimet, Paris, France/The Bridgeman Art Library/Getty Images

the duke by putting into practice the political ideas that he had learned from the ancient sages and worthies. Although Confucius never realized his political dream, his conception of politics as moral persuasion became more and more influential.

The concept of "heaven" (*tian*), unique in Zhou cosmology, was compatible with that of the Lord on High

(Shangdi) in the Shang dynasty. Lord on High may have referred to the ancestral progenitor of the Shang royal lineage, but heaven to the Zhou kings, although also ancestral, was a more generalized anthropomorphic god. The Zhou belief in the mandate of heaven (the functional equivalent of the will of the Lord on High) differed from the divine right of kings in that there was no guarantee that the descendants of the Zhou royal house would be entrusted with kingship, for, as written in the *Shujing* ("Classic of History"), "heaven sees as the people see [and] hears as the people hear"; thus the virtues of the kings were essential for the maintenance of their power and authority. This emphasis on benevolent rulership, expressed in numerous bronze inscriptions, was both a reaction to the collapse of the Shang dynasty and an affirmation of a deep-rooted worldview.

Partly because of the vitality of the feudal ritual system and partly because of the strength of the royal household itself, the Zhou kings were able to control their kingdom for several centuries. In 771 BCE, however, they were forced to move their capital eastward to present-day Luoyang to avoid barbarian attacks from Central Asia. Real power thereafter passed into the hands of feudal lords. Since the surviving line of the Zhou kings continued to be recognized in name, they still managed to exercise some measure of symbolic control. By Confucius's time, however, the feudal ritual system had been so fundamentally undermined that the political crises also precipitated a profound sense of moral decline: the centre of symbolic control could no longer hold the kingdom, which had devolved from centuries of civil war into 14 feudal states.

Confucius's response was to address himself to the issue of learning to be human. In so doing he attempted to redefine and revitalize the institutions that for centuries had been vital to political stability and social order: the family, the school, the local community, the state, and the kingdom. Confucius did not accept the status quo, which held that wealth and power spoke the loudest. He felt that virtue, both as a personal quality and as a requirement for leadership, was essential for individual dignity, communal solidarity, and political order.

ANALECTS

The *Lunyu* (*Analects*), the most revered sacred scripture in the Confucian tradition, was probably compiled by the succeeding generations of Confucius's disciples. Based primarily on the Master's sayings, preserved in both oral and written transmissions, it captures the Confucian spirit in form and content in the same way that the Platonic dialogues embody Socratic pedagogy.

The *Analects* has often been viewed by the critical modern reader as a collection of unrelated reflections randomly put together. This impression may have resulted from the unfortunate perception of Confucius as a mere commonsense moralizer who gave practical advice to students in everyday situations. If readers approach the *Analects* as a communal memory, a literary device on the part of those who considered themselves beneficiaries of the Confucian Way to continue the Master's memory and to transmit his form of life as a living tradition, they come close to why it has been so revered in China for centuries. Interchanges with various historical figures and his disciples are used to show Confucius in thought and action, not as an isolated individual but as the centre of relationships. Actually the sayings of the *Analects* reveal Confucius's personality—his ambitions, his fears, his joys, his commitments, and above all his self-knowledge.

The purpose, then, in compiling these distilled statements centring on Confucius seems not to have been to present an argument or to record an event but to offer an invitation to readers to take part in an ongoing conversation. Through the *Analects* Confucians for centuries learned to reenact the awe-inspiring ritual of participating in a conversation with Confucius.

One of Confucius's most significant personal descriptions is the short autobiographical account of his spiritual development found in the *Analects*:

> *At 15 I set my heart on learning; at 30 I firmly took my stand; at 40 I had no delusions; at 50 I knew the mandate of heaven; at 60 my ear was attuned; at 70 I followed my heart's desire without overstepping the boundaries. (2:4)*

Confucius's life as a student and teacher exemplified his idea that education was a ceaseless process of self-realization. When one of his students reportedly had difficulty describing him, Confucius came to his aid:

> *Why did you not simply say something to this effect: he is the sort of man who forgets to eat when he engages himself in vigorous pursuit of learning, who is so full of joy that he forgets his worries, and who does not notice that old age is coming on? (7:18)*

Confucius was deeply concerned that the culture (*wen*) he cherished was not being transmitted and that the learning (*xue*) he propounded was not being taught. His strong sense of mission, however, never interfered with his ability to remember what had been imparted to him, to learn without flagging, and to teach without growing weary. What he demanded of himself was strenuous:

> *It is these things that cause me concern: failure to cultivate virtue, failure to go deeply into what I have learned, inability to move up to what I have heard to be right, and inability to reform myself when I have defects. (7:3)*

What he demanded of his students was the willingness to learn: "I do not enlighten anyone who is not eager to learn, nor encourage anyone who is not anxious to put his ideas into words (7:8).

The community that Confucius created was a scholarly fellowship of like-minded men of different ages and different backgrounds from different states. They were attracted to Confucius because they shared his vision and to varying degrees took part in his mission to bring moral order to an increasingly fragmented world. This mission was difficult and even dangerous. Confucius himself suffered from joblessness, homelessness, starvation, and occasionally life-threatening violence. Yet his faith in the survivability of the culture that he cherished and the workability of the approach to teaching that he propounded was so steadfast that he convinced his followers as well as himself that heaven was on their side. When Confucius's life was threatened in Kuang, he said:

> *Since the death of King Wen [founder of the Zhou dynasty] does not the mission of culture (wen) rest here in me? If heaven intends this culture to be destroyed, those who come after me will not be able to have any part of it. If heaven does not intend this culture to be destroyed, then what can the men of Kuang do to me? (9:5)*

This expression of self-confidence informed by a powerful sense of mission may give the impression that there was presumptuousness in Confucius's self-image. Confucius, however, made it explicit that he was far from attaining sagehood and that all he really excelled in was "love of learning" (5:27). To him, learning not only broadened his knowledge and deepened his self-awareness but also defined who he was. He frankly admitted that he was not born endowed with knowledge, nor did he belong to the class of men who could transform society without knowledge. Rather, he reported that he used his ears widely and followed what was good in what he had heard and used his eyes widely and retained in his mind what he had seen. His learning constituted "a lower level of knowledge" (7:27), a practical level that was presumably accessible to the majority of human beings. In this sense Confucius was neither a prophet with privileged access to the divine nor a philosopher who had already seen the truth but a teacher of humanity who was also an advanced fellow traveler on the way to self-realization.

As a teacher of humanity Confucius stated his ambition in terms of concern for human beings: "To bring comfort to the old, to have trust in friends, and to cherish the young" (5:25). Confucius's vision of the way to develop a moral community began with a holistic reflection on the human condition. Instead of dwelling on abstract speculations such as man's condition in the state of nature, Confucius sought to understand the actual situation of a given time and to use that as his point of departure. His aim was to restore trust in government and to transform society into a flourishing moral community by cultivating a sense of humanity in politics and society. To achieve that aim, the creation of a scholarly community, the fellowship of *junzi* (exemplary persons), was essential. In the words of Confucius's disciple Zengzi, exemplary persons

> must be broad-minded and resolute, for their burden is heavy and their road is long. They take humanity as their burden. Is that not heavy? Only with death does their road come to an end. Is that not long? (8:7)

The fellowship of *junzi* as moral vanguards of society, however, did not seek to establish a radically different order. Its mission was to redefine and revitalize those institutions that for centuries were believed to have maintained social solidarity and enabled people to live in harmony and prosperity. An obvious example of such an institution was the family.

It is related in the *Analects* that Confucius, when asked why he did not take part in government, responded by citing a passage from the ancient *Shujing* ("Classic of History"), "Simply by being a good son and friendly to his brothers a man can exert an influence upon government!" to show that what a person does in the confines of his home is politically significant (2:21). This maxim is based on the Confucian conviction that cultivation of the self is the root of social order and that social order is the basis for political stability and enduring peace.

The assertion that family ethics is politically efficacious must be seen in the context of the Confucian conception of politics as "rectification" (*zheng*). Rulers should begin by rectifying their own conduct; that is, they are to be examples who govern by moral leadership and exemplary teaching rather than by force. Government's responsibility is not only to provide food and security but also to educate the people. Law and punishment are the minimum requirements for order; the higher goal of social harmony, however, can only be attained by virtue expressed through ritual performance. To perform rituals, then, is to take part in a communal act to promote mutual understanding.

One of the fundamental Confucian values that ensures the integrity of ritual performance is *xiao* (filial piety). Indeed, Confucius saw filial piety as the first step toward moral excellence, which he believed lay in the attainment of the cardinal virtue, *ren* (humanity). To learn to embody the family in the mind and heart is to become able to move beyond self-centredness or, to borrow from modern psychology, to transform the enclosed private ego into an open self. Filial piety, however, does not demand unconditional submissiveness to parental authority but recognition of and reverence for the source of life. The purpose of filial piety, as the ancient Greeks expressed it, is to enable both parent and child to flourish.

Confucians see it as an essential way of learning to be human.

Confucians, moreover, are fond of applying the family metaphor to the community, the country, and the cosmos. They prefer to address the emperor as the son of heaven (*tianzi*), the king as ruler-father, and the magistrate as the father-mother official because to them the family-centred nomenclature implies a political vision. When Confucius said that taking care of family affairs is itself active participation in politics, he had already made it clear that family ethics is not merely a private concern; the public good is realized by and through it.

Confucius defined the process of becoming human as being able to "discipline yourself and return to ritual" (12:1). The dual focus on the transformation of the self (Confucius is said to have freed himself from four things: "opinionatedness, dogmatism, obstinacy, and egoism" [9:4]) and on social participation enabled Confucius to be loyal (*zhong*) to himself and considerate (*shu*) of others (4:15). It is easy to understand why the Confucian "golden rule" is "Do not do unto others what you would not want others to do unto you!" (15:23). Confucius's legacy, laden with profound ethical implications, is captured by his "plain and real" appreciation that learning to be human is a communal enterprise:

Persons of humanity, in wishing to establish themselves, also establish others, and in wishing to enlarge themselves, also enlarge others. The ability to take as analogy what is near at hand can be called the method of humanity. (6:30)

FORMATION OF THE CLASSICAL CONFUCIAN TRADITION

According to Hanfeizi (d. 233 BCE), shortly after Confucius's death his followers split into eight distinct schools, all claiming to be the legitimate heir to the Confucian legacy. Presumably each school was associated with or inspired by one or more of Confucius's disciples. Yet the Confucians did not exert much influence in the 5th century BCE. Although the reverent Yan Yuan (or Yan Hui), the faithful Zengzi, the talented Zigong, the erudite Zixia, and others may have generated a great deal of enthusiasm among the second generation of Confucius's students, it was not at all clear at the time that the Confucian tradition was to emerge as the most powerful one in Chinese history.

Mencius (Mengzi; c. 371–c. 289 BCE) complained that the world of thought in the early Warring States period (475–221 BCE) was dominated by the collectivism of Mozi and the individualism of Yang Zhu (440–c. 360 BCE). The historical situation a century after Confucius's death clearly shows that the Confucian attempt to moralize politics was not working; the disintegration of the Zhou feudal ritual system and the rise of powerful hegemonic states reveal that wealth and power spoke the loudest. The hermits (the early Daoists), who left the world to create a sanctuary in nature in order to lead a contemplative life, and the realists (proto-Legalists), who played the dangerous game of assisting ambitious kings to gain wealth and power so that they could influence the political process, were actually determining the intellectual agenda. The Confucians refused to be identified with the interests of the ruling minority because their social consciousness impelled them to serve as the conscience of the people. They were in a dilemma. Although they wanted to be actively involved in politics, they could not accept the status quo as the legitimate arena in which to exercise authority and power. In short, they were in the world but not of it; they could not leave the world, nor could they effectively change it.

MENCIUS: THE PARADIGMATIC CONFUCIAN INTELLECTUAL

Mencius is known as the self-styled transmitter of the Confucian Way. Educated first by his mother and then allegedly by a student of Confucius's grandson, Mencius brilliantly performed his role as a social critic, a moral philosopher, and a political activist. He argued that cultivating a class of scholar-officials who would not be directly involved in agriculture, industry, and commerce was vital to the well-being of the state. In his sophisticated argument against the physiocrats (those who advocated the supremacy of agriculture), he intelligently employed the idea of the division of labour to defend those who labour with their minds, observing that service is as important as productivity. To him Confucians served the vital interests of the state as scholars not by becoming bureaucratic functionaries but by assuming the responsibility of teaching the ruling minority humane government (*renzheng*) and the kingly way (*wangdao*). In dealing with feudal lords, Mencius conducted himself not merely as a political adviser but also as a teacher of kings. Mencius made it explicit that a true person cannot be corrupted by wealth, subdued by power, or affected by poverty.

To articulate the relationship between Confucian moral idealism and the concrete social and political realities of his time, Mencius began by exposing as impractical the prevailing ideologies of Mozi's collectivism and Yang Zhu's individualism. Mozi's collectivism rested on the advocacy of loving everyone. Mencius contended, however, that the result of the Mohist admonition to treat a stranger as intimately as one's own father would be to treat one's own father as indifferently as one would treat a stranger. Yang Zhu, on the other hand, advocated the primacy of the self. Mencius contended, however, that excessive attention to self-interest would lead to political disorder.

Indeed, in Mohist collectivism fatherhood becomes a meaningless concept, and so does kingship in Yang Zhu's individualism.

Mencius's strategy for social reform was to change the language of profit, self-interest, wealth, and power by making it part of a moral discourse, with emphasis on rightness, public-spiritedness, welfare, and influence. Mencius, however, was not arguing against profit. Rather, he instructed the feudal lords to look beyond the narrow horizon of their palaces and to cultivate a common bond with their ministers, officers, clerks, and the seemingly undifferentiated masses. Only then, Mencius contended, would they be able to preserve their profit, self-interest, wealth, and power. He encouraged them to extend their benevolence and warned them that this was crucial for the protection of their families.

Mencius's appeal to the common bond among all people as a mechanism of government was predicated on his strong "populist" sense that the people are more important than the state and the state more important than the king and that the ruler who does not act in accordance with the kingly way is unfit to rule. Mencius insisted that an unfit ruler should be criticized, rehabilitated, or, as the last resort, deposed. Since "heaven sees as the people see; heaven hears as the people hear," revolution, or literally the change of the mandate (*geming*), in severe cases is not only justifiable but is a moral imperative.

Mencius's "populist" conception of politics was predicated on his philosophical vision that human beings can perfect themselves through effort and that human nature (*xing*) is good. While he acknowledged the role of biological and environmental factors in shaping the human condition, he insisted that human beings become moral by willing to be so. According to Mencius, willing entails the transformative moral act insofar as the propensity of humans to be good is activated whenever they decide to bring it to their conscious attention.

Mencius taught that all people have the spiritual resources to deepen their self-awareness and strengthen their bonds with others. Biologic and environmental constraints notwithstanding, people always have the freedom and the ability to refine and enlarge their heaven-endowed nobility (their "great body"). The possibility of continuously refining and enlarging the self is vividly illustrated in Mencius's description of degrees of excellence:

Those who are admirable are called good (shan). Those who are sincere are called true (xin). Those who are totally genuine are called beautiful (mei). Those who radiate this genuineness are called great (da). Those whose greatness transforms are called sagely (sheng). Those whose sageliness is unfathomable are called spiritual (shen). (VIIB:25)

Furthermore, Mencius asserted that if people fully realize the potential of their hearts, they will understand their nature; by understanding their nature, they will know heaven. Learning to be fully human, in this Mencian perspective, entails the cultivation of human sensitivity to embody the whole cosmos as one's lived experience:

> All myriad things are here in me. There is no greater joy for me than to find, on self-examination, that I am true to myself. Try your best to treat others as you would wish to be treated yourself, and you will find that this is the shortest way to humanity. (VIIA:4)

XUNZI: THE TRANSMITTER OF CONFUCIAN SCHOLARSHIP

If Mencius brought Confucian moral idealism to fruition, Xunzi (c. 300–c. 230 BCE) conscientiously transformed Confucianism into a realistic and systematic inquiry on the human condition, with special reference to ritual and authority. Widely acknowledged as the most eminent of the notable scholars who congregated in Jixia, the capital of the wealthy and powerful Qi state in the mid-3rd century BCE, Xunzi distinguished himself in erudition and by the quality of his argumentation. His critique of the so-called 12 philosophers gave an overview of the intellectual life of his time. His penetrating insight into the limitations of virtually all the major currents of thought propounded by his fellow thinkers helped to establish the Confucian school as a dominant political and social force. His principal adversary, however, was Mencius, and he vigorously attacked Mencius's view that human nature is good as naive moral optimism.

True to the Confucian and, for that matter, Mencian spirit, Xunzi underscored the centrality of self-cultivation. He defined the process of Confucian education, from exemplary person (junzi) to sage, as a ceaseless endeavour to accumulate knowledge, skills, insight, and wisdom. In contrast to Mencius, Xunzi stressed that human nature is evil. Because he saw human beings as prone by nature to pursue the gratification of their passions, he firmly believed in the need for clearly articulated social constraints. Without constraints, social solidarity, the precondition for human well-being, would be undermined. The most serious flaw he perceived in the Mencian commitment to the goodness of human nature was the practical consequence of neglecting the necessity of ritual and authority for the well-being of society. For Xunzi, as for Confucius before him, becoming moral is hard work.

Xunzi singled out the cognitive function of the heart-and-mind (xin), or human rationality, as the basis for morality. People become moral by voluntarily harnessing their desires and passions to act in accordance with society's norms. Although this is alien to human nature, it is perceived by the heart-and-mind as necessary for both survival and well-being. It is the construction of the moral mind as a human artifact, as a "second nature." Like Mencius, Xunzi believed in the perfectibility of all human beings through self-cultivation, in humanity and rightness as cardinal virtues, in humane government as the kingly way, in social harmony, and in education. But his view of how these could actually be achieved was diametrically opposed to that of Mencius. The Confucian project, as shaped by Xunzi, defines learning as socialization. The authority of ancient sages and worthies, the classical tradition, conventional norms, teachers, governmental rules and regulations, and political officers are all important for this process. A cultured person is by definition a fully socialized member of the human community, who has successfully sublimated his instinctual demands for the public good.

Xunzi's tough-minded stance on law, order, authority, and ritual seems precariously close to that of the Legalists, whose policy of social conformism was designed exclusively for the benefit of the ruler. His insistence on objective standards of behaviour may have ideologically contributed to the rise of authoritarianism, which resulted in the dictatorship of the Qin (221–207 BCE). As a matter of fact, two of the most influential Legalists, the theoretician Hanfeizi from the state of Han and the Qin minister Li Si (c. 280–208 BCE), were his pupils. Yet Xunzi was instrumental in the continuation of Confucianism as a scholarly enterprise. His naturalistic interpretation of heaven, his sophisticated understanding of culture, his insightful observations on the epistemological aspect of the mind and social function of language, his emphasis on moral reasoning and the art of argumentation, his belief in progress, and his interest in political institutions so significantly enriched the Confucian heritage that he was revered by the Confucians as the paradigmatic scholar for more than three centuries.

THE CONFUCIANIZATION OF POLITICS

The short-lived dictatorship of the Qin marked a brief triumph of Legalism. In the early years of the Western Han (206 BCE–25 CE), however, the Legalist practice of absolute power of the emperor, complete subjugation of the peripheral states to the central government, total uniformity of thought, and ruthless enforcement of law were replaced by the Daoist practice of reconciliation and noninterference. This practice is commonly known in history as the Huang-Lao method, referring to the art of rulership attributed to the Yellow Emperor (Huangdi) and the mysterious founder of Daoism, Laozi. Although a few Confucian thinkers, such as Lu Jia and Jia Yi, made important policy recommendations, Confucianism before the emergence of Dong Zhongshu (c. 179–c. 104 BCE) was not particularly influential. Nonetheless, the gradual

Confucianization of Han politics began soon after the founding of the dynasty.

By the reign of Wudi (the Martial Emperor, 141–87 BCE), who inherited the task of consolidating power in the central Han court, Confucianism was deeply entrenched in the central bureaucracy. It was manifest in such practices as the clear separation of the court and the government, often under the leadership of a scholarly prime minister, the process of recruiting officials through the dual mechanism of recommendation and selection, the family-centred social structure, the agriculture-based economy, and the educational network. Confucian ideas were also firmly established in the legal system as ritual became increasingly important in governing behaviour, defining social relationships, and adjudicating civil disputes. Yet it was not until the prime minister Gungsun Hong (d. 121 BCE) had persuaded Wudi to announce formally that the *ru* school alone would receive state sponsorship that Confucianism became an officially recognized imperial ideology and state cult.

As a result Confucian Classics became the core curriculum for all levels of education. In 136 BCE Wudi set up at court five Erudites of the Five Classics (see The Five Classics on p. 77) and in 124 BCE assigned 50 official students to study with them, thus creating a de facto imperial university. By 50 BCE enrollment at the university had grown to an impressive 3,000, and by 1 CE a hundred students a year were entering government service through the examinations administered by the state. In short, those with a Confucian education began to staff the bureaucracy. In the year 58 all government schools were required to make sacrifices to Confucius, and in 175 the court had the approved version of the Classics, which had been determined by scholarly conferences and research groups under imperial auspices for several decades, carved on large stone tablets. (These stelae, which were erected at the capital, are today well preserved in the museum of Xi'an.) This act of committing to permanence and to public display the content of the sacred scriptures symbolized the completion of the formation of the classical Confucian tradition.

DONG ZHONGSHU: THE CONFUCIAN VISIONARY

Like Sima Qian, Dong Zhongshu (c. 179–c. 104 BCE) also took the *Chunqiu* absolutely seriously. His own work, *Chunqiufanlu* ("Luxuriant Gems of the Spring and Autumn Annals"), however, is far from being a book of historical judgment. It is a metaphysical treatise in the spirit of the *Yijing*. A man extraordinarily dedicated to learning (he is said to have been so absorbed in his studies that for three years he did not even glance at the garden in front of him) and strongly committed to moral idealism (one of his often-quoted dicta is "rectifying rightness without scheming for profit; enlightening his Way without calculating efficaciousness"), Dong was instrumental

THE FIVE CLASSICS

The compilation of the Wujing *("The Five Classics") was a concrete manifestation of the coming of age of the Confucian tradition. The inclusion of both pre-Confucian texts, the* Shujing *("Classic of History") and the* Shijing *("Classic of Poetry"), and contemporary Qin-Han material, such as certain portions of the* Liji *("Record of Rites"), suggests that the spirit behind the establishment of the core curriculum for Confucian education was ecumenical. The Five Classics can be described in terms of five visions: metaphysical, political, poetic, social, and historical.*

The metaphysical vision, expressed in the Yijing *("Classic of Changes"), combines divinatory art with numerological technique and ethical insight. According to the philosophy of change, the cosmos is a great transformation occasioned by the constant interaction of two complementary as well as conflicting vital energies, yin and yang. The world, which emerges out of this ongoing transformation, exhibits both organismic unity and dynamism. The exemplary person, inspired by the harmony and creativity of the cosmos, must emulate this pattern by aiming to realize the highest ideal of "unity of man and heaven"* (tianrenheyi) *through ceaseless self-exertion.*

The political vision, contained in the Shujing, *presents kingship in terms of the ethical foundation for a humane government. The legendary Three Emperors (Yao, Shun, and Yu) all ruled by virtue. Their sagacity, xiao (filial piety), and dedication to work enabled them to create a political culture based on responsibility and trust. Their exemplary lives taught and encouraged the people to enter into a covenant with them so that social harmony could be achieved without punishment or coercion. Even in the Three Dynasties (Xia, Shang, and Zhou) moral authority, as expressed through ritual, was sufficient to maintain political order. The human continuum, from the undifferentiated masses to the enlightened people, the nobility, and the sage-king, formed an organic unity as an integral part of the great cosmic transformation. Politics means moral persuasion, and the purpose of the government is not only to provide food and maintain order but also to educate.*

The poetic vision, contained in the Shijing, *underscores the Confucian valuation of common human feelings. The majority of verses give voice to emotions and sentiments of communities and persons from all levels of society expressed on a variety of occasions. The basic theme of this poetic world is mutual responsiveness. The tone as a whole is honest rather than earnest and evocative rather than expressive.*

The social vision, contained in the Liji, *shows society not as an adversarial system based on contractual relationships but as a community of trust with emphasis on communication. Society organized by the four functional occupations—the scholar, farmer, artisan, and merchant—is, in the true sense of the word, a cooperation. As a contributing member of the cooperation each person is obligated to recognize the existence of others and to serve the public good. It is the king's duty to act kingly and the father's duty to act fatherly. If the king or father fails to behave properly, he cannot expect his minister or son to act in accordance with ritual. It is in this sense that a chapter in the* Liji *entitled the "Great Learning" specifies, "From the son of heaven to the commoner, all must regard self-cultivation as the root." This pervasive consciousness of duty features prominently in all Confucian literature on ritual.*

The historical vision, presented in the Chunqiu *("Spring and Autumn Annals"), emphasizes the significance of collective memory for communal self-identification. Historical consciousness is a defining characteristic of Confucian thought. By defining himself as a lover of antiquity and a transmitter of its values, Confucius made it explicit that a sense of history is not only desirable but is necessary for self-knowledge. Confucius's emphasis on the importance of history was in a way his reappropriation of the ancient Sinitic wisdom that reanimating the old is the best way to attain the new. Confucius may not have been the author of the* Chunqiu, *but it seems likely that he applied moral judgment to political events in China proper from the 8th to the 5th century BCE. In this unprecedented procedure he assumed a godlike role in evaluating politics by assigning ultimate historical praise and blame to the most powerful and influential political actors of the period. Not only did this practice inspire the innovative style of the grand historian Sima Qian (c. 145–c. 87 BCE) but it was also widely employed by others writing dynastic histories in imperial China.*

in developing a characteristically Han interpretation of Confucianism.

Despite Wudi's pronouncement that Confucianism alone would receive imperial sponsorship, Daoists, yin-yang cosmologists, Legalists, shamanists, practitioners of seances, healers, magicians, geomancers, and others all contributed to the cosmological thinking of the Han cultural elite. Indeed, Dong himself was a beneficiary of this intellectual syncretism, for he freely tapped the spiritual resources of his time in formulating his own worldview: that human actions have cosmic consequences.

Dong's inquiries on the meaning of the five agents (metal, wood, water, fire, and earth), the correspondence of human beings and the numerical categories of heaven, and the sympathetic activation of things of the same kind, as well as his studies of cardinal Confucian values such as humanity, rightness, ritual, wisdom, and trustworthiness, enabled him to develop an elaborate worldview integrating Confucian ethics with naturalistic cosmology. What Dong accomplished was not merely a theological justification for the emperor as the "son of heaven"; rather, his theory of mutual responsiveness between heaven and humanity provided the Confucian scholars with a higher law by which to judge the conduct of the ruler.

Despite Dong's immense popularity, his worldview was not universally accepted by Han Confucian scholars. A reaction in favour of a more rational and moralistic approach to the Confucian Classics, known as the "Old Text" school, had already set in before the fall of the Western Han. Yang Xiong (c. 53 BCE–18 CE) in the *Fayan* ("Model Sayings"), a collection of moralistic aphorisms in the style of the *Analects*, and the *Taixuanjing* ("Classic of the Supremely Profound Principle"), a cosmological speculation in the style of the *Yijing*, presented an alternative worldview. This school, claiming its own recensions of authentic classical texts allegedly rediscovered during the Han period and written in an "old" script before the Qin unification, was widely accepted in the Eastern Han (25–220 CE). As the institutions of the Erudites and the Imperial University expanded in the Eastern Han, the study of the Classics became more refined and elaborate. Confucian scholasticism, however, like its counterparts in Talmudic and biblical studies, became too professionalized to remain a vital intellectual force.

Yet Confucian ethics exerted great influence on government, schools, and society at large. Toward the end of the Han as many as 30,000 students attended the Imperial University. All public schools throughout the land offered regular sacrifices to Confucius, and he virtually became the patron saint of education. Many Confucian temples were also built. The imperial courts continued to honour Confucius from age to age; a Confucian temple eventually stood in every one of the 2,000 counties. As a result, the teacher, together with heaven, earth, the emperor, and parents, became one of the most respected authorities in traditional China.

CONFUCIAN ETHICS IN THE DAOIST AND BUDDHIST CONTEXT

Incompetent rulership, faction-ridden bureaucracy, a mismanaged tax structure, and domination by eunuchs toward the end of the Eastern Han first prompted widespread protests by the Imperial University students. The high-handed policy of the court to imprison and kill thousands of them and their official sympathizers in 169 CE may have put a temporary stop to the intellectual revolt, but the downward economic spiral made the life of the peasantry unbearable. The peasant rebellion led by Confucian scholars as well as Daoist religious leaders of faith-healing sects, combined with open insurrections of the military, brought down the Han dynasty and thus put an end to the first Chinese empire. As the imperial Han system disintegrated, barbarians invaded from the north. The plains of northern China were fought over, despoiled, and controlled by rival groups, and a succession of states was established in the south. This period of disunity, from the early 3rd to the late 6th century, marked the decline of Confucianism, the upsurge of neo-Daoism, and the spread of Buddhism.

The prominence of Daoism and Buddhism among the cultural elite and the populace in general, however, did not mean that the Confucian tradition had disappeared. In fact, Confucian ethics was by then virtually inseparable from the moral fabric of Chinese society. Confucius continued to be universally honoured as the paradigmatic sage. The outstanding Daoist thinker Wang Bi (226–249) argued that Confucius, by not speculating on the nature of the dao, had an experiential understanding of it superior to Laozi's. The Confucian Classics remained the foundation of all literate culture, and sophisticated commentaries were produced throughout the age. Confucian values continued to dominate in such political institutions as the central bureaucracy, the recruitment of officials, and local governance. The political forms of life also were distinctively Confucian. When a barbarian state adopted a sinicization policy, notably the case of the Northern Wei (386–534/535), it was by and large Confucian in character. In the south systematic attempts were made to strengthen family ties by establishing clan rules, genealogical trees, and ancestral rituals based on Confucian ethics.

The reunification of China by the Sui (581–618) and the restoration of lasting peace and prosperity by the Tang (618–907) gave a powerful stimulus to the revival of Confucian learning. The publication of a definitive, official edition of the *Wujing* with elaborate commentaries and subcommentaries and the implementation of Confucian rituals at all levels of governmental practice, including the compilation of the famous Tang legal code, were two outstanding examples of Confucianism in practice.

An examination system was established based on literary competence. This system made the mastery of Confucian Classics a prerequisite for political success and was, therefore, perhaps the single most important institutional innovation in defining elite culture in Confucian terms.

The Tang dynasty, nevertheless, was dominated by Buddhism and, to a lesser degree, by Daoism. The philosophical originality of the dynasty was mainly represented by monk-scholars such as Jizang (549–623), Xuanzang (602–664), and Zhiyi (538–597). An unintended consequence in the development of Confucian thought in this context was the prominent rise of the metaphysically significant Confucian texts, notably *Zhongyong* ("Doctrine of the Mean") and *Yizhuan* ("The Great Commentary of the Classic of Changes"), which appealed to some Buddhist and Daoist thinkers. A sign of a possible Confucian turn in the Tang was Li Ao's (d. c. 844) essay on "Returning to Nature" that foreshadowed features of Song (960–1279) Confucian thought. The most influential precursor of a Confucian revival, however, was Han Yu (768–824). He attacked Buddhism from the perspectives of social ethics and cultural identity and provoked interest in the question of what actually constitutes the Confucian Way. The issue of *Daotong*, the transmission of the Way or the authentic method to repossess the Way, has stimulated much discussion in the Confucian tradition since the 11th century.

CONFUCIAN REVIVAL

The Buddhist conquest of China and the Chinese transformation of Buddhism, a process entailing the introduction, domestication, growth, and appropriation of a distinctly Indian form of spirituality, lasted for at least six centuries. Since Buddhist ideas were introduced to China via Daoist categories and since the development of the Daoist religion benefited from having Buddhist institutions and practices as models, the spiritual dynamics in medieval China were characterized by Buddhist and Daoist values. The reemergence of Confucianism as the leading intellectual force thus involved both a creative response to the Buddhist and Daoist challenge and an imaginative reappropriation of classical Confucian insights. Furthermore, after the collapse of the Tang dynasty, the grave threats to the survival of Chinese culture from the Khitan, the Juchen (Jin), and later the Mongols prompted the literati to protect their common heritage by deepening their communal critical self-awareness. To enrich their personal knowledge as well as to preserve China as a civilization-state, they explored the symbolic and spiritual resources that made Confucianism a living tradition.

SONG MASTERS

The Song dynasty (960–1279) was militarily weak and much smaller than the Tang, but its cultural splendour and economic prosperity were unprecedented in Chinese, if not human, history. The Song's commercial revolution produced flourishing markets, densely populated urban centres, elaborate communication networks, theatrical performances, literary groups, and popular religions—developments that tended to remain unchanged into the 19th century. Technological advances in agriculture, textiles, lacquer, porcelain, printing, maritime trade, and weaponry demonstrated that China excelled in the fine arts as well as in the sciences. The decline of the aristocracy, the widespread availability of printed books, the democratization of education, and the full implementation of the examination system produced a new social class, the gentry, noted for its literary proficiency, social consciousness, and political participation. The outstanding members of this class, such as the classicists Hu Yuan (993–1059) and Sun Fu (992–1057), the reformers Fan Zhongyan (989–1052) and Wang Anshi (1021–86), the writer-officials Ouyang Xiu (1007–72) and Su Shi (pen name of Su Dongpo; 1037–1101), and the statesman-historian Sima Guang (1019–86), contributed to the revival of Confucianism in education, politics, literature, and history and collectively to the development of a scholarly official style, a way of life informed by Confucian ethics.

The Confucian revival, understood in traditional historiography as the establishment of the lineage of *Daoxue* ("Learning of the Way"), nevertheless can be traced through a line of Neo-Confucian thinkers from Zhou Dunyi (1017–73) by way of Shao Yong (1011–77), Zhang Zai (1020–77), the brothers Cheng Hao (1032–85) and Cheng Yi (1033–1107), and the great synthesizer Zhu Xi (1130–1200). These men developed a comprehensive humanist vision in which cultivation of the self was integrated with social ethics and moral metaphysics. In the eyes of the Song literati this new philosophy faithfully restored the classical Confucian insights and successfully applied them to the concerns of their own age.

Zhou Dunyi ingeniously articulated the relationship between the "great transformation" of the cosmos and the moral development of human beings. In his metaphysics, humanity, as the recipient of the highest excellence from heaven, is itself a centre of cosmic creativity. He developed this all-embracing humanism by a thought-provoking interpretation of the Daoist diagram of Taiji ("Great Ultimate"). Shao Yong elaborated on the metaphysical basis of human affairs, insisting that a disinterested numerological mode of analysis is most appropriate for understanding the "supreme principles governing the world." Zhang Zai, on the other hand, focused on the omnipresence of *qi* ("vital energy"). He also advocated the oneness of *li* ("principle"; comparable to the idea of Natural Law) and the multiplicity of its manifestations, which is created as the principle expresses itself through the "vital energy." As an article of faith he pronounced in the "Western Inscription": "Heaven is my father and Earth is my mother, and even such a small being as I finds a central abode in their midst. Therefore that which fills the cosmos I regard as my body and that which directs the cosmos I consider as my nature. All people are my brothers and sisters, and all things are my companions."

This theme of mutuality between heaven and human beings, consanguinity between man and man, and harmony between man and nature was brought to fruition in Cheng Hao's definition of humanity as "forming one body with all things." To him the presence of *tianli* ("heavenly principle") in all things as well as in human nature enables the human mind to purify itself in a spirit of reverence. Cheng Yi, following his brother's lead, formulated the famous dictum, "self-cultivation requires reverence; the extension of knowledge consists in the investigation of things." By making special reference to *gewu* ("investigation of things"), he raised doubts about the appropriateness of focusing exclusively on the illumination of the mind in self-cultivation, as his brother seems to have done. The learning of the mind as advocated by Cheng Hao and the learning of the principle as advocated by Cheng Yi became two distinct modes of thought in Song Confucianism.

Zhu Xi, clearly following Cheng Yi's School of Principle and implicitly rejecting Cheng Hao's School of Mind, developed a method of interpreting and transmitting the Confucian Way that for centuries defined Confucianism not only for the Chinese but for the Koreans and the Japanese as well. If, as quite a few scholars have advocated, Confucianism represents a distinct form of East Asian spirituality, it is the Confucianism shaped by Zhu Xi. Zhu Xi virtually reconstituted the Confucian tradition, giving it new structure, new texture, and new meaning. He was more than a synthesizer; through conscientious appropriation and systematic interpretation he gave rise to a new Confucianism, known as Neo-Confucianism in the West but often referred to as *lixue* ("Learning of the Principle") in modern China.

The "Doctrine of the Mean" and the "Great Learning," two chapters in the *Liji*, had become independent treatises and, together with the *Analects* and *Mencius*, had been included in the core curriculum of Confucian education for centuries before Zhu Xi's birth. But by putting them into a particular sequence, the "Great Learning," the *Analects*, *Mencius*, and the "Doctrine of the Mean," synthesizing their commentaries, interpreting them as a coherent humanistic vision, and calling them the Four Books (*Sishu*), Zhu Xi fundamentally restructured the Confucian scriptural tradition. The Four Books, placed above the Five Classics, became the central texts for both primary education and civil service examinations in traditional China from the 14th century. Thus they have exerted far greater influence on Chinese life and thought in the past 600 years than any other work.

As an interpreter and transmitter of the Confucian Way, Zhu Xi identified which early Song masters belonged to the lineage of Confucius and Mencius. His judgment, later widely accepted by governments in East Asia, was based principally on philosophical insight. Zhou Dunyi, Zhang Zai, and the Cheng brothers, the select four, were Zhu Xi's cultural heroes. Shao Yong and Sima Guang were originally on his list, but Zhu Xi apparently changed his mind, perhaps because of Shao's excessive metaphysical speculation and Sima's obsession with historical facts.

Up until Zhu Xi's time the Confucian thinking of the Song masters was characterized by a few fruitfully ambiguous concepts, notably the Great Ultimate, principle, vital energy, nature, mind, and humanity. Zhu Xi defined the process of the investigation of things as a rigorous discipline of the mind to probe the principle in things. He recommended a twofold method of study: to cultivate a sense of reverence and to pursue knowledge. This combination of morality and wisdom made his pedagogy an inclusive approach to humanist education. Reading, sitting quietly, ritual practice, physical exercise, calligraphy, arithmetic, and empirical observation all had a place in his pedagogical program. Zhu Xi reestablished the White Deer Grotto in present Jiangxi province as an academy. It became the intellectual centre of his age and provided an instructional model for all schools in East Asia for generations to come.

Zhu Xi was considered the preeminent Confucian scholar in Song China, but his interpretation of the Confucian Way was seriously challenged by his contemporary, Lu Jiuyuan (Lu Xiangshan, 1139–93). Claiming that he appropriated the true wisdom of Confucian teaching by reading Mencius, Lu criticized Zhu Xi's theory of the investigation of things as fragmented and ineffective empiricism. Instead he advocated a return to Mencian moral idealism by insisting that establishing the "great body" (i.e., heaven-endowed nobility) is the primary precondition for self-realization. To him the learning of the mind as a quest for self-knowledge provided the basis upon which the investigation of things assumed its proper significance. Lu's confrontation with Zhu Xi in the famous meeting at the Goose Lake Temple in 1175 further convinced him that Confucianism as Zhu Xi had shaped it was not Mencian. Although Lu's challenge remained a minority position for some time, his learning of the mind later became a major intellectual force in Ming China (1368–1644) and Tokugawa Japan (1603–1867).

CONFUCIAN LEARNING IN JIN, YUAN, AND MING

For about 150 years, from the time the Song court moved its capital to the South and reestablished itself there in 1127, North China was ruled by three conquest dynasties, the Liao (907–1125), Xi Xia (1038–1227), and Jin (1115–1234). Although the bureaucracies and political cultures of both Liao and Xi Xia were under Confucian influence, no discernible

intellectual developments helped to further the Confucian tradition there. In the Juchen Jin dynasty, however, despite the paucity of information about the Confucian renaissance in the Southern Song, the Jin scholar-officials continued the classical, artistic, literary, and historiographic traditions of the North and developed a richly textured cultural form of their own. Zhao Bingwen's (1159–1232) combination of literary talent and moral concerns and Wang Roxu's (1174–1243) scholarship in Classics and history, as depicted in Yuan Haowen's (1190–1257) biographical sketches and preserved in their collected works, compared well with the high standards set by their counterparts in the South.

When the Mongols reunited China in 1279, the intellectual dynamism of the South profoundly affected the northern style of scholarship. Although the harsh treatment of scholars by the conquest Yuan (Mongol) dynasty (1206–1368) seriously damaged the well-being of the scholarly community, outstanding Confucian thinkers nevertheless emerged throughout the period. Some opted to purify themselves so that they could repossess the Way for the future; some decided to become engaged in politics to put their teaching into practice.

Xu Heng (1209–81) took a practical approach. Appointed by Kublai, the Great Khan in Marco Polo's *Description of the World*, as the president of the Imperial Academy and respected as the leading scholar in the court, Xu conscientiously introduced Zhu Xi's teaching to the

Mongols. He assumed personal responsibility for educating the sons of the Mongol nobility to become qualified teachers of Confucian Classics. His erudition and skills in medicine, legal affairs, irrigation, military science, arithmetic, and astronomy enabled him to be an informed adviser to the conquest dynasty. He set the tone for the eventual success of the Confucianization of Yuan bureaucracy. In fact, it was the Yuan court that first officially adopted the Four Books as the basis of the civil service examination, a practice that was to be observed until 1905. Thanks to Xu Heng, Zhu Xi's teaching prevailed in the Mongol period, but it was significantly simplified.

The hermit-scholar Liu Yin (1249–93), on the other hand, allegedly refused Kublai Khan's summons in order to maintain the dignity of the Confucian Way. To him education was for self-realization. Loyal to the Jin culture in which he was reared and faithful to the Confucian Way that he had learned from the Song masters, Liu Yin rigorously applied philological methods to classical studies and strongly advocated the importance of history. Although true to Zhu Xi's spirit, by taking seriously the idea of the investigation of things, he put a great deal of emphasis on the learning of the mind. Liu Yin's contemporary, Wu Zheng (1249–1333), further developed the learning of the mind. He fully acknowledged the contribution of Lu Jiuyuan to the Confucian tradition, even though as an admirer of Xu Heng he considered himself a follower of Zhu Xi. Wu assigned himself the challenging task of harmonizing the difference between Zhu and Lu. As a result, he reoriented Zhu's balanced approach to morality and wisdom to accommodate Lu's existential concern for self-knowledge. This prepared the way for the revival of Lu's learning of the mind in the Ming (1368–1644).

The thought of the first outstanding Ming Confucian scholar, Xue Xuan (1389–1464), already revealed the turn toward moral subjectivity. Although a devoted follower of Zhu Xi, Xue's *Records of Reading* clearly shows that he considered the cultivation of "mind and nature" to be particularly important. Two other early Ming scholars, Wu Yubi (1391–1469) and Chen Xianzhang (1428–1500), helped to define Confucian education for those who studied the Classics not simply in preparation for examinations but as learning of the "body and mind." They cleared the way for Wang Yangming (1472–1529), the most influential Confucian thinker after Zhu Xi.

As a critique of excessive attention to philological details characteristic of Zhu Xi's followers, Wang Yangming allied himself with Lu Jiuyuan's learning of the mind. He advocated the precept of uniting thought and action. By focusing on the transformative power of the will, he inspired a generation of Confucian students to return to the moral idealism of Mencius. His own personal example of combining teaching with bureaucratic routine, administrative responsibility, and leadership in military campaigns demonstrated that he was a man of deeds.

Despite his competence in practical affairs, Wang's primary concern was moral education, which he felt had to be grounded in the "original substance" of the mind. This he later identified as *liangzhi* ("good conscience"), by which he meant innate knowledge or a primordial existential awareness possessed by every human being. He further suggested that good conscience as the heavenly principle is inherent in all beings from the highest spiritual forms to grass, wood, bricks, and stone. Because the universe consists of vital energy informed by good conscience, it is a dynamic process rather than a static structure. Human beings can learn to regard heaven and earth and the myriad things as one body by extending their good conscience to embrace an ever-expanding network of relationships.

Wang Yangming's dynamic idealism, as Wing-tsit Chan, the late dean of Chinese philosophy in North America, characterized it, set the Confucian agenda for several generations in China. His followers, such as the communitarian Wang Ji (1498–1583), who devoted his long life to building a community of the like-minded, and the radical individualist Li Zhi (1527–1602), who proposed to reduce all human relationships to friendship, broadened Confucianism to accommodate a variety of lifestyles.

Among Wang's critics, Liu Zongzhou (1578–1645) was perhaps the most brilliant. His *Human Schemata (Renpu)* offered a rigorous phenomenological description of human mistakes as a corrective to Wang Yangming's moral

optimism. Liu's student Huang Zongxi (1610–95) compiled a comprehensive biographical history of Ming Confucians based on Liu's writings. One of Huang's contemporaries, Gu Yanwu (1613–82), was also a critic of Wang Yangming. He excelled in his studies of political institutions, ancient phonology, and classical philology. While Gu was well-known in his time and honoured as the patron saint of "evidential learning" in the 18th century, his contemporary Wang Fuzhi (1619–92) was discovered 200 years later as one of the most sophisticated original minds in the history of Confucian thought. His extensive writings on metaphysics, history, and the Classics made him a thorough critic of Wang Yangming and his followers.

AGE OF CONFUCIANISM: QING CHINA

The Confucianization of Chinese society reached its apex during the Qing (1644–1911/12) when China was again ruled by a conquest (Manchu) dynasty. The Qing emperors outshone their counterparts in the Ming in presenting themselves as exemplars of Confucian kingship. They transformed Confucian teaching into a political ideology, indeed a mechanism of control. Jealously guarding their imperial prerogatives as the ultimate interpreters of Confucian truth, they undermined the freedom of scholars to transmit the Confucian Way by imposing harsh measures, such as literary inquisition. It was Gu Yanwu's classical scholarship rather than his insights on political reform that inspired the 18th-century evidential scholars. Dai Zhen, the most philosophically-minded philologist among them, couched his brilliant critique of Song learning in his commentary on "The Meanings of Terms in the *Book of Mencius.*" Dai Zhen was one of the scholars appointed by the Qianlong emperor in 1773 to compile an imperial manuscript library. This massive scholarly attempt, *The Complete Library of the Four Treasures,* is symbolic of the grandiose intent of the Manchu court to give an account of all the important works of the four branches of learning—the Classics, history, philosophy, and literature—in Confucian culture. The project comprised more than 36,000 volumes with comments on about 10,230 titles, employed as many as 15,000 copyists, and took 20 years to complete. The Qianlong emperor and the scholars around him may have expressed their cultural heritage in a definitive form, but the Confucian tradition was yet to encounter its most serious threat.

MODERN TRANSFORMATION

At the time of the first Opium War (1839–42) East Asian societies had been Confucianized for centuries. The continuous growth of Mahayana Buddhism throughout Asia and the presence of Daoism in China, shamanism in Korea, and Shintōism in Japan did not undermine the power of Confucianism in government, education, family rituals, and social ethics. In fact, Buddhist monks were often messengers of Confucian values, and the coexistence of Confucianism with Daoism, shamanism, and Shintōism actually characterized the syncretic East Asian religious life. The impact of the West, however, so fundamentally challenged the Confucian roots in East Asia that for some time it was widely debated whether or not Confucianism could remain a viable tradition in modern times.

Beginning in the 19th century, Chinese intellectuals' faith in the ability of Confucian culture to withstand the impact of the West became gradually eroded. This loss of faith may be perceived in Lin Zexu's (1785–1850) moral indignation against the British, followed by Zeng Guofan's (1811–72) pragmatic acceptance of the superiority of Western technology, Kang Youwei's (1858–1927) sweeping recommendation for political reform, and Zhang Zhidong's (1837–1909) desperate, eclectic attempt to save the essence of Confucian learning, which, however, eventually led to the anti-Confucian iconoclasm of the so-called May Fourth Movement in 1919. The triumph of Marxism-Leninism as the official ideology of the People's Republic of China in 1949 relegated Confucian rhetoric to the background. The modern Chinese intelligentsia, however, maintained unacknowledged, sometimes unconscious, continuities with the Confucian tradition at every level of life—behaviour, attitude, belief, and commitment. Indeed, Confucianism remains an integral part of the psycho-cultural construct of the

This statue of Chinese philosopher Confucius stands in front of the Confucius Temple in Beijing. Liu Jin/AFP/Getty Images

contemporary Chinese intellectual as well as of the Chinese farmer.

The emergence of Japan and other newly industrialized Asian countries (e.g., South Korea, Taiwan, and Singapore) as the most dynamic region of economic development since World War II has generated much scholarly interest. Labeled the "Sinitic World in Perspective," "The Second Case of Industrial Capitalism," the "Eastasia Edge," or "the Challenge of the Post-Confucian States," this phenomenon has raised questions about how the typical East Asian institutions, still suffused with Confucian values—such as a paternalistic government, an educational system based on competitive examinations, the family with emphasis on loyalty and cooperation, and local organizations informed by consensus—have adapted themselves to the imperatives of modernization.

Some of the most creative and influential intellectuals in contemporary China have continued to think from Confucian roots. Xiong Shili's ontological reflection, Liang Shuming's cultural analysis, Feng Youlan's reconstruction of the learning of the principle, He Lin's new interpretation of the learning of the mind, Tang Junyi's philosophy of culture, Xu Fuguan's social criticism, and Mou Zongsan's moral metaphysics are noteworthy examples. Although some of the most articulate intellectuals in the People's Republic of China criticize their Confucian heritage as the embodiment of authoritarianism, bureaucratism, nepotism, conservatism, and male chauvinism, others in China, Taiwan, Singapore, and North America have imaginatively established the relevance of Confucian humanism to China's modernization. The revival of Confucian studies in South Korea, Taiwan, Hong Kong, and Singapore has been under way for more than a generation, though Confucian scholarship in Japan remains unrivaled. Confucian thinkers in the West, inspired by religious pluralism and liberal democratic ideas, have begun to explore the possibility of a third epoch of Confucian humanism. They uphold that its modern transformation, as a creative response to the challenge of the West, is a continuation of its classical formulation and its medieval elaboration. Scholars in mainland China have also begun to explore the possibility of a fruitful interaction between Confucian humanism and democratic liberalism in a socialist context.

CHAPTER 5

DAOISM

Daoism—also called Taoism—is an indigenous religio-philosophical tradition that has shaped Chinese life for more than 2,000 years. In the broadest sense, a Daoist attitude toward life can be seen in the accepting and yielding, the joyful and carefree sides of the Chinese character, an attitude that offsets and complements the moral and duty-conscious, austere and purposeful character ascribed to Confucianism. Daoism is also characterized by a positive, active attitude toward the occult and the metaphysical (theories on the nature of reality), whereas the agnostic, pragmatic Confucian tradition considers these issues of only marginal importance, although the reality of such issues is, by most Confucians, not denied.

Daoism arose out of the promotion of *dao* (which means the way, or the path) as the social ideal. More strictly defined, Daoism includes: the ideas and attitudes peculiar to the *Daodejing* ("Classic of the Way of Power"), the *Zhuangzi*, the *Liezi*, and related writings; the Daoist religion, which is concerned with the ritual worship of the Dao; and those who identify themselves as Daoists. The figure who stands behind all forms of Daoism is Laozi, who is traditionally regarded as the author of the classic text known as the *Laozi*, or the *Daodejing*.

Daoist thought permeates Chinese culture, including many aspects not usually considered Daoist. In Chinese religion, the Daoist tradition—often serving as a link between the Confucian tradition and folk tradition—has generally been more popular and spontaneous than the official (Confucian) state cult and less diffuse and shapeless than folk religion.

LAOZI AND THE *DAODEJING*

The first mention of Laozi is found in another early classic of Daoist speculation, the *Zhuangzi* (4th–3rd century BCE), so called after the name of its author. In this work Laozi is described as being one of Zhuangzi's own teachers, and the same book contains many of the Master's (Laozi's) discourses, generally introduced by the questions of a disciple. The *Zhuangzi* also presents seven versions of a meeting of Laozi and Confucius. Laozi is portrayed as the elder and his Daoist teachings confound his celebrated interlocutor. The *Zhuangzi* also gives the only account of Laozi's death. Thus, in this early source, Laozi appears as a senior contemporary of Confucius (6th–5th century BCE) and a renowned Daoist master, a curator of the archives at the court of the Zhou dynasty (c. 1046–256 BCE), and, finally, a mere mortal.

The first consistent biographical account of Laozi is found in the "Records of the Historian" (*Shiji*)—China's first universal history (2nd century BCE)—of Sima Qian. This concise résumé has served as the classical source on the philosopher's life. Laozi's family name was Li, his given name Er; and he occupied the post of archivist at the Zhou court. He is said to have instructed Confucius on points of ceremony. Observing the decline of the Zhou dynasty, Laozi left the court and headed west. At the request of Yin Xi, the guardian of the frontier pass, he wrote his treatise on the Dao in two scrolls. He then left China behind, and what became of him is not known. The historian quotes variant accounts, including one that attributed to Laozi an exceptional longevity; the narrative terminates with the genealogy of eight generations of Laozi's supposed descendants. With passing references in other early texts, this constitutes the body of information on the life of the sage as of the 2nd century BCE; it is presumably legendary.

Modern scholarship has little to add to the *Shiji* account, and the *Daodejing*, regarded by many scholars as a compilation that reached its final form only in the 3rd century BCE, rather than the work of a single author, stands alone, with all its attractions and enigmas, as the fundamental text of both philosophical and religious Daoism.

The work's 81 brief sections contain only about 5,000 characters in all, from which fact derives still another of its titles, *Laozi's Five Thousand Words*. The text itself appears in equal measure to express a profound quietism and anarchistic views on government. It is consequently between the extremes of meditative introspection and political application that its many and widely divergent interpreters have veered.

The *Daodejing* was meant as a hand-book for the ruler. He should be a sage whose actions pass so unnoticed that his very existence remains unknown. He imposes no restrictions or prohibitions on his subjects; "so long as I love qui-etude, the people will of themselves go straight. So long as I act only by inactiv-ity, the people will of themselves become prosperous." His simplicity makes the Ten Thousand Things passionless and still, and peace follows naturally. He does not teach them discrimination, vir-tue, or ambition because "when intellect emerges, the great artifices begin. When discord is rife in families, 'dutiful sons' appear. When the State falls into anarchy, 'loyal subjects' appear." Thus, it is better to banish wisdom, righteousness, and ingenuity, and the people will benefit a hundredfold.

Therefore the Sage rules by empty-ing their hearts (minds) and filling their bellies, weakening their wills and strengthening their bones, ever striving to make the people knowledgeless and desireless.

The word "people" in this passage more likely refers not to the common people but to those nobles and intellectu-als who incite the ruler's ambition and aggressiveness.

War is condemned but not entirely excluded: "Arms are ill-omened instru-ments," and the sage uses them only when he cannot do otherwise. He does not glory in victory; "he that has conquered in battle is received with rites of mourning."

The book shares certain constants of classical Chinese thought but clothes them in an imagery of its own. The sacred aura surrounding kingship is here rationalized and expressed as "inaction" (*wuwei*), demanding of the sovereign no more than right cosmological ori-entation at the centre of an obedient universe. Survivals of archaic notions concerning the compelling effect of renunciation—which the Confucians sanctified as ritual "deference" (*rang*)—are echoed in the recommendation to "hold to the role of the female," with an eye to the ultimate mastery that comes of passivity.

It is more particularly in the func-tion attributed to the Dao, or Way, that this little tract stands apart. The term "dao" was employed by all schools of thought. The universe has its dao; there is a dao of the sovereign, his royal mode of being, while the dao of man com-prises continuity through procreation. Each of the schools, too, had its own dao, its way or doctrine. But in the *Daodejing*, the ultimate unity of the uni-versal Dao itself, is proposed as a social ideal. It is this idealistic peculiarity that seems to justify later historians and bib-liographers in their assignment of the term Daoist to the *Daodejing* and its successors.

From a literary point of view, the *Daodejing* is distinguished for its highly compressed style. Unlike the dialec-tic or anecdotal composition of other contemporary treatises, it articulates its cryptic subject matter in short, concise statements. More than half of these are in rhyme, and close parallelism recurs throughout the text. No proper name occurs anywhere. Although its historical enigmas are apparently insoluble, there is abundant testimony to the vast influence exercised by the book since the earliest times and in surprisingly varied social contexts. Among the classics of speculative Daoism, it alone holds the distinction of having become a scripture of the esoteric Daoist movements, which developed their own interpretations of its ambiguities and transmitted it as a sacred text.

INTERPRETATION OF ZHUANGZI

Pseudohistorical knowledge of the sage Zhuangzi is even less well defined than that of Laozi. Most of Sima Qian's brief portrait of the man is transparently drawn from anecdotes in the *Zhuangzi* itself and as such has no necessary basis in fact. The *Zhuangzi*, however, is valuable as a monument of Chinese literature and because it contains considerable documentary material, describing numerous speculative trends and spiritual practices of the Warring States period (475–221 BCE).

Whereas the *Daodejing* is addressed to the sage-king, the *Zhuangzi* is the earliest surviving Chinese text to present a philosophy for private life, a wisdom for the individual. Zhuangzi is said to have preferred the doctrine of Laozi over all others; many of his writings strike the reader as metaphorical illustrations of the terse sayings of the "Old Master."

Whereas Laozi in his book as well as in his life (in legend) was concerned with Daoist rule, Zhuangzi, some generations later, rejected all participation in society. He compared the servant of state to the well-fed decorated ox being led to sacrifice in the temple and himself to the untended piglet blissfully frolicking in the mire.

Here there is none of the *Daodejing*'s studied density. The rambling *Zhuangzi* opens with a sprightly fable, illustrating the incomprehension of small wildfowl of the majestic splendour of a gigantic bird. Other such parables demonstrate the relativity of all values: the sliding scales of size, utility, beauty, and perfection. There is a colloquy between the Lord of the Yellow River and the God of the Eastern Ocean, in which the complacent self-satisfaction of the lesser spirit is shaken by his unexpected meeting with inconceivable vastness. Humble artisans are depicted, who, through the perfect mastery of their craft, exemplify for their social superiors the art of mastering life. Life and death are equated, and the dying are seen to welcome their approaching transformation as a fusion with the Dao. A succession of acquiescent cripples exclaims in rapture on the strange forms in which it has pleased heaven to shape them. Those involved in state ritual are brought onstage only to be mocked, and the propositions of contemporary logic-choppers are drawn into the unending whirl of paradox, spun out to their conclusions, and so abolished. Such are a few aspects of this wild kaleidoscope of unconventional thought, a landmark in Chinese literature. Its concluding chapter is a systematic account of the preeminent thinkers of the time, and the note of mock despair on which it closes typifies the *Zhuangzi*'s position regarding the more formal, straitlaced ideologies that it parodies.

Among the strange figures that people the pages of *Zhuangzi* are a very special class of spiritualized being. Dwelling far apart from the turbulent world of men, dining on air and sipping the dew, they share none of the anxieties of ordinary folk and have the smooth, untroubled faces of children. These "supreme persons," or "perfect persons," are immune to the effects of the elements, untouched by heat and cold. They possess the power of flight and are described as mounting upward with a fluttering motion. Their effortless existence was the ultimate in autonomy, the natural spontaneity that *Zhuangzi* ceaselessly applauds. These striking portraits may have been intended to be allegorical, but whatever their original meaning, these Immortals (*xian*), as they came to be called, were to become the centre of great interest. Purely literary descriptions of their freedom, their breathtaking mobility, and their agelessness were construed as practical objectives by later generations. By a variety of practices, people attempted to attain these qualities in their own persons, and in time *Zhuangzi*'s unfettered paragons of liberty were to see themselves classified according to kind and degree in a hierarchy of the heavenly hosts.

BASIC CONCEPTS OF DAOISM

Certain concepts of ancient agrarian religion have dominated Chinese thought uninterruptedly from before the formation of the philosophic schools until the first radical break with tradition and the overthrow of dynastic rule at the beginning of the 20th century, and they are thus not specifically Daoist. The most important of these concepts are (1) the continuity between nature and human beings, or the interaction between the world and human society; (2) the rhythm of constant flux and transformation in the universe and the return or reversion of all things to the Dao from which they emerged; and (3) the worship of ancestors, the cult of heaven, and the divine nature of the sovereign.

COSMOLOGY

What Laozi calls the "constant Dao" in reality is nameless. The name (*ming*) in ancient Chinese thought implied an evaluation assigning an object its place in a hierarchical universe. The Dao is outside these categories.

It is something formlessly fashioned, that existed before heaven *and earth . . . Its name (*ming*) we do not know; Dao is the byname that we give it. Were I forced to say to what class of things it belongs I should call it Immense.*

Dao is the "imperceptible, indiscernible," about which nothing can be predicated but that latently contains the forms, entities, and forces of all particular phenomena: "It was from the Nameless that heaven and earth sprang; the Named is the mother that rears the Ten Thousand Things, each after its kind." The Nameless (*wuming*) and the Named (*youming*), Nothing (*wu*) and Something (*you*), are interdependent and "grow out of one another."

Nothing (*wu*) and Dao are not identical; *wu* and *you* are two aspects of the constant Dao: "in its mode of being Unseen, we will see its mysteries; in the mode of the Seen, we will see its boundaries."

Nothing does not mean "Nothingness" but rather indeterminacy, the absence of perceptible qualities; in Laozi's view it is superior to Something. It is the Void (that is, empty incipience) that harbours in itself all potentialities and without which even Something lacks its efficacy.

Emptiness realized in the mind of the Daoist who has freed himself from all obstructing notions and distracting passions makes the Dao act through him without obstacle. An essential characteristic that governs the Dao is spontaneity (*ziran*), the what-is-so-of-itself, the self-so, the unconditioned. The Dao, in turn, governs the cosmos: "The ways of heaven are conditioned by those of the Dao, and the ways of Dao by the Self-so."

This is the way of the sage who does not intervene but possesses the total power of spontaneous realization that is at work in the cosmos; of proper order in the world, "everyone, throughout the country, says 'It happened of its own accord' (*ziran*)."

MICROCOSM-MACROCOSM CONCEPT

The conception of the cosmos common to all Chinese philosophy is neither materialistic nor animistic (a belief system centring on soul substances); it can be called magical or even alchemical. The universe is viewed as a hierarchically organized organism in which every part reproduces the whole. The human being is a microcosm (small world) corresponding rigorously to this macrocosm (large world); the body reproduces the plan of the cosmos. Between humans and the world there exists a system of correspondences and participations that the ritualists, philosophers, alchemists, and physicians have described but certainly not invented. This originally magical feeling of the integral unity of mankind and the natural order has always characterized the Chinese mentality, and the Daoists especially have elaborated upon it. The five organs of the body and its orifices and the dispositions, features, and passions of humans correspond to the

Fishing in a Mountain Stream, *detail of an ink drawing on silk by Xu Daoning, 11th century. The drawing suggests the Daoist concept of harmony of the universe and the relative role of humankind in the universal order; in the Nelson-Atkins Museum of Art, Kansas City, Missouri.* Courtesy of the Nelson Gallery-Atkins Museum, Kansas City, Missouri (Nelson Fund)

five directions, the five holy mountains, the sections of the sky, the seasons, and the Five Phases (*wuxing*), which in China are not material but are more like five fundamental phases of any process in space-time. Whoever understands the human experience thus understands the structure of the cosmos. The physiologist knows that blood circulates because rivers carry water and that the body has 360 articulations because the ritual year has 360 days. In religious Daoism the interior of the body is inhabited by the same gods as those of the macrocosm. Adepts often search for their divine teacher in all the holy mountains of China until they finally discover him in one of the "palaces" inside their heads.

RETURN TO THE DAO

The law of the Dao as natural order refers to the continuous reversion of everything to its starting point. Anything that develops extreme qualities will invariably revert to the opposite qualities: "Reversion is the movement of the Dao" (*Laozi*). Everything issues from the Dao and ineluctably returns to it; Undifferentiated Unity becomes multiplicity in the movement of the Dao. Life and death are contained in this continuing transformation from Nothing into Something and back to Nothing, but the underlying primordial unity is never lost.

For society, any reform means a type of return to the remote past; civilization is considered a degradation of the natural order, and the ideal is the return to an original purity. For the individual, wisdom is to conform to the rhythm of the cosmos. The Daoist mystics, however, not only adapt themselves ritually and physiologically to the alternations of nature but create a void inside themselves that permits them to return to nature's origin. Laozi, in trance, "wandered freely in the origin of all things." Thus, in ecstasy he escaped the rhythm of life and death by contemplating the ineluctable return: "Having attained perfect emptiness, holding fast to stillness, I can watch the return of the ever active Ten Thousand Things." The number 10,000 symbolizes totality.

CHANGE AND TRANSFORMATION

All parts of the cosmos are attuned in a rhythmical pulsation. Nothing is static; all things are subjected to periodical mutations and transformations that represent the Chinese view of creation. Instead of being opposed with a static ideal, change itself is systematized and made intelligible, as in the theory of the Five Phases and in the 64 hexagrams of the *Yijing* (*Book of Changes*), which are basic recurrent constellations in the general flux. An unchanging unity (the constant Dao) was seen as underlying the kaleidoscopic plurality.

Zhuangzi's image for creation was that of the activity of the potter and the bronze caster: "to shape and to transform" (*zaohua*). These are two phases of the same process: the imperceptible Dao shapes the cosmos continuously out of primordial chaos; the perpetual transformation of the cosmos by the alternations of yin and yang, or complementary energies (seen as night and day or as winter and summer), is nothing but the external aspect of the same Dao. The shaping of the Ten Thousand Things by the Supreme Unity and their transformation by yin and yang are both simultaneous and perpetual. Thus, the sage's ecstatic union is a "moving together with the Dao; dispersing and concentrating, his appearance has no consistency." United with the constant Dao, the sage's outer aspect becomes one of ungraspable change. Because the gods can become perceptible only by adapting to the mode of this changing world, their apparitions are "transformations" (*bianhua*); and the magician (*huaren*) is believed to be one who transforms rather than one who conjures out of nothing.

CONCEPTS OF
THE HUMAN IN SOCIETY

The power acquired by the Daoist is *de*, the efficacy of the Dao in the human experience, which is translated as "virtue." Laozi viewed it, however, as different from Confucian virtue:

> *Persons of superior virtue are not virtuous, and that is why they have virtue. Persons of inferior [Confucian] virtue never stray from virtue, and that is why they have no virtue.*

The "superior virtue" of Daoism is a latent power that never lays claim to its achievements; it is the "mysterious power" (*xuande*) of Dao present in the heart of the sage—"persons of superior virtue never act (*wuwei*), and yet there is nothing they leave undone."

WUWEI

Wuwei is neither an ideal of absolute inaction nor a mere "not-overdoing." It is actions so well in accordance with things that their authors leave no traces of themselves in their work: "Perfect activity leaves no track behind it; perfect speech is like a jade worker whose tool leaves no mark." It is the Dao that "never acts, yet there is nothing it does not do." There is no true achievement without *wuwei* because every deliberate intervention in the natural course of things will sooner or

A Tall Pine and Daoist Immortal, *ink and colour on silk hanging scroll with self-portrait* (bottom centre) *by Chen Hongshou, 1635, Ming dynasty; in the National Palace Museum, Taipei, Taiwan.* National Palace Museum, Taipei, Taiwan

later turn into the opposite of what was intended and will result in failure.

Those sages who practice *wuwei* live out of their original nature before it was tampered with by knowledge and restricted by morality; they have reverted to infancy (that is, the undiminished vitality of the newborn state); they have "returned to the state of the Uncarved Block (*pu*)." *Pu* is uncut and unpainted wood, simplicity. Society carves this wood into specific shapes for its own use and thus robs the individual piece of its original totality. "Once the uncarved block is carved, it forms utensils (that is, instruments of government); but when the Sages use it, they would be fit to become Chiefs of all Ministers. This is why the great craftsman (ruler) does not carve (rule)."

SOCIAL IDEAL OF PRIMITIVISM

Any willful human intervention is believed to be able to ruin the harmony of the natural transformation process. The spontaneous rhythm of the primitive agrarian community and its un-self-conscious symbiosis with nature's cycles is thus the Daoist ideal of society.

In the ideal society there are no books; the *Laozi* (*Daodejing*) itself would not have been written but for the entreaty of Yin Xi, the guardian of the pass, who asked the "Old Master" to write down his thoughts. In the Golden Age, past or future, knotted cords are the only form of records. The people of this age are "dull and unwitting, they have no desire; this is called uncarved simplicity. In uncarved simplicity the people attain their true nature."

Zhuangzi liked to oppose the heaven-made and the man-made; that is, nature and society. He wanted humans to renounce all artificial "cunning contrivances" that facilitate their work but lead to "cunning hearts" and agitated souls in which the Dao will not dwell. Man should equally renounce all concepts of measure, law, and virtue. "Fashion pecks and bushels for people to measure by and they will steal by peck and bushel." He blamed not only the culture heroes and inventors praised by the Confucians but also the sages who shaped the rites and rules of society.

That the unwrought substance was blighted in order to fashion implements—this was the crime of the artisan. That the Way (Dao) and its Virtue (de) were destroyed in order to create benevolence and righteousness—this was the fault of the sage.

Even "coveting knowledge" is condemned because it engenders competition and "fight to the death over profit."

IDEAS OF KNOWLEDGE AND LANGUAGE

Characteristic of Zhuangzi are his ideas of knowledge and language developed under the stimulus of his friend and opponent, the philosopher Hui Shi.

Because, in the Daoist view, all beings and everything are fundamentally one, opposing opinions can arise only when people lose sight of the Whole and regard their partial truths as absolute. They are then like the frog at the bottom of the well who takes the bit of brightness he sees for the whole sky. The closed systems—i.e., the passions and prejudices into which petty minds shut themselves—hide the Dao, the "Supreme Master" who resides inside themselves and is superior to all distinctions.

Thus, Zhuangzi's authentic persons fully recognize the relativity of notions such as "good and evil" and "true and false." They are neutral and open to the extent that they offer no active resistance to any would-be opponent, whether it be a person or an idea. "When you argue, there are some things you are failing to see. In the greatest Dao nothing is named; in the greatest disputation, nothing is said."

The person who wants to know the Dao is told: "Do not meditate, do not cogitate . . . Follow no school, follow no way, and then you will attain the Dao"; discard knowledge, forget distinctions, reach no-knowledge. "Forget" indicates that distinctions had to be known first. The original ignorance of the child is distinguished from the no-knowledge of the sage who can "sit in forgetfulness."

The mystic does not speak because declaring unity, by creating the duality of the speaker and the affirmation, destroys it. Those who speak about the Dao (like Zhuangzi himself) are "wholly wrong. For he who knows does not speak; he who speaks does not know." Zhuangzi was aware of the fact that, in speaking about it, he could do no more than hint at the way toward the all-embracing and intuitive knowledge.

IDENTITY OF LIFE AND DEATH

Mystic realization does away with the distinction between the self and the world. This idea also governs Zhuangzi's attitude toward death. Life and death are but one of the pairs of cyclical phases, such as day and night or summer and winter. "Since life and death are each other's companions, why worry about them? All things are one." Life and death are not in opposition but merely two aspects of the same reality, arrested moments out of the flux of the ongoing mutations of everything into everything. Human beings are no exception: "They go back into the great weaving machine: thus all things issue from the Loom and return to the Loom."

Viewed from the single reality experienced in ecstasy, it is just as difficult to distinguish life from death as it is to distinguish the waking Zhuangzi from the dreaming butterfly. Death is natural, and men ought neither to fear nor to desire it. Zhuangzi's attitude thus is one of serene acceptance.

RELIGIOUS GOALS OF THE INDIVIDUAL

The Confucian sage (*sheng*) is viewed as a ruler of antiquity or a great sage who taught humanity how to return to the rites of antiquity. Daoist sagehood, however, is internal (*neisheng*), although it can become manifest in an external royalty (*waiwang*) that brings the world back to the Way by means of quietism: variously called "non-intervention" (*wuwei*), "inner cultivation" (*neiye*), or "art of the heart and mind" (*xinshu*).

Whereas worldly ambitions, riches, and (especially) discursive knowledge scatter persons and drain their energies, sages "embrace Unity" or "hold fast to the One" (*baoyi*); that is, they aspire to union with the Dao in a primordial undivided state underlying consciousness. "Embracing Unity" also means that they maintain the balance of yin and yang within themselves and the union of their spiritual (*hun*) and vegetative (*po*) souls, the dispersion of which spells death; Daoists usually believe there are three *hun* and seven *po*. The spiritual souls tend to wander (in dreams), and any passion or desire can result in loss of soul. To retain and harmonize one's souls is important for physical life as well as for the unification of the whole human entity. Cleansed of every distraction, sages create inside themselves a void that in reality is plenitude. Empty of all impurity, they are full of the original energy (*yuanqi*), which is the principle of life that in the ordinary person decays from the moment of birth on.

Because vital energy and spirituality are not clearly distinguished, old age in itself becomes a proof of sagehood. Aged Daoist sages become sages because they have been able to cultivate themselves throughout a long existence; their longevity in itself is the proof of their sageliness and union with the Dao. Externally they have a healthy, flourishing appearance; inside they contain an ever-flowing source of energy that manifests itself in radiance and in a powerful, beneficial influence on their surroundings, which is the charismatic efficacy (*de*) of the Dao.

The mystic insight of Zhuangzi made him scorn those who strove for longevity and immortality through physiological practices. Nevertheless, physical immortality was a Daoist goal probably long before and alongside the unfolding of Daoist mysticism. Adepts of immortality have a choice between many methods that are all intended to restore the pure energies possessed at birth by the infant whose perfect vital force Laozi admired. Through these methods, adepts become Immortals (*xian*) who live 1,000 years in this world if they so choose and, once satiated with life, "ascend to heaven in broad daylight." This is the final apotheosis of those Daoists who transform their bodies into pure yang energy.

Zhuangzi's descriptions of the indescribable Dao, as well as of those who have attained union with the Dao, are invariably poetic. Perfect persons have identified their life rhythms so completely with the rhythm of the forces of nature that they have become indistinguishable from them and share their immortality and infinity, which is above the cycle of ordinary life and death. They are "pure spirit. They feel neither the heat of the brushlands afire nor the cold of the waters in flood"; nothing can startle or frighten them. They are not magically invulnerable (as the adepts of physical immortality would have it), but they are "so cautious in shunning and approaching, that nothing can do them injury."

"Persons like this ride the clouds as their carriages and the sun and moon as their steeds." The theme of the spiritual wandering (yuanyou), which can be traced back to the shamanistic soul journey, crops up wherever Zhuangzi speaks of the perfect persons.

Those who let themselves be borne away by the unadulterated energies of heaven and earth and can harness the six composite energies to roam through the limitless, whatever need they henceforth depend on?

These wanderings are journeys within oneself; they are roamings through the Infinite in ecstasy. Transcending the ordinary distinctions of things and one with the Dao, "the Perfect Person has no self, the Holy Person has no merit, the Sage has no fame." They lives inconspicuously

in society, and whatever applies to the Dao applies to them.

SYMBOLISM AND MYTHOLOGY

Daoists prefer to convey their ecstatic insights in images and parables. The Dao is low and receiving as a valley, soft and life-giving as water, and it is the "mysterious female," the source of all life, the Mother of the Ten Thousand Things. Human beings should become weak and yielding as water that overcomes the hard and the strong and always takes the low ground; they should develop their male and female sides but "prefer femininity," "feed on the mother," and find within themselves the well that never runs dry. Dao is also the axis, the ridgepole, the pivot, and the empty centre of the hub. The sage is the "useless tree" or the huge gourd too large to be fashioned into implements. A frequent metaphor for the working of the Dao is the incommunicable ability to be skillful at a craft. Skilled artisans do not ponder their actions, but, in union with the dao of their subjects, they do their work reflexively and without conscious intent.

Much ancient Chinese mythology has been preserved by the Daoists, who drew on it to illustrate their views. A chaos (hundun) myth is recorded as a metaphor for the undifferentiated primal unity; the mythical emperors (Huangdi and others) are extolled for wise Daoist rule or blamed for introducing harmful civilization. Dreams of mythical paradises and journeys on clouds and flying dragons are metaphors for the wanderings of the soul, the attainment of the Dao, and the identity of dream and reality.

Daoists have transformed and adapted some ancient myths to their beliefs. Thus, the Queen Mother of the West (Xiwangmu), who was a mountain spirit, pestilence goddess, and tigress, became a high deity—the Fairy Queen of all Immortals.

EARLY ECLECTIC CONTRIBUTIONS: YIN-YANG, *QI*, AND OTHER IDEAS

Yin and yang literally mean "dark side" and "sunny side" of a hill. They are mentioned for the first time in the *Xice*, or "Appended Explanations" (c. 4th century BCE), an appendix to the *Yijing* (*Book of Changes*): "A succession of yin and yang is called the Dao."

YIN AND YANG

Yin and yang are two complementary, interdependent phases alternating in space and time; they are emblems evoking the harmonious interplay of all pairs of opposites in the cosmos.

First conceived by musicians, astronomers, or diviners and then propagated by a school that came to be named after them, yin and yang became the common stock of all Chinese philosophy. The Daoist treatise *Huainanzi* (book of "Master Huainan") describes how the one

"Primordial Breath" (*yuanqi*) split into the light ethereal yang breath, which formed heaven; and the heavier, cruder yin breath, which formed earth. The diversifications and interactions of yin and yang produced the Ten Thousand Things.

The warm breath of yang accumulated to produce fire, the essence of which formed the sun. The cold breath of yin accumulated to produce water, the essence of which became the moon.

QI

Yin and yang are often referred to as two "breaths" (*qi*). *Qi* means air, breath, or vapour—originally the vapour arising from cooking cereals. It also came to mean a cosmic energy. The Primordial Breath is a name of the chaos (state of Unity) in which the original life force is not yet diversified into the phases that the concepts yin and yang describe.

All persons have a portion of this primordial life force allotted to them at birth, and their task is not to dissipate it through the activity of the senses but to strengthen, control, and increase it in order to live out the full span of their lives.

WUXING

Another important set of notions associated with the same school of yin-yang are the "Five Phases" (*wuxing*) or "powers" (*wude*): water, fire, wood, metal, earth. They are also "breaths" (i.e., active energies), the idea of which enabled the philosophers to construct a coherent system of correspondences and participations linking all phenomena of the macrocosm and the microcosm. Associated with spatial directions, seasons of the year, colours, musical notes, animals, and other aspects of nature, they also correspond, in the human body, to the five inner organs. The Daoist techniques of longevity are grounded in these correspondences. The idea behind such techniques was that of nourishing the inner organs with the essences corresponding to their respective phases and during the season dominated by the latter.

YANG ZHU AND THE *LIEZI*

Yang Zhu (c. 400 BCE) is representative of the early pre-Daoist recluses, "those who hid themselves" (*yinshi*), who, in the *Analects* of Confucius, ridiculed Confucius's zeal to improve society. Yang Zhu held that each individual should value his own life above all else, despise wealth and power, and not agree to sacrifice even a single hair of his head to benefit the whole world. The scattered sayings of Yang Zhu in pre-Han texts are much less hedonistic than his doctrine as it is presented in the *Liezi* (book of "Master Lie").

Liezi was a legendary Daoist master whom Zhuangzi described as being able to "ride the wind and go soaring around with cool and breezy skill." In many old legends Liezi is the paragon of the spiritual traveler. The text named after him (of uncertain date) presents a philosophy that views natural changes as a pattern that can serve as a model for human activities.

GUANZI AND *HUAINANZI*

In the several Daoist chapters of the *Guanzi* (book of "Master Guan"), another text of uncertain date, emphasis is placed on "the art of the heart (mind)"; the heart governs the body as the chief governs the state. If the organs and senses submit to it, the heart can achieve a desirelessness and emptiness that make it a pure receptacle of the "heart inside the heart," a new soul that is the indwelling Dao.

The *Huainanzi* is a compilation of essays written by different learned magicians (*fangshi*) at the court of their patron, the prince of Huainan. Although lacking in unity, it is a compendium of the knowledge of the time that had been neglected by the less speculative scholars of the new state Confucianism. The *Huainanzi* discusses the most elaborate cosmology up to that time, the position of human beings in the macrocosm, the proper ordering of society, and the ideal of personal sagehood.

DAOISM IN CHINESE CULTURE

Unlike Confucianism, which is concerned with human society and the social responsibilities of its members, Daoism emphasizes nature and what is natural and spontaneous in the human experience. The two traditions, "within society" and "beyond society," balance and complement each other.

This classic definition is generally correct concerning orthodox Han Confucianism; it neglects some aspects of Confucian thought, such as the speculations on the *Yijing*, that are considered to be among the Confucian Classics and the prophetic occult (*chanwei*) commentaries to the classics. As far as Daoism is concerned, this definition neglects the social thought of the Daoist philosophers and the political aspects of Daoist religion. Chinese Buddhism has been viewed not as a Sinicized Indian religion but as flowers on the tree of Chinese religions that blossomed under Indian stimulus and that basically maintained their Chinese character.

The first mention of Buddhism in China (65 CE) occurs in a Daoist context, at the court of a member of the imperial family known for his devotion to the doctrines of Huang-Lao. The Indian religion was at first regarded as a foreign variety of Daoism; the particular Buddhist texts chosen to be translated during the Han period reveal the Daoist preoccupation of the earliest converts with rules of conduct and techniques of meditation. Early translators employed Daoist expressions as equivalents for Buddhist technical terms. Thus, the Buddha, in achieving enlightenment (*bodhi*), was described as having "obtained the Dao"; the Buddhist saints (*arhat*) become perfected Immortals (*zhenren*); and "non-action" (*wuwei*) was used to render nirvana (the

Buddhist state of bliss). A joint sacrifice to Laozi and the Buddha was performed by the Han emperor in 166 CE. During this period occurred the first reference to the notion that Laozi, after vanishing into the west, became the Buddha. This theory enjoyed a long and varied history. It claimed that Buddhism was a debased form of Daoism, designed by Laozi as a curb on the violent natures and vicious habits of the "western barbarians," and as such was entirely unsuitable for Chinese consumption. A variant theory even suggested that, by imposing celibacy on Buddhist monks, Laozi intended the foreigners' extinction. In approximately 300 CE, the Daoist scholar Wang Fou composed a "Classic of the Conversion of the Barbarians" (*Huahujing*), which was altered and expanded in subsequent centuries to encompass new developments in the continuing debate. Although there is no evidence that the earliest Daoist organization, literature, or ceremonies were in any way indebted to Buddhism, by the 4th century there was a distinct Buddhist influence upon the literary form of Daoist scriptures and the philosophical expression of the most eminent Daoist masters.

The process of interaction, however, was a mutual one, Daoism participating in the widening of thought because of the influence of a foreign religion and Buddhism undergoing a partial "Daoicization" as part of its adaptation to Chinese conditions. The Buddhist contribution is particularly noticeable in the developing conceptions of the afterlife;

Buddhist ideas of purgatory had a most striking effect not only on Daoism but especially on Chinese popular religion. On a more profound level the ultimate synthesis of Daoism and Buddhism was realized in the Chan (Japanese Zen) tradition (from the 7th century on), into which the paradoxes of the ancient Daoist mystics were integrated. Likewise, the goal of illumination in a single lifetime, rather than at the end of an indefinite succession of future existences, was analogous to the religious Daoist's objective of immortality as the culmination of his present life.

Chan Buddhism deeply influenced Neo-Confucianism, the renaissance of Confucian philosophy in Song times (960–1279), which in Chinese is called "Learning of the Way" (daoxue). In this movement Confucianism acquired a universal dimension beyond a concern for society. Neo-Confucian thought often seems as Daoist as the so-called neo-Daoist philosophy and literature seem Confucian.

As early as the Tang dynasty, there are traces of the syncretism of the "Three Religions" (sanjiao), which became a popular movement in Song and Ming China. A mixture of Confucian ethics, the Daoist system of merits, and the Buddhist concept of reincarnation produced such "books on goodness" (shanshu) as the Ganyingpian ("Tract on Actions and Retributions"). The school of the "Three Religions" was rejected by most Confucians and Buddhists but received wide support in Daoist circles. Many Daoist masters of those periods transmitted neidan and other techniques of inner cultivation to their disciples while at the same time preaching the moralism of the "Three Religions" to outsiders.

DAOIST CONTRIBUTIONS TO CHINESE SCIENCE

Daoist physiological techniques have, in themselves, no devotional character. They have the same preoccupations as physicians: to preserve health and to prolong physical life. Medicine developed independently from about the 1st century CE, but many Daoist faith healers and hygienists added to medical knowledge.

The earliest surviving medical book, the Huangdineijing, or "The Yellow Emperor's Esoteric Classic" (3rd century BCE?), presents itself as the teachings of a legendary Celestial Master addressed to the Yellow Emperor.

Experiments with minerals, plants, and animal substances, inspired to some extent by Daoist dietetics and by the search for the elixir of life, resulted in the 52 chapters of pharmacopoeia called Bencaogangmu, or "Great Pharmacopoeia" (16th century).

This interest in science is considered a reflection of the Daoist emphasis on direct observation and experience of the nature of things, as opposed to Confucian reliance on the authority of tradition. Zhuangzi declared that tradition tells what was good for a bygone age but not what is good for the present.

The Daoist secret of efficacy is to follow the nature of things; this does not imply scientific experimentation but rather a sensitivity and skill obtained by "minute concentration on the Dao running through natural objects of all kinds." This knowledge and skill cannot be handed down but is that which the men of old took with them when they died (*Zhuangzi*). The image for it is the skill of the artisan admired by the Daoists in their numerous parables on wheelwrights, meatcutters, sword makers, carvers, animal tamers, and musicians.

Though extolling the intuitive comprehension and skillful handling of matter, the Daoists did not observe nature in the Western sense and rejected technology out of their aversion to the artificial. Any new idea or discovery in China was phrased as "what the old masters really meant." This ideology of rediscovery makes it hard to study the evolution of scientific thought. Some progress over the ages (for example, in alchemy) can be seen, but the Daoist contribution to Chinese science might be smaller than it has been assumed.

DAOIST IMAGERY

Daoist literature manifests such richness and variety that scholars tend naturally to seek the symbolic modes of expression that served as points of unity within its historical diversity. No image is more fundamental to all phases of Daoism than that of the child. *Daodejing* praises the infant's closeness to the Dao in its freedom from outside impressions, and *Zhuangzi* describes the spiritual beings nurtured on primal substances, air and dew, as having the faces of children. Thus many of the spirits, both indwelling and celestial, in the esoteric system are described as resembling newborn babes, while the Immortals who appear in visions, though hundreds of years old, are at most adolescent in appearance. Other persistent images are those of mountain and cavern. Present in the older texts, they are carried over, with particular connotations, into the later works. The mountain as a meeting place of heaven and earth, gods and men, and master and disciple (as already in *Zhuangzi*), takes on a vast downward extension. Beneath the mountains are the great "cavern-heavens" (*dongtian*) of esoteric Daoism, a hierarchy staffed by numerous Immortals. Thus, for example, while Maoshan is only some 400 metres (1,300 feet) high to the gaze of the profane, the initiate knows that its luminous grottoes plunge thousands of metres into the earth. And *light* is everywhere in Daoist revelation: spirits and paradises alike gleam with brilliance unknown in the world of men.

INFLUENCE ON SECULAR LITERATURE

Already during the Warring States period and the early Han, Daoism had made its appearance in the works of the other schools. Both direct quotations and patent imitations were frequent, and citations from *Daodejing* and *Zhuangzi* abound throughout later Chinese literature, as do reminiscences of both their style and their content. Esoteric Daoist writings, too, held great fascination for men of letters. Their response might vary from a mere mention of the most celebrated Immortals to whole works inspired directly by specific Daoist texts and practices. Many a poet recorded his search, real or metaphorical, for Immortals or transcendent herbs or described his attempts at compounding an elixir. A certain number of technical terms became touchstones of poetic diction. The revealed literature of Maoshan came to have the greatest effect on secular writings. As works of great literary refinement, the *Lives of the Perfected* directly inspired a very famous tale, the *Intimate Life of Emperor Wu of Han* (*Han Wudi neizhuan;* late 6th century), which in highly polished terms describes the visit to the emperor of a goddess, the Queen Mother of the West. This work, in turn, made a decisive contribution to the development of Tang romantic fiction. Literary accounts of fantastic marvels also drew heavily on the wonders of Maoshan hagiography and topography. The Maoshan influence on Tang poetry was no less important. Precise references to the literature of the sect abound in the poems of the time, while many of the greatest poets, such as Li Bai, were formally initiated into the Maoshan organization. As awareness of these influences increases, scholars are faced with the intriguing question of the possible religious origins of whole genres of Chinese literature.

INFLUENCE ON THE VISUAL ARTS

A number of early Chinese books of spiritual interest claim to have been inspired by pictures seen on the walls of local temples. A similar tradition attaches to the *Lives of the Immortals,* which is said to derive from a pictorial work called *Portraits of the Immortals.* As has been noted, the Immortals were depicted on Han mirrors. Other illustrative materials were in close relation to the earliest esoteric Daoist literature. Graphic guides existed from early times to aid in the identification of sacred minerals and plants, particularly mushrooms. A later specimen of such a work is to be found in the Daoist Canon. This practical aspect of Daoist influence resulted in the exceptionally high technical level of botanical and mineralogical drawing that China soon attained. In calligraphy, too, Daoists soon set the highest standard. One of the greatest of all calligraphers, Wang Xizhi (*c.* 303–361), was an adherent of the Way of the Celestial Master, and one of his most renowned works was a transcription of the *Book of the Yellow Court.* The efficacy of talismans, in particular, depended on the precision of the strokes from which they were created. Figure painting was another field in which Daoists excelled. China's celebrated painter Gu Kaizhi, a

Daoist nuns and monks pray for world peace in Hong Kong on March 21, 2009, as part of a festival marking the birthday of Laozi, believed to be Daoism's father. Ted Aljibe/AFP/ Getty Images

practicing Daoist, left an essay containing directions for painting a scene in the life of the first Celestial Master, Zhang Daoling. Many works on Daoist themes, famous in their time but now lost, have been attributed to other great early masters. Of these, some may have been painted for use in ritual, and religious paintings of the Daoist pantheon are still produced today. The Daoist scriptures, with their instructions for visualization

of the spiritual hierarchy, including details of apparel and accoutrements, are ready-made painter's manuals. Finally, the language of speculative Daoism was pressed into service as the basic vocabulary of Chinese aesthetics. Consequently, many secular artists attempted to express their own conceptions of the "natural spontaneity" of *Zhuangzi* and *Laozi*'s "spirit of the valley." Here Daoism found still wider imaginative extension, and the efforts of these painters are embodied in those magnificent landscapes that have come to be thought of as most characteristically Chinese.

DAOISM IN
THE MODERN ERA

The principal refuge of Daoism in the 20th and 21st centuries was on Taiwan. Its establishment on the island is doubtless contemporary with the great emigration from the opposite mainland province of Fujian in the 17th and 18th centuries. The religion, however, has received new impetus since the 63rd celestial master, Zhang Enbu, took refuge there in 1949.

On Taiwan, Daoism may still be observed in its traditional setting, distinct from the manifestations of popular religion that surround it. Hereditary Daoist priests (Taiwanese *saigong*), called "blackheads" (*wutou*) from their headgear, are clearly set off from the exorcists (*fashi*) or "redheads" (*hongtou*) of the ecstatic cults. Their lengthy rites are still held, now known under the term *jiao* ("offering"), rather than the medieval *jai* ("retreat"). The liturgy chanted, in expanded Song form, still embodies elements that can be traced back to Zhang Daoling's sect. The religion has enjoyed a renaissance since the 1960s, with great activity being carried on in temple building and restoration.

CHAPTER 6

BUDDHISM

Buddhism is a religion and philosophy that developed from the teachings of the Buddha (Sanskrit: "awakened one"), a teacher who lived in northern India between the mid-6th and the mid-4th centuries BCE (before the Common Era). Spreading from India to Central and Southeast Asia, China, Korea, and Japan, Buddhism has played a central role in the spiritual, cultural, and social life of Asia, and during the 20th century it spread to the West.

Ancient Buddhist scripture and doctrine developed in several closely related literary languages of ancient India, especially in Pali and Sanskrit. In this chapter Pali and Sanskrit words that have gained currency in English are treated as English words and are rendered in the form in which they appear in English-language dictionaries. Exceptions occur in special circumstances—as, for example, in the case of the Sanskrit term *dharma* (Pali: *dhamma*), which has meanings that are not usually associated with the English "dharma." Pali forms are given in the sections on the core teachings of early Buddhism that are reconstructed primarily from Pali texts and in sections that deal with Buddhist traditions in which the primary sacred language is Pali. Sanskrit forms are given in the sections that deal with Buddhist traditions whose primary sacred language is Sanskrit and in other sections that deal with traditions whose primary sacred texts were translated from Sanskrit into a Central or East Asian language such as Tibetan or Chinese.

CULTURAL CONTEXT

Buddhism arose in northeastern India sometime between the late 6th century and the early 4th century BCE, a period of great social change and intense religious activity. There is disagreement among scholars about the dates of the Buddha's birth and death. Many modern scholars believe that the historical Buddha lived from about 563 to about 483 BCE. Many others believe that he lived about 100 years later (from about 448 to 368 BCE). At this time in India, there was much discontent with Brahmanic (Hindu high-caste) sacrifice and ritual. In northwestern India there were ascetics who tried to create a more personal and spiritual religious experience than that found in the Vedas (Hindu sacred scriptures). In the literature that grew out of this movement, the Upanishads, a new emphasis on renunciation and transcendental knowledge can be found. Northeastern India, which was less influenced by the Aryans who had developed the main tenets and practices of the Vedic Hindu faith, became the breeding ground of many new sects. Society in this area was troubled by the breakdown of tribal unity and the expansion of several petty kingdoms. Religiously, this was a time of doubt, turmoil, and experimentation.

A proto-Samkhya group (i.e., one based on the Samkhya school of Hinduism founded by Kapila) was already well established in the area. New sects abounded, including various skeptics (e.g., Sanjaya Belatthiputta), atomists (e.g., Pakudha Kaccayana), materialists (e.g., Ajita Kesakambali), and antinomians (i.e., those against rules or laws—e.g., Purana Kassapa). The most important sects to arise at the time of the Buddha, however, were the Ajivikas (Ajivakas), who emphasized the rule of fate (*niyati*), and the Jains, who stressed the need to free the soul from matter. Although the Jains, like the Buddhists, have often been regarded as atheists, their beliefs are actually more complicated. Unlike early Buddhists, both the Ajivikas and the Jains believed in the permanence of the elements that constitute the universe, as well as in the existence of the soul.

Despite the bewildering variety of religious communities, many shared the same vocabulary—*nirvana* (transcendent freedom), *atman* ("self" or "soul"), *yoga* ("union"), *karma* ("causality"), *Tathagata* ("one who has come" or "one who has thus gone"), *buddha* ("enlightened one"), *samsara* ("eternal recurrence" or "becoming"), and *dhamma* ("rule" or "law")—and most involved the practice of yoga. According to tradition, the Buddha himself was a yogi—that is, a miracle-working ascetic.

Buddhism, like many of the sects that developed in northeastern India at the time, was constituted by the presence of a charismatic teacher, by the teachings this leader promulgated, and by a community of adherents that was often made up of renunciant members and lay supporters. In the case of Buddhism, this pattern is reflected in the Triratna—i.e., the "Three Jewels" of Buddha (the teacher), *dharma* (the teaching), and *sangha* (the community).

In the centuries following the founder's death, Buddhism developed in two directions represented by two different groups. One was called the Hinayana (Sanskrit: "Lesser Vehicle"), a term given to it by its Buddhist opponents. This more conservative group, which included what is now called the Theravada (Pali: "Way of the Elders") community, compiled versions of the Buddha's teachings that had been preserved in collections called the *Sutta Pitaka* and the *Vinaya Pitaka* and retained them as normative. The other major group, which calls itself the Mahayana (Sanskrit: "Greater Vehicle"), recognized the authority of other teachings that, from the group's point of view, made salvation available to a greater number of people. These supposedly more advanced teachings were expressed in sutras that the Buddha purportedly made available only to his more advanced disciples.

As Buddhism spread, it encountered new currents of thought and religion. In some Mahayana communities, for example, the strict law of karma (the belief that virtuous actions create pleasure in the future and nonvirtuous actions create pain) was modified to accommodate new emphases on the efficacy of ritual actions and devotional practices. During the second half of the 1st millennium CE, a third major Buddhist movement, Vajrayana (Sanskrit: "Diamond Vehicle"), or Esoteric Buddhism, developed in India. This movement was influenced by gnostic and magical currents pervasive at that time, and its aim was to obtain spiritual liberation and purity more speedily.

Despite these vicissitudes, Buddhism did not abandon its basic principles. Instead, they were reinterpreted, rethought, and reformulated in a process that led to the creation of a great body of literature. This literature includes the Pali *Tipitaka* ("Three Baskets")—the *Sutta Pitaka* ("Basket of Discourse"), which contains the Buddha's sermons; the *Vinaya Pitaka* ("Basket of Discipline"), which contains the rule governing the monastic order; and the *Abhidhamma Pitaka* ("Basket of Special [Further] Doctrine"), which contains doctrinal systematizations and summaries. These Pali texts have served as the basis for a long and very rich tradition of commentaries that were written and preserved by adherents of the Theravada community. The Mahayana and Vajrayana/Esoteric traditions have accepted as Buddhavacana ("the word of the Buddha") many other sutras and tantras, along with extensive treatises and commentaries based on these texts. Consequently, from the first sermon of the Buddha at Sarnath to the most recent derivations, there is an indisputable continuity—a development or metamorphosis around a central nucleus—by virtue of which Buddhism is differentiated from other religions.

LIFE OF THE BUDDHA

The teacher known as the Buddha lived in northern India sometime between the mid-6th and the mid-4th centuries before the Common Era. In ancient India the title *buddha* referred to an enlightened being who has awakened from the sleep of ignorance and achieved freedom from suffering. According to the various traditions of Buddhism, buddhas have existed in the past and will exist in the future. Some Buddhists believe that there is only one buddha for each historical age, others that all beings will become buddhas because they possess the buddha nature (*tathagatagarbha*).

The historical figure referred to as the Buddha (whose life is known largely through legend) was born on the northern edge of the Ganges River basin, an area on the periphery of the ancient civilization of North India, in what is today southern Nepal. He is said to have lived for 80 years. His family name was Gautama (in Sanskrit) or Gotama (in Pali), and his given name was Siddhartha (Sanskrit: "he who achieves his aim") or Siddhatta (in Pali). He is frequently called Shakyamuni, "the sage of the Shakya clan." In Buddhist texts he is most commonly addressed as Bhagavat (often translated as "Lord"), and he refers to himself as the Tathagata, which can mean both "one who has thus come" and "one who has thus gone." Traditional sources on the date of his death—or, in the language of the tradition, his "passage into nirvana"—range from 2420 to 290 BCE. Scholarship in the 20th century limited this range considerably, with opinion generally divided between those who believed he lived from about 563 to 483 BCE and those who believed he lived about a century later.

Information about his life derives largely from Buddhist texts, the earliest of which were produced shortly before the beginning of the Common Era and thus several centuries after his death. According to the traditional accounts, however, the Buddha was born into the ruling Shakya clan and was a member of the Kshatriya, or warrior, caste. His mother, Maha Maya, dreamt one night that an elephant entered her womb, and 10 lunar months later, while she was strolling in the garden of Lumbini, her son emerged from under her right arm. His early life was one of luxury and comfort, and his father protected him from exposure to the ills of the world, including old age, sickness, and death. At age 16 he married the princess Yashodhara, who would eventually bear him a son. At 29, however, the prince had a profound experience when he first observed the suffering of the world while on chariot

Buddhist guardian deity, three-colour painted ceramic sculpture from Zhongbaocun, near Xi'an, Shaanxi province, China, 8th century, Tang dynasty; in the Shaanxi Provincial Museum, Xi'an, China. Wang Lu/ChinaStock Photo Library

rides outside the palace. He resolved then to renounce his wealth and family and live the life of an ascetic. During the next six years, he practiced meditation with several teachers and then, with five companions, undertook a life of extreme self-mortification. One day, while bathing in a river, he fainted from weakness and therefore concluded that mortification was not the path to liberation from suffering. Abandoning the life of extreme asceticism, the prince sat in meditation under a tree and received enlightenment, sometimes identified with understanding the Four Noble Truths.

Dream of Maya presaging the Buddha's birth, marble relief from Nagarjunikonda, Andhra Pradesh state, India, Amaravati school, c. 3rd century CE; in the India Museum, Kolkata. P. Chandra

For the next 45 years, the Buddha spread his message throughout northeastern India, established orders of monks and nuns, and received the patronage of kings and merchants. At the age of 80, he became seriously ill. He then met with his disciples for the last time to impart his final instructions and passed into nirvana. His body was then cremated and the relics distributed and enshrined in stupas (funerary monuments that usually contained relics), where they would be venerated.

The Buddha's place within the tradition, however, cannot be understood by focusing exclusively on the events of his life and time (even to the extent that they are known). Instead, he must be viewed within the context of Buddhist theories of time and history. Among these theories is the belief that the universe is the product of karma, the law of the cause and effect of actions. The beings of the universe are reborn without beginning in six realms as gods, demigods, humans, animals, ghosts, and hell beings. The cycle of rebirth, called samsara (literally "wandering"), is regarded as a domain of suffering, and the Buddhist's ultimate goal is to escape from that suffering. The means of escape remains unknown until, over the course of millions of lifetimes, a person perfects himself, ultimately gaining the power to discover the path out of samsara and then revealing that path to the world.

A person who has set out to discover the path to freedom from suffering and then to teach it to others is called a bodhisattva. A person who has discovered that path, followed it to its end, and taught it to the world is called a buddha. Buddhas are not reborn after they die but enter a state beyond suffering called nirvana (literally "passing away"). Because buddhas appear so rarely over the course of time and because only they reveal the path to liberation from suffering, the appearance of a buddha in the world is considered a momentous event.

The story of a particular buddha begins before his birth and extends beyond his death. It encompasses the millions of lives spent on the path toward enlightenment and Buddhahood and the persistence of the buddha through his teachings and his relics after he has passed into nirvana. The historical Buddha is regarded as neither the first nor the last buddha to appear in the world. According to some traditions he is the 7th buddha, according to another he is the 25th, and according to yet another he is the 4th. The next buddha, Maitreya, will appear after Shakyamuni's teachings and relics have disappeared from the world.

Although the Buddha did not leave any written works, various versions of his teachings were preserved orally by his disciples. In the centuries following his death, hundreds of texts (called sutras) were attributed to him and would subsequently be translated into the languages of Asia.

SPREAD TO CENTRAL ASIA AND CHINA

The spread of Buddhism into Central Asia is still not completely understood. However murky the details may be, it is clear that the trade routes that ran from northwestern India to northern China facilitated both the introduction of Buddhism to Central Asia and the maintenance, for many centuries, of a flourishing Buddhist culture there.

By the beginning of the Common Era, Buddhism had probably been introduced into Eastern Turkistan. According to tradition, a son of Asoka founded the kingdom of Khotan around 240 BCE. The grandson of this king supposedly introduced Buddhism to Khotan, where it became the state religion. Other accounts indicate that the Indo-Scythian king Kaniska of the Kushan (Kusana) dynasty, which ruled in northern India, Afghanistan, and parts of Central Asia in the 1st to 2nd century CE, encouraged the spread of Buddhism into Central Asia. Kaniska purportedly called an important Buddhist council and patronized the Gandhara school of Buddhist art, which introduced Greek and Persian elements into Buddhist iconography. In the northern part of Chinese Turkistan, Buddhism spread from Kuqa (Kucha) to the kingdoms of Agnidesa (Karashahr), Gaochang (Torpan), and Bharuka (Aksu). According to Chinese travelers who visited Central Asia, the Hinayanists were strongest in Turpan, Shanshan, Kashi (Kashgar), and Kuqa, while Mahayana strongholds were located in Yarkant (Yarkand) and Hotan (Khotan).

In Central Asia there was a confusing welter of languages, religions, and cultures, and, as Buddhism interacted with these various traditions, it changed and developed. Shamanism, Zoroastrianism, Nestorian Christianity, and Islam all penetrated these lands and coexisted with Buddhism. Some of the Mahayana bodhisattvas, such as Amitabha, may have been inspired in part by Zoroastrianism. There is also evidence of some syncretism between Buddhism and Manichaeism, an Iranian dualistic religion that was founded in the 3rd century CE.

Buddhism flourished in parts of Central Asia until the 11th century, particularly under the patronage of the Uighur Turks. But with the successful incursions of Islam (beginning in the 7th century CE) and the decline of the Tang dynasty (618–907) in China, Central Asia ceased to be the important crossroads of Indian and Chinese trade and culture that it once had been. Buddhism in the area gradually became a thing of the past.

CHINA

Although there are reports of Buddhists in China as early as the 3rd century BCE, Buddhism was not actively propagated there until the early centuries of the Common Era. According to tradition, Buddhism was introduced into China after the Han emperor Mingdi (reigned 57/58–75/76 CE) dreamed of a flying golden deity in what was interpreted as a vision of the Buddha. The emperor dispatched emissaries to India who returned to China with the *Sutra in Forty-two Sections*, which was deposited in a temple outside the capital of Louyang. However this may be, Buddhism most likely entered China gradually, first primarily through Central Asia and later by way of the trade routes around and through Southeast Asia.

THE EARLY CENTURIES

Buddhism in China during the Han dynasty was deeply coloured with magical practices, which made it compatible with popular Chinese Daoism, an integral component of contemporary folk religion. Instead of the doctrine of no-self, early Chinese Buddhists seem to have taught the indestructibility of the soul. Nirvana became a kind of immortality. They also taught the theory of karma, the values of charity and compassion, and the need to suppress the passions. Until the end of the Han dynasty, there was a virtual symbiosis between Daoism and Buddhism, and both religions advocated similar ascetic practices as a means of attaining immortality. It was widely believed that Laozi, the founder of Daoism, had been reborn in India as the Buddha. Many Chinese emperors worshiped Laozi and the Buddha on the same altar. The first translations of Buddhist sutras into Chinese—namely, those dealing with topics such as breath control and mystical concentration—utilized a Daoist vocabulary to make them intelligible to the Chinese.

After the Han period, Buddhist monks were often used by non-Chinese emperors in the north of China for their political-military counsel and their skill in magic. At the same time, in the south Buddhism penetrated the philosophical and literary circles of the gentry. One of the most important contributions to the growth of Buddhism in China during this period was the work of translation. The greatest of the early translators was the learned monk Kumarajiva, who had studied the Hindu Vedas, the occult sciences,

These statues are located in the Longmen caves Buddhist shrine in Luoyang, Henan province, China. Andrea Pistolesi/The Image Bank/Getty Images

and astronomy, as well as the Hinayana and Mahayana sutras before he was taken to the Chinese court in 401 CE.

During the 5th and 6th centuries CE, Buddhist schools from India were established in China, and new, specifically Chinese schools were formed. Buddhism was a powerful intellectual force in China; monastic establishments proliferated; and Buddhism became established among the peasantry. Thus, it is not surprising that, when the Sui dynasty (581–618) established its rule over a reunified China, Buddhism flourished as a state religion.

DEVELOPMENTS DURING THE TANG DYNASTY (618–907)

The golden age of Buddhism in China occurred during the Tang dynasty. Although the Tang emperors were usually Daoists themselves, they favoured Buddhism, which had become extremely popular. Under the Tang the government extended its control over the monasteries and the ordination and legal status of monks. From this time forward, the Chinese monk styled himself simply *chen* ("subject").

During this period several Chinese schools developed their own distinctive approaches and systematized the vast body of Buddhist texts and teachings. There was a great expansion in the number of Buddhist monasteries and the amount of land they owned. It was also during this period that many scholars made pilgrimages to India and returned with texts

and spiritual and intellectual inspiration that greatly enriched Buddhism in China. Buddhism was never able to replace Daoism and Confucianism, however, and in 845 the emperor Wuzong began a major persecution. According to records, 4,600 Buddhist temples and 40,000 shrines were destroyed, and 260,500 monks and nuns were forced to return to lay life.

BUDDHISM AFTER THE TANG

Buddhism in China never recovered completely from the great persecution of 845. It did maintain much of its heritage, however, and it continued to play a significant role in the religious life of China. On one hand, Buddhism retained its identity as Buddhism and generated new forms of expression. These included texts such as the *you lu* ("recorded sayings") of famous teachers, which were oriented primarily toward monks, as well as more literary creations such as the *Journey to the West* (written in the 16th century) and *Dream of the Red Chamber* (18th century). On the other hand, Buddhism coalesced with the Confucian, Neo-Confucian, and Daoist traditions to form a complex multireligious ethos within which all three traditions were more or less comfortably encompassed.

The various schools that retained the greatest vitality in China were the Chan school (better known in the West by its Japanese name, Zen), which was noted for its emphasis on meditation, and the Pure Land tradition, which emphasized Buddhist devotion. The former school was most influential among the cultured elite, especially through the arts. Chan artists during the Song dynasty (960–1279) had a decisive impact on Chinese landscape painting. Artists used images of flowers, rivers, and trees, executed with sudden, deft strokes, to evoke an insight into the flux and emptiness of all reality. The Pure Land tradition was most influential among the population as a whole and was sometimes associated with secret societies and peasant uprisings. But the two seemingly disparate traditions were often very closely linked. In addition, they were mixed with other Buddhist elements such as the so-called "masses for the dead" that had originally been popularized by the practitioners of Esoteric Buddhism.

A reform movement aimed at revitalizing the Chinese Buddhist tradition and adapting its teachings and institutions to modern conditions took shape during the early 20th century. However, the disruptions caused by the Sino-Japanese War (1937–45) and the subsequent establishment of a communist government in China (1949) were not helpful to the Buddhist cause. During the Cultural Revolution (especially 1966–69), Buddhist temples and monasteries suffered massive destruction, and the Buddhist community was the victim of severe repression. After 1976 the Chinese government pursued a more tolerant policy, and Buddhism began to show new life. The extent and depth of continuing Buddhist vitality, however, is difficult to determine.

SANGHA, SOCIETY, AND STATE

Buddhists have always recognized the importance of community life, and over the centuries there has developed a distinctive symbiotic relationship between monks (and in some cases nuns) and the lay community. The relationship between the monastics and the laity has differed from place to place and from time to time, but throughout most of Buddhist history both groups have played an essential role in the process of constituting and reconstituting the Buddhist world. Moreover, both the monastics and the laity have engaged in a variety of common and complementary religious practices that have expressed Buddhist orientations and values, structured Buddhist societies, and addressed the soteriological and practical concerns of individuals.

MONASTIC INSTITUTIONS

The *sangha* is the assembly of Buddhist monks (and in some contexts nuns) that has, from the origins of Buddhism, authoritatively studied, taught, and preserved the teachings of the Buddha. In their communities monastics have been responsible for providing an example of the ideal mode of Buddhist life, for teaching Buddhist principles and practices to the laity, for generating and participating in basic ritual activities, for offering "fields of merit" that enable lay members of the community to improve their spiritual condition, for providing protection against evil forces (particularly though

Young Tai pupils studying in a Buddhist monastery. S.E. Hedin/
Ostman Agency

live apart from worldly concerns, a situation that has usually been believed necessary or at least advisable in order to follow the path that leads most directly to release.

SANGHAS

According to scholars of early Buddhism, at the time of the Buddha there were numerous mendicants in northeastern India who wandered and begged individually or in groups. They had forsaken the life of a householder and the involvement with worldly affairs that this entails in order to seek a pattern of belief and practice that would meaningfully explain life and offer salvation. When such a seeker met someone who seemed to offer such a salvific message, he would accept him as a teacher (guru) and wander with him. The situation of these mendicants is summed up in the greeting with which they met other religious wanderers. This greeting asked, "Under whose guidance have you accepted religious mendicancy? Who is your master (sattha)? Whose dhamma is agreeable to you?"

According to early Buddhist texts, the Buddha established an order of

not exclusively supernatural forces), and for maintaining a variety of other services that have varied over time and place. In exchange for their contributions, the monastics have received veneration and support from the laity, who thereby earn merit, advance their own well-being, and contribute to the well-being of others (including, in many cases, the ancestors of the living).

Besides serving as the centre of Buddhist learning, meditation, ritual activity, and teaching, the monastery offers the monk or nun an opportunity to

male monastics early on in his ministry and outlined the rules and procedures for governing their common life. These texts also report that later in his career he reluctantly agreed to a proposal made by his aunt Mahapajapati and supported by his favourite disciple, Ananda, to establish an order of nuns. The Buddha then set down rules and procedures for the order of the nuns and for the relationship between the order of nuns and the order of monks. (In the discussion that follows, the emphasis will be on the order of monks.)

The various mendicant groups interrupted their wanderings during the rainy season (*vassa*) from July through August. At this time they gathered at various rain retreats (*vassavasa*), usually situated near villages, where they would beg for their daily needs and continue their spiritual quest. The Buddha and his followers may well have been the first group to found such a yearly rain retreat.

After the Buddha's death his followers did not separate but continued to wander and enjoy the rain retreat together. In their retreats the Buddha's followers probably built their own huts and lived separately, but their sense of community with other Buddhists led them to gather at the time of the full and new moons to recite the *patimokkha*, a declaration of their steadfastness in observing the monastic discipline. This occasion, in which the laity also participated, was called the *uposatha*.

Within several centuries of the Buddha's death, the *sangha* came to include two different monastic groups.

One group retained the wandering mode of existence. The other, much larger, group gave up the forest life and settled in permanent monastic settlements (*viharas*); it is the earliest truly cenobitic monastic group about which any knowledge exists.

There appear to be two major reasons for the change in the mode of living of most Buddhist monks. First, the Buddha's followers were able, through their common loyalty to the Buddha and his teachings, to build up a certain coherent organization. Second, as acts of piety, the laity gave gifts of land and raised buildings in which the followers of the Buddha might live permanently, assured of a supply of the staples of life and also able to fulfill the Buddha's directive to minister to the laity. In this manner small *viharas* were established in northeastern India and adjoining areas into which Buddhism spread.

In all Buddhist countries monasteries served as centres of teaching, learning, and outreach. Different types of monastic establishments developed in particular areas and in particular contexts. In several regions there were at least two types of institutions. There were a few large public monasteries that usually functioned in greater or lesser accord with classical Buddhist norms. There were also many smaller monasteries, often located in rural areas, that were much more loosely regulated. Often these were hereditary institutions in which the rights and privileges of the abbot were passed on to an adopted disciple. In areas where clerical marriage was practiced—for example, in medieval Sri Lanka, in certain Tibetan areas, and in post-Heian Japan—a tradition of blood inheritance developed.

INTERNAL ORGANIZATION OF THE *SANGHA*

The transformation of the *sangha* from a group of wandering mendicants, loosely bound together by their commitment to the Buddha and his teachings, to monks living closely together in a permanent monastery necessitated the development of rules and a degree of hierarchical organization. It appears that the earliest organization within Indian monasteries was democratic in nature. This democratic character arose from two important historical factors. First, the Buddha did not, as was the custom among the teachers of his time, designate a human successor. Instead, the Buddha taught that each monk should strive to follow the path that he had preached. This decision placed every monk on the same footing. There could be no absolute authority vested in one person, for the authority was the *dhamma* that the Buddha had taught. Second, the region in which Buddhism arose was noted for a system of tribal democracy, or republicanism, that had existed in the past and was preserved by some groups during the Buddha's lifetime. Within this tradition each polity had an elected assembly that decided important issues.

This tradition, which was consonant with the antiauthoritarian nature of the Buddha's teaching, was adopted by the early *sangha*. When an issue arose, all the monks of the monastery assembled. The issue was put before the body of monks and discussed. If any solution was forthcoming, it had to be read three times, with silence signifying acceptance. If there was debate, a vote might be taken or the issue referred to committee or to arbitration by the elders of a neighbouring monastery. As the *sangha* developed, a certain division of labour and hierarchical administration was adopted. The abbot became the head of this administrative hierarchy and was vested with power over monastic affairs. In many countries there developed state-controlled hierarchies, which enabled kings and other political authorities to exert a significant amount of control over the monks and their activities.

The antiauthoritarian character of Buddhism, however, continued to assert itself. In China, for instance, the abbot referred all important questions to the assembled monks, who had elected him their leader. Similarly, in Southeast Asian countries there has traditionally been a popular distaste for hierarchy, which makes it difficult to enforce rules in the numerous almost-independent monasteries.

As the Buddhist *sangha* developed, specific rules and rites were enacted that differ very little in Buddhist monasteries even today. The rules by which the monks are judged and the punishments that should be assessed are found in the *vinaya* texts (*vinaya* literally means "that which leads"). The *Vinaya Pitaka* of the Theravada canon contains precepts that were supposedly given by the Buddha as he judged a particular situation. While in many cases the Buddha's authorship may be doubted, the attempt is made to refer all authority to the Buddha and not to one of his disciples. The heart of the *vinaya* texts is the *patimokkha*, which became a list of monastic rules.

Ideally, the *patimokkha* is recited by the assembled monks every fortnight, with a pause after each one so that any monk who has transgressed this rule may confess and receive his punishment. While the number of rules in the *patimokkha* differs in the various schools, with 227, 250, and 253, respectively, in the Pali, Chinese, and Tibetan canons, the rules are essentially the same. The first part of the *patimokkha* deals with the four gravest sins, which necessarily lead to expulsion from the monastery. They are sexual intercourse, theft, murder, and exaggeration of one's miraculous powers. The other rules, in seven sections, deal with transgressions of a lesser nature, such as drinking or lying.

In China, which follows the Mahayana and Vajrayana traditions of Buddhism, there was traditionally a stage of one year before the aspirant could become a novice. This was a year of probation, during which the aspirant did not receive tonsure and remained subject to governmental taxation and service while receiving instructions and performing menial tasks within the monastery. At the end of this period, the aspirant had to pass a test, which included the recitation of part of a well-known sutra—the length depending upon whether the applicant was male or female—and a discussion of various doctrinal questions. In China usually only those who were of exceptional character or who were affiliated with the government progressed beyond the novice stage.

According to *vinaya* rules, entry into the *sangha* is an individual affair that depends on the wishes of the individual and his family. In some Buddhist countries, however, ordination was often under the control of the state, which conducted the examinations to determine entry or advancement in the *sangha*. In certain situations ordination could be obtained through the favour of high officials or through the purchase of an ordination certificate from the government. At times the government engaged in the selling of ordination certificates in order to fill its treasury.

The life of a Buddhist monk originally involved wandering, poverty, begging, and strict sexual abstinence. The monks were supposed to live only on alms, to wear clothes made from cloth taken from rubbish heaps, and to possess only three robes, one girdle, an alms bowl, a razor, a needle, and a water strainer for filtering insects from drinking water (so as not to kill or imbibe them). In all schools, however, begging has become merely a symbolic gesture used to teach humility or compassion or to raise funds for special purposes. Also, the growth of large monasteries has often led to compromises on the rule of poverty. While the monk might technically give up his property before entering the monastery—though even this rule is sometimes relaxed—the community of monks might inherit wealth and receive lavish gifts of land. The acquisition of wealth has often led to the attainment of temporal power. This factor, in addition to the self-governing nature of Buddhist monasteries and the early Buddhist connection with Indian kingship, has influenced the interaction of the *sangha* and the state.

SOCIETY AND STATE

Buddhism is sometimes inaccurately described as a purely monastic, otherworldly religion. In the earliest phases of the tradition, the Buddha was pictured as a teacher who addressed not only renouncers but lay householders. Moreover, although he is not depicted in the early texts as a social reformer, the Buddha does address issues of social order and responsibility. Perhaps the most famous early text on this topic is the *Sigalovada Sutta*, which has been called the "householder's *vinaya*."

Throughout their history Buddhists have put forth varying forms of social ethics based on notions of karmic justice (the "law" that good deeds will be rewarded with happy results while evil deeds will entail suffering for the one who does them); the cultivation of virtues such as self-giving, compassion, and evenhandedness; and the fulfillment of responsibilities to parents, teachers, rulers, and so on. Moreover, Buddhists have formulated various notions of cosmogony, cosmology, and soteriology that have provided legitimacy for the social hierarchies and political orders with which they have been associated. For the most part, Buddhism has played a conservative, moderating role in the social and political organization of various Asian societies, but the tradition has also given rise to more radical and revolutionary movements.

Over the course of Buddhism's long history, the relationship between the Buddhist community and state authority has taken many forms. The early Buddhist *sangha* in India appears to have been treated by Indian rulers as a self-governing unit not subject to their power unless it proved subversive or was threatened by internal or external disruption.

In China, Buddhism has been seen as a foreign religion, as a potential competitor with the state, and as a drain on national resources of men and wealth. These perceptions have led to sharp persecutions of Buddhism and to rules curbing its influence. Some of the rules attempted to limit the number of monks and to guarantee governmental influence in ordination through state examinations and the granting of ordination certificates. At other times, such as during the early centuries of the

Tang dynasty (618–907), Buddhism was virtually a state religion. The government created a commissioner of religion to earn merit for the state by erecting temples, monasteries, and images in honour of the Buddha.

Only in Tibet did Buddhists establish a theocratic polity that lasted for an extended period of time. Beginning in the 12th century, Tibetan monastic groups forged relationships with the powerful Mongol khans that often gave them control of governmental affairs. In the 17th century the Dge-lugs-pa school, working with the Mongols, established a monastic regime that was able to maintain almost continual control until Tibet's incorporation into the People's Republic in the 1950s.

During the premodern period the various Buddhist communities in Asia developed working relationships with the sociopolitical systems in their particular areas. As a result of Western colonial incursions, and especially after the establishment of new political ideologies and political systems during the 19th and 20th centuries, these older patterns of accommodation between Buddhism and state authority were seriously disrupted. In other cases, as in the Tibet, an autonomous region, strong tensions remained.

MAHAYANA: THE MAIN CHINESE TRADITION

Mahayana Buddhism is both a system of metaphysics dealing with the basic structure and principles of reality and, primarily, a theoretical propaedeutic to the achievement of a desired state. Arising in India in the 1st century CE, it spread to Central Asia, China, Japan, mainland Southeast Asia, Java, Sumatra, and even Sri Lanka. Its teachings involved basic shifts in doctrine and approach, though there were precedents in earlier schools. It taught that neither the self nor the *dharmas* exist. Moreover, for the elite arhat ideal, it substituted the bodhisattva, one who vows to become a buddha and delays entry into nirvana to help others. In Mahayana, love for creatures is exalted to the highest; a bodhisattva is encouraged to offer the merit he derives from good deeds for the good of others. The tension between morality and mysticism that agitated India also influenced the Mahayana.

BASIC TEACHINGS

In the Mahayana tradition the Buddha is viewed as a supramundane being. He multiplies himself and is often reflected in a pentad of buddhas—Vairocana, Aksobhya, Ratnasambhava, Amitabha, and Amoghasiddhi—who reveal various doctrines and elaborate liturgies and sometimes take the place of Shakyamuni.

As the tradition developed, there emerged new texts that were considered by Mahayana adherents to be Buddhavacana ("the word or words of the Buddha"). This new literature went far beyond the ancient canons and was believed to be the highest revelation,

ZHENYAN

During the 7th, 8th, and 9th centuries, Indian Esoteric Buddhism spread to Southeast Asia and East Asia. In East Asia, especially China, Esoteric Buddhism became established in the Zhenyan ("True Word") school.

According to the Zhenyan tradition, Esoteric Buddhism was taken from India to China by three missionary monks who translated the basic Zhenyan texts. The first monk, Shubhakarasimha, arrived in China in 716, and he translated the Mahavairocana-sutra *and a closely related ritual compendium, the* Susiddhikara, *into Chinese. The other two monks, Vajrabodhi and his disciple Amoghavajra, arrived in 720 and produced two abridged translations of the* Sarvatathagatatattvasamgraha *("Symposium of Truth of All the Buddhas"), also known as the* Tattvasamgraha.

Between the arrival of Shubhakarasimha and the great persecution of 845, the Zhenyan school enjoyed amazing success. The tradition of Shubhakarasimha and the Mahavairocana-sutra *merged with that of Vajrabodhi and the* Tattvasamgraha. *The Chinese disciples of this new tradition, such as Huiguo, contributed to an emerging Zhenyan synthesis. The combination of sophisticated doctrinal instruction and miracle-working powers supposedly conferred by the Esoteric rituals enabled Zhenyan leaders to gain the confidence of the court, especially of Emperor Daizong (762–779), who rejected Daoism in favour of Zhenyan Buddhism.*

Although Zhenyan lost its position of prominence in China after the persecution of 845, it maintained spiritual vitality and communal visibility through the Song dynasty (960–1279). Moreover, the Zhenyan school contributed a great deal that has endured in the larger fabric of Chinese religion.

superseding earlier texts. In this literature the teaching is thought to operate on various levels, each adapted to the intellectual capacity and karmic propensities of those who hear it.

BODHISATTVA IDEAL

The purpose of the bodhisattva is to achieve enlightenment and to fulfill the vow to become a buddha. The bodhisattva also foregoes entrance into nirvana in order to remain in the world as long as there are creatures to be saved from suffering.

Beginning with the vow to become a buddha, the career of a bodhisattva, according to some texts, traverses 10 stages or spiritual levels (*bhumi*) and achieves purification through the practice of the 10 perfections (*paramitas*). These levels elevate the bodhisattva to Buddhahood. The first six levels are preliminary, representing the true practice of the six perfections (generosity, morality, patience, vigour, concentration, and wisdom). Even though further purification and fortification must be achieved in the following stages, irreversibility occurs as soon as the seventh stage has been reached and the bodhisattva has assumed the true buddha nature. This is the moment when he engages in activity aimed at fulfilling the obligations of a bodhisattva. The difference between this and the preceding six stages is that now the activity is explained as an innate and spontaneous impulse manifested with conscious constraint and therefore not subject to doubt. Everything is now uncreated, ungenerated; thus, the body of the bodhisattva becomes identified more and more completely with the essential body (*dharma-kaya*), with Buddhahood, and with omniscience.

THREE BUDDHA BODIES

The three bodies (*tri-kaya*; i.e., modes of being) of the Buddha are rooted in Hinayana teachings concerning the physical body, the mental body, and the body of the law. The theory of the three bodies was a subject of major discussion for the Mahayana, becoming part of the salvation process and assuming central significance in doctrine. The emanation body (*nirmana-kaya*) is the form of the Buddha that appears in the world to teach

Avalokiteshvara, the compassionate bodhisattva, shown as a sympathetic figure with 11 heads and 8 arms, symbolic of his ability to sense humankind's needs everywhere in the universe. In the Rijksmuseum voor Volkenkunde, Leiden, Netherlands. Courtesy of Rijksmuseum voor Volkenkunde, Leiden, The Netherlands

people the path to liberation. The enjoyment (or bliss) body (*sambhoga-kaya*) is the celestial body of the Buddha to which contemplation can ascend. In the heavenly regions, or Pure Lands, the enjoyment body teaches the bodhisattva doctrines that are unintelligible to those who are unenlightened. The unmanifested body of the law (*dharma-kaya*) already appears in the *Saddharmapundarika*, or *Lotus Sutra*, a transitional text of great importance to Mahayana devotional schools. In many Mahayana texts buddhas are infinite and share an identical nature—the *dharma-kaya*.

As anticipated in ancient schools, the Buddha is the law (*dharma*) and is identified with an eternal *dharma*, enlightenment (*bodhi*), and nirvana. In later schools real existence is opposed to the mere appearance of existence, and voidness, the "thingness of things," an undefinable condition, present and immutable within the Buddhas, is stressed. All is in the *dharma-kaya*, the third body and expression of ultimate reality; nothing is outside it, just as nothing is outside space; transcendence and immanence come together. Other schools posit a presence that is innate within all human beings, even if it is not perceived. It is like a gem hidden in dross, which shines in its purity as soon as the veil of ignorance has been removed.

New Revelations

New revelations are made on earth and in heavenly paradises by Shakyamuni and other buddhas. The teaching is expounded uninterruptedly in the universe because worlds and paradises are infinite and all buddhas are consubstantial with the essential body. They speak to assemblies of *shravakas* (disciples), bodhisattvas, gods, and demons. The authors of the new doctrines revealed their religious enthusiasm in various highly expressive ways, filling their works with phantasmagoria of celestial choruses, fabulous visions in which shine flashes of new speculations, and trains of thought influenced by Indian speculative and mystical traditions. The texts, from which new trends spring, overflow with repetitions and modulate the same arguments with a variety of readings.

Mahayana thinkers faced the daunting challenge of producing a completely logical arrangement of this prolix literature, some of which had legendary origins. The *Prajnaparamita* ("Perfection of Wisdom") and the *Avatamsaka-sutras* ("Flower Ornament Sutra"), for instance, are said to have been concealed by the *nagas*, demigods that live in miraculous palaces in an underground kingdom. There are various *Prajnaparamita* texts, ranging from 100,000 verses (the *Shatasahasrika*) to only a few lines (the *Prajnaparamitahrdaya-sutra*, famous in English as the *Heart Sutra*). The fundamental assumption of the *Prajnaparamita* is expounded in a famous verse: "like light, a mirage, a lamp, an illusion, a drop of water, a dream, a lightning flash; thus must all compounded things be considered." Not only is there no "self," but all things lack a real nature (*svabhava*) of their own. The *Prajnaparamita-sutras* announce that the world as it appears to us does not exist, that reality is the indefinable "thingness of things" (*tathata*; *dharmanam dharmata*), that voidness (*shunyata*) is an absolute "without signs or characteristics" (*animitta*).

Mahayana Schools and Their Texts

The Mahayana tradition encompasses a great many different schools, including the Madhyamika; the Yogacara or Vijnanavada (Vijnaptamatrata); the Avatamsaka school, which recognized the special importance of the *Avatamsaka Sutra*; a number of different schools that recognized the special authority of the *Saddharmapundarika* (*Lotus Sutra*); various Pure Land devotional schools; and several Dhyana ("Meditation") schools.

Madhyamika (Sanlun/Sanron)

The Madhyamika ("Doctrine of the Middle Way") system, also known as Shunyavada ("Theory of Negativity or Relativity"), held both subject and object to be unreal and systematized the doctrine of *shunyata* ("cosmic emptiness") contained in the *Prajnaparamita* literature.

Along with his disciple Aryadeva, the Indian philosopher Nagarjuna (c. 150–250 CE) is recognized as the founder and principal exponent of the Madhyamika system.

Nagarjuna is the presumed author of the voluminous *Mahaprajnaparamita-shastra* ("The Great Treatise on the Perfection of Wisdom"), preserved in its Chinese translation (402–405) by Kumarajia, and the *Mulamadhyamakakarika* (more commonly known as *Madhyamika Karika*; "Fundamentals of the Middle Way"), which is considered by many to be the Madhyamika work par excellence. The main work of Aryadeva, the *Catuhshataka*, criticizes other forms of Buddhism and the classical Sanskrit philosophical systems.

Nagarjuna and his followers sought a middle position, devoid of name and character and beyond all thought and words. They used rigorous logic to demonstrate the absurdity of various philosophical positions, including those of Hindus and other Buddhists. Assuming that contradiction is proof of error, Nagarjuna took any point of view that would reveal the error of his opponents. He did not, however, accept the opposing point of view but used it only as a means to expose the relativity of the system he was attacking. Because he was willing to refute his first position, he could claim adherence to no doctrine. Moreover, Nagarjuna attempted to prove that all worldly thought is empty (*shunya*) or relative and that the true path is that of the middle, the path that is between or, more correctly, above extremes. This belief has been called the doctrine of emptiness of all things, which posits that all things lack essential characteristics and exist only in relation to conditions surrounding them.

Nagarjuna presented this middle path above extremes in his statement of the Eightfold Path of Buddhism:

Nothing comes into being, nor does anything disappear. Nothing is eternal, nor has anything an end. Nothing is identical, nor is anything differentiated. Nothing moves here, nor does anything move there.

In presenting these pairs of opposites, Nagarjuna taught that anything that can be conceptualized or put into words is relative. This led to the Madhyamika identification of nirvana and samsara, which are empty concepts with the truth lying somewhere beyond.

After the world's emptiness or relativity has been proved, the question arises of how one is to go beyond this position. Nagarjuna answered with the doctrine of the two truths, explaining that humans can gain salvation and are not irreconcilably caught in this world, which can be used as a ladder leading to the absolute. In his doctrine the relative truth is of this existence. This leads first to the realization that all things are empty of *subhava* ("own being") and then to the intuition of an absolute truth beyond all conceptions. The link between these two truths—the relative and the absolute—is the Buddha. He experienced the absolute truth, which is *nisprapanca*—i.e., inexplicable in speech and unrealizable in ordinary thought—and yet he returned to point to this truth in the phenomenal world.

By following this path, one can be saved. Thus, Nagarjuna taught that through the middle path of Madhyamika, which is identified as the Buddha's true teachings, one is guided to an experience beyond affirmation and negation, being and non-being. Madhyamika is a philosophy that can rightly be called a doctrine of salvation, for it claims to present humans with a system that leads to rescue from their situation.

The Madhyamika school divided into two subtraditions in the 5th and 6th centuries. The Prasangika school, which emphasized a more negative form of argumentation, was founded by Buddhapalita (*c.* 470–540), who wrote many works, including a commentary on Nagarjuna's *Madhyamika Karika*. The school was continued by Candrakirti, a famous logician of the 7th century and author of a commentary on the *Madhyamika Karika*, and by Shantideva (*c.* 650–750), whose *Shiksa-samuccaya* ("Summary of Training") and *Bodhicaryavatara* ("The Coming of the Bodhisattva Way of Life") are among the most popular Mahayana literary works.

The Svatantrika school, which utilized a syllogistic mode of argumentation, was founded by Bhavaviveka, a contemporary of Buddhapalita and author of a commentary on the *Madhyamika Karika*. Santiraksita, a great scholar who wrote the *Tattvasamgraha* ("Summary of Essentials") and the *Madhyamikalankara Karika* ("Verses on the Ornament of the Madhyamika Teaching"), continued the school. Both the Svatantrika tradition and the Prasangika tradition strongly influenced Buddhist philosophy in Tibet.

The missionary translator Kumarajiva took the Madhyamika school to China from India in the 5th century. Three of the texts that he translated from Sanskrit into Chinese—the *Madhyamika Karika* and the *Dvadashamukha-shastra* or *Dvadasha-dvara-shastra* ("The Twelve Topics or Gates Treatise") of Nagarjuna and the *Shata-shastra* ("One Hundred Verses Treatise") of Aryadeva—became the basic texts of the Chinese Sanlun (Japanese: Sanron), or "Three Treatise," school of Madhyamika. Although this school was challenged by the Silun, or "Four Treatise," school, which also accepted the *Mahaprajnaparamita-shastra* as a basic text, Sanlun regained preeminence as a result of the teachings of Sengzhao, Kumarajiva's disciple, and later of Jizang. Both of these Chinese Madhyamika masters commented on Nagarjuna's thesis in numerous influential works.

YOGACARA/VIJNANAVADA (FAXIANG/HOSSŌ)

The Yogacara (or Vijnanavada) school was founded, according to tradition, by the brothers Asanga and Vasubandhu (4th/5th century CE) and by Sthiramati (6th century), who systematized doctrines found in the *Lankavatara-sutra* and the *Mahayana-shraddhotpada-shastra* (attributed to Ashvaghosa but probably written in Central Asia or in China). Later Mahayana and Esoteric Buddhism include doctrines that were to be influenced by Yogacara teaching.

The special characteristics of Yogacara are its emphasis on meditation and a broadly psychological analysis, which contrasts with the other great Mahayana system, Madhyamika, where the emphasis is on logical analysis and dialectic. Its central doctrine, however, is that only consciousness (*vijnanamatra*; hence the name Vijnanavada) is real and that eternal things do not exist. Thought or mind is the ultimate reality, and nothing exists outside the mind, according to this school. The common view that external things exist is due to an error that can be removed by a meditative or yogic process that brings an inner concentration and tranquility and a complete withdrawal or "revulsion" from fictitious externalities.

Alaya-vijnana ("store" or "storehouse consciousness") is postulated as the receptacle of the imprint of thoughts and deeds, the *vasana* (literally, "dwelling") of various karmic seeds (*bijas*). The "seeds" develop into touch, mental activity, feeling, perception, and will, corresponding to the five *skandhas* ("aggregates"; parts of an individual personality). This is followed first by the emergence of ideation (*manas*), which sets off the self or mind from the world, and then by the realization that objects exist only through the sense perceptions and thought of subject. The store consciousness must be purged of its subject-object duality and restored to its pure state. This pure state is equivalent to the absolute "suchness" (*tathata*), to Buddhahood, to the undifferentiated.

Corresponding to false imagination (*vikalpa*), right knowledge, and suchness are the three modes of being: the mere fictions of false imagination; the relative existence of things, under certain conditions or aspects; and the perfect mode of being. Corresponding to this threefold version of the modes of being and awareness is the *tri-kaya* doctrine of the Buddha (the apparitional body, the enjoyment body, and the *dharma* body), a doctrine that was systematized by Yogacara thinkers.

The Yogacara school was represented in China primarily by the Faxiang (or Dharmalaksana; also Weishi) school, called Hossō in Japan. Paramartha, an Indian missionary-teacher, introduced the basic Yogacara teachings to China in the 6th century, and his translation of the *Mahayana-samparigraha-shastra* provided the foundation for the Silun school. Silun was succeeded as the major vehicle of Yogacara thought in China by the Faxiang school, which was founded by Xuanzang, the 7th-century Chinese pilgrim-translator, and his main disciple, Kuiji. Xuanzang went to India, where he studied the works of Dharmapala (d. 561) and taught at the Vijnanavada centre at Valabhi. When he returned to China, he translated Dharmapala's *Vijnapti-matrata-siddhi* and many other works and taught doctrines that were based on those of Dharmapala and other Indian teachers. Xuanzang's teachings were expressed systematically in *Fayuanyilinzhang* and *Weishishuji*, the basic texts of the Faxiang school.

Faxiang, the Chinese translation of *dharmalaksana* (Sanskrit: "characteristic of *dharma*"), refers to the school's basic emphasis on the peculiar characteristics (*dharmalaksana*) of the *dharmas* that make up the world that appears in human ideation. According to Faxiang teaching, there are five categories of *dharmas*: 8 mental *dharmas* (*cittadharma*), comprising the 5 sense consciousnesses, cognition, the cognitive faculty, and the store consciousness; 51 mental functions or capacities, dispositions, and activities (*caitashikadharma*); 11 elements concerned with material forms or appearances (*rupa-dharma*); 24 things, situations, and processes not associated with the mind—e.g., time, becoming (*cittaviprayuktasamskara*); and 6 noncreated or nonconditioned elements (*asamskrtadharma*)—e.g., space or suchness (*tathata*).

In *Chengweishilun* ("Treatise on the Establishment of the Doctrine Consciousness Only"), Xuanzang explained how there can be a common empirical world for different individuals who construct or ideate particular objects and who possess distinct bodies and sensory systems. According to Xuanzang, the universal "seeds" in the store consciousness account for the common appearance of things, and particular "seeds" account for the differences.

According to traditional accounts, Faxiang was first taken to Japan by Dōshō, a Japanese priest who visited China, studied under Xuanzang, and established the teaching (now called Hossō) at Gangō

Monastery. It was also taken there by other priests, Japanese and Korean, who studied in China under Xuanzang, Kuiji, or their disciples. Thus, the Japanese claim to have received the Hossō teaching in a direct line from its originators, and it continues to have a living and significant role in Japanese Buddhism.

AVATAMSAKA (HUAYAN/KEGON)

Unlike the Faxiang (Hossō) school, which concentrated on the differentiating characteristics of things and the separation of facts and principles, the Avatamsaka school (called Huayan in China, Kegon in Japan) stressed the sameness of things, the presence of absolute reality in them, and the identity of facts and ultimate principles. It took its name from the *Mahavaipulya-Buddhavatamsaka-sutra* ("The Great and Vast Buddha Garland Sutra"), often called simply the *Avatamsaka-sutra* ("Wreath Sutra" or "Garland Sutra").

According to legend, the *Avatamsaka-sutra* was first preached by the buddha Vairocana shortly after his enlightenment but was replaced with simpler doctrines because it proved incomprehensible to his hearers. The sutra tells of the pilgrimage of a young man in a quest to realize *dharmadhatu* ("totality" or "universal principle"). Three Chinese versions and one Sanskrit original (the *Gandavyuha*), which contains the last section only, are extant. There is no trace of an Indian sectarian development, and the school is known only in its Chinese and Japanese forms.

The forerunner of the Avatamsaka or Huayan school in China was the Dilun school, which was based on the *Shiyidijinglun* or *Dilun*, an early 6th-century translation of the *Dashabhumika-sutra* ("Sutra on the Ten Stages"). Since this work, which concerns the path of a bodhisattva to Buddhahood, was part of the *Avatamsaka-sutra* (which came to circulate independently), Dilun adherents readily joined the Huayan school that was thought to have been established in the late 6th century by Dushun (Fashun), the first patriarch (d. 640). The real founder of the school, however, was the third patriarch, Fazang (also called Xianshou; died 712), who systematized its teachings; hence, it is sometimes called the Xianshou school. The school developed further under Fazang's student Chengguan (d. *c.* 820 or *c.* 838), who wrote important commentaries on the *Avatamsaka-sutra*. After the death of the fifth and final patriarch, Zongmi, in 841, Huayan declined because of the general suppression of Buddhism in China in 845. Despite its decline, the school greatly influenced the development of Neo-Confucianism (a significant movement in Chinese thought beginning in the 11th century) and is regarded by many as the most highly developed form of Chinese Buddhist thought.

The Avatamsaka school was introduced into Japan by pupils of Fazang and by an Avatamsaka missionary from central India during the period from about 725 to 740. Known in Japan as the Kegon school, it has exerted an important influence in Japanese Buddhism that has continued to the present day.

The school's most significant doctrine is the theory of causation by *dharma-dhatu* ("totality" or "universal principle"), according to which all elements arise simultaneously, the whole of things creates itself, ultimate principles and concrete manifestations are interfused, and the manifestations are mutually identical. Thus, in Fazang's *Essay on the Golden Lion*, written for the empress Wu Hou, gold is the essential nature or principle (Chinese: *li*), and lion is the particular manifestation or form (Chinese: *shi*). Moreover, as gold, each part or particle expresses the whole lion and is identical with every other part or particle. This model suggests that all phenomena in the universe are expressions of the ultimate suchness or voidness while at the same time retaining their phenomenal character; each phenomenon is both "all" and "one." All the constituents of the world (the *dharmas*) are interdependent and possess a sixfold nature: universality, speciality, similarity, diversity, integration, and differentiation.

The ideal expressed in this doctrine is a harmonious totality of things leading to the perfectly enlightened buddha. The buddha nature is present potentially in all things. There are an infinite number of buddhas and buddha realms. There are myriads of buddhas in every grain of sand and a buddha realm at the tip of a hair.

The universe is fourfold: a world of factual, practical reality; a world of principle or theory; a world of principle and facts harmonized; and a world of factual realities interwoven and mutually identified. The first three aspects are the particular emphases of other Buddhist schools. The fourth aspect—emphasizing the harmonious whole—is the distinctive doctrine that represents the perfect knowledge that was attained by the buddha Vairocana and is communicated in the *Avatamsaka-sutra*.

TIANTAI/TENDAI

The school known as Tiantai in China and Tendai in Japan is one of the most important schools in Chinese and Japanese Buddhism. It is significant for its doctrines, which in many respects are similar to those of the Huayan/Kegon school, and for its influence on devotion. The school's doctrines and practices are focused on the Indian or Central Asian *Saddharmapundarika-sutra* ("Lotus of the True Law Sutra") as well as on the *Mahaparinirvana* and *Mahaprajnaparamita-sutras*.

Sometimes called Lotus (Fahua in Chinese; Hokke in Japanese), this school, which apparently had no separate development in India, took its name from the mountain in southeastern China where the basic interpretation of the *Lotus Sutra* was first propounded in the 6th century. The origins of the school, however, are to be found in the early 5th century when the original text of the Sanskrit sutra was translated into Chinese by Kumarajiva and was then taught in North China by the monks and first patriarchs, Huiwen and Huisi. The latter's student Zhiyi, who established a famous monastery on Mount Tiantai ("Heavenly Terrace"), is regarded as the true founder of the school because he propounded the systematic interpretation of Lotus doctrines that came to be widely accepted. His interpretation spread to Japan in the early 9th century, where Saichō (known posthumously as Dengyō Daishi), a Buddhist priest who studied the teachings first in Japan and then on Mount Tiantai, founded a Japanese Tendai school. He also founded a monastery on Mount Hiei that became one of Japan's greatest centres of Buddhist learning.

Along with the Esoteric Buddhist school of Shingon, with which it was closely connected, Tendai became one of the most important influences on Japanese religious culture. Tendai has been markedly syncretistic, incorporating the teachings of various Buddhist schools and those of Shintō, the indigenous Japanese religion, into its traditions.

The *Lotus Sutra*, which is recognized by Tiantai and Tendai as the locus of the most exalted Buddhist teaching, emphasizes the notion of the one way (or "vehicle" or "career") for attaining salvation (Buddhahood). It claims to be the definitive and complete teaching of the Buddha, who is depicted as a transcendent eternal being, preaching to arhats, gods, bodhisattvas, and other figures, using all sorts of sermons, lectures, imaginative parables, and miracles. The Lotus is an object of devotion in this school, and those who preach, recite, or hear it are believed to accrue religious merit.

In the Lotus the three ways of salvation supposedly preached by the Buddha are adjusted to the level and situation of the hearers: *shravakayana*, the way of the disciples (*shravakas*), appropriate for becoming an arhat; *pratyeka-buddhayana*, the way of those who aim at salvation for themselves alone; and *bodhisattvayana*, the way of those (the bodhisattvas) who, on the point of attaining salvation, give it up to work for the salvation of all other beings. All are forms of the one way, the *buddhayana*, and the aim for all is to become a buddha.

The Tiantai/Tendai tradition divides the Buddha's teachings into five periods. The first immediately followed the Buddha's enlightenment, when, without success, he preached the *Avatamsaka-sutra* (or *Huayan/Kegon Sutra*). The second is the so-called Deer Park period, when he preached the *Agamas* (Hinayana scriptures) to those with ordinary human capacities. In the third or Fangdeng ("broad and equal") period, he preached the *Vaipulya* or early Mahayana teachings, which were intended for all persons. During the fourth period he preached the *Mahaprajnaparamita*, or Ta-pan-jo-po-lo-mi-to, doctrines concerning absolute voidness and the falsity of all distinctions. Finally, in the *Saddharmapundarika* and *Mahaparinirvana* ("Wisdom") period, he taught the identity of contrasts, the unity of the three "vehicles," and the ultimate authority of the *Lotus Sutra*.

Central to Tiantai/Tendai doctrine is the threefold truth principle (following

Nagarjuna's [?] commentary on the *Mahaprajnaparamita*), according to which all things are void, without substantial reality; all things have temporary existence; and all things are in the mean or middle state, synthesizing voidness and temporary existence, being both at once. The three truths are a harmonious unity, mutually including one another, and the mean or middle truth is equivalent to the absolute suchness. The world of temporary appearances is thus the same as absolute reality.

Tiantai/Tendai propounds an elaborate cosmology of 3,000 realms. There are 10 basic realms, respectively, of buddhas, bodhisattvas, *pratyeka buddhas*, *shravakas*, heavenly beings, fighting spirits (*asuras*), human beings, hungry spirits or ghosts (*pretas*), beasts, and depraved hellish beings. Each realm, however, includes the other 9 and their characteristics, and counting these together thus yields 100 realms. Each of these in turn is characterized by the 10 features of suchness manifested through phenomena—form, nature, substance, power, action, cause, condition, effect, compensation, and ultimacy—which thus brings the total to 1,000 realms. Finally, each of these realms is divided into living beings, space, and the aggregates (*skandhas*); hence, the whole of things consists of 3,000 realms.

These realms interpenetrate one another and are immanent in one moment of thought: "one thought is the three thousand worlds." The universe is not produced by thought or consciousness but is manifest in it, as is the absolute suchness: hence, the central importance of concentration (*chih*) and insight (*kuan*) that leads to a realization of the unity of things and their manifestation of the ultimate.

PURE LAND

The main text of the Pure Land schools is the *Sukhavativyuha-sutra* ("Pure Land Sutra"). Written in northwestern India probably before the beginning of the 2nd century CE, the *Sukhavativyuha* exists in two original versions, a longer one that emphasizes good works and a shorter version that emphasizes faith and devotion alone. This sutra tells of a monk, Dharmakara, who heard the preaching of Lokeshvararaja Buddha aeons ago and asked to become a buddha. After millions of years of study, Dharmakara vowed, among other things, to establish a Pure or Happy Land (Sanskrit: Sukhavati; Chinese: Qingtu; Japanese: Jōdo), also known as the Western Paradise, if he achieved Buddhahood. In this Pure Land no evil would exist, the people would be long-lived, they would receive whatever they desired, and from there they might attain nirvana. Dharmakara then revealed in a series of 48 vows the means by which this Pure Land can be reached. Several vows emphasize meditation and good works on earth as a prerequisite, but the 18th one (a famous vow in the later development of Pure Land schools) states that, if one merely calls the name of the

Buddha at the moment of death, then one will be reborn in the Pure Land.

Dharmakara, it is believed, attained Buddhahood and is known as the buddha Amitabha (Sanskrit: "Infinite Light"; Chinese: Emituofo; Japanese: Amida) or the buddha Amitayus (Sanskrit: "Infinite Lifespan"). He is flanked in the Pure Land he created in fulfillment of his vows by Avalokitesvara (Chinese: Guanyin; Japanese: Kannon) on his left and Mahasthamaprapta on his right, who assist Amitabha in bringing the faithful to salvation.

By the 3rd century CE, the Amitabhist doctrine had spread from India to China, where a school based on it gradually became the most popular form of Buddhism. Followers of the Tendai school took Amitabhist teachings to Japan, where they attempted to weld the many sects of Buddhism into one system. By the 13th century CE, the Pure Land sect had separated from the Tendai school and spread among the common people of Japan through the work of two outstanding figures, Hōnen and Shinran.

The basic doctrines of the Pure Land schools emphasize the importance of devotion. Pure Land leaders teach that a person reaches salvation not by individual effort or the accumulation of merit but through faith in the grace of the buddha Amitabha. The main practice of those who follow the Pure Land teachings is not the study of the texts or meditation on the Buddha but rather the constant invocation of the name Amitabha, a practice based on the 18th vow of Dharmakara. Furthermore, in Pure Land Buddhism the attainment of nirvana is not the most prominent goal; it is rather to become reborn in the Pure Land of Amitabha.

These doctrines and the practice of invoking the name Amitabha—called *nembutsu* in Japanese and *nianfo* in Chinese—became popular in China and Japan, where it was believed that the world had reached the decadent age, the so-called "latter days of the law" in which Buddhist doctrines were unclear and humans lacked the purity of heart or determination to attain salvation by their efforts. Therefore, the only hope was to be saved by the grace of Amitabha. This doctrine of grace became more and more radical, until individual actions were said by some to play no part in the attainment of salvation.

Tanluan and the other 6th–7th-century Chinese Pure Land patriarchs, Daochuo and Shandao, were among those who rejected the role of works in salvation. Originally a follower of Daoism, Tanluan, while searching for the elixir of immortality, was converted to the Pure Land doctrine by an Indian monk. Dedicating his life to the spread of this doctrine, Tanluan preached the invocation of the name Amitabha and declared that even evil persons were eligible for the Pure Land if they sincerely uttered the *nembutsu*. He warned, however, that the lowest hell awaited those who reviled the Buddhist *dharma*.

Tanluan was followed by Daochuo, who argued that, because his was the age of the final decline predicted in Buddhist scriptures, people must take the "easy path" to salvation. They must trust Amitabha completely, for they are no longer able to follow the more difficult path of the saints. His disciple Shandao, believed by some Japanese Pure Land adherents to be the incarnation of Amida, shaped the doctrines of the later forms of Pure Land Buddhism. He distributed many copies of the *Pure Land Sutra* and wrote a commentary in which he taught that rebirth in the Western Paradise is made possible by invoking Amida. The *nembutsu* must be supplemented, however, by the chanting of sutras, meditation on the Buddha, worshiping of buddha images, and singing his praises.

The work of Shandao inspired Hōnen, the founder of the Pure Land sect (Jōdo-shu) in Japan, to declare that in this evil period people must put complete faith in the saving grace of Amida and constantly invoke his name. Hōnen expressed his beliefs in the treatise *Senchaku hongan nembutsu-shu* (1198), which was popular among the common people, as were his teachings generally. The treatise was burned by the monks of Mount Hiei, and his teachings were vigorously opposed by the established Buddhist priesthood. Indeed, opposition to Hōnen was so great that his rivals forced him into exile from 1206 to 1211.

Hōnen's disciple Shinran, who was exiled at the same time, was the founder of True Pure Land (Jōdo Shinshu or Shin), a more radical Amida school. Shinran married with Hōnen's consent, which thus suggests that one need not be a monk to attain the Pure Land. In Shinran's teachings, which he popularized by preaching in Japanese villages, he rejected all sutras except the *Pure Land Sutra*, as well as the vows of Dharmakara in that sutra that stress individual merit. Basing his doctrines on the 18th vow, Shinran discouraged any attempt to accumulate merit, for he felt that this stood in the way of absolute faith and dependence on Amida. Furthermore, he rejected Hōnen's practice of continual invocation of Amida, believing that the *nembutsu* need be said only once in order to attain salvation and that repetition of it should be regarded as praise of Amida and not as affecting one's salvation. Thus, Shinran established the total ascendancy of the doctrine of grace. He also founded what would become the Shin school, the largest single Buddhist school in contemporary Japan. Throughout its history the Shin school has actively promoted music, dance, and drama and, since the late 19th century, has engaged in extensive educational and social welfare programs.

A third Pure Land sect grew up around the itinerant teacher Ippen. He traveled throughout Japan, advocating the chanting of Amida's name at set intervals throughout the day; hence, his school was called the Ji ("Times") school, or Jishū.

Dhyana (Chan/Zen)

The Dhyana (Sanskrit: "Meditation") school of Buddhism emphasizes meditation as the way to awareness of ultimate reality, an important practice of Buddhism from its origin in India and one found in other Indian schools, such as Yogacara. Chan, which was also influenced by Daoism, promotes special meditation training techniques and doctrines. Despite Indian influences, Chan is generally considered a specifically Chinese product, a view reinforced by the fact that 4th–5th-century Chinese Buddhist monks, such as Huiyuan and Sengzhao, taught beliefs and practices similar to those of the Chan school before the traditional date of its arrival in China.

Most Chinese texts name a South Indian monk, Bodhidharma, who arrived in China about 520 CE, as the founder of the Chan school. Bodhidharma is regarded as the first Chan patriarch and the 28th patriarch of the Indian meditation school. The Indian school began with the monk Kashyapa, who received Buddha Shakyamuni's supreme teaching, which is found in the *Lankavatara-sutra* ("Descent to the Island of Lanka"). The sutra teaches that all beings possess a buddha nature, often equated with *shunya* (Sanskrit: "the void") in Chan, and that realization of this fact is enlightenment (Chinese: Wu; Japanese: satori). The truly enlightened one cannot explain this ultimate truth or reality, nor can books, words, concepts, or teachers, for it is beyond the ordinary duality of subject and object and must be realized in direct personal experience.

Bodhidharma was succeeded as patriarch of the Chan school by Huike, and this line of transmission continued to the fifth patriarch, Hengren, in the 7th century. After Hengren's death a schism occurred between the adherents of the Northern school of Shenxiu, which held that enlightenment must be attained gradually, and the Southern school of Huineng, which taught that true wisdom, as undifferentiated, must be attained suddenly and spontaneously. Huineng's Southern school claimed to de-emphasize rituals and the study of texts and to rely on teaching passed from master to pupil. Some proponents of the Southern school also adopted an iconoclastic attitude toward the Buddha, maintaining that if all things contain the buddha nature, then the Buddha could rightfully be equated with a dung heap. The Southern school overcame its rival, and standard Chinese Chan texts therefore name Huineng as the true and only sixth patriarch. Huineng's *Liuzu Tanching* (Chinese: "Platform Scripture of the Sixth Patriarch") became a key text of the Chan school.

In the 9th century, the Linzi (Japanese: Rinzai) and Caodong (Japanese: Sōtō) branches of the Southern school emerged. The former relied heavily on the *gong'an* (Japanese: *koan*), a paradoxical question or aphorism that was intended to reveal that all conceptualization is wrong and thus leads to enlightenment. The *gong'an* was often accompanied by shouts and slaps from the master to provoke anxiety in the student and, from this, an instant realization of the truth. The Caodong/Sōtō school emphasized the practice of "silent illumination" or "just sitting" (Chinese: *zuochan*; Japanese: *zazen*), which involved sitting in silent meditation under the direction of a master and purging the mind of all notions and concepts.

Both schools followed the doctrine of Huaihai, who taught that a monk who would not work should not eat and that work (as well as everything else) should be done spontaneously and naturally. The emphasis on work made the Chan schools self-sufficient and saved them from the worst effects of the government purge of supposedly parasitic Buddhist monks in 845. The emphasis on spontaneity and naturalness stimulated the development of a Chan aesthetic that profoundly influenced later Chinese painting and writing. The relative success of the Chan tradition in subsequent Chinese history is demonstrated by the fact that virtually all Chinese monks eventually came to belong to one of the two Chan lineages.

Chan (Zen) Buddhism was introduced into Japan as early as the 7th century but flowered only in the 12th and 13th centuries, most notably in the work of the monks Eisai and Dōgen. By the mid-20th century, Zen had become one of the best-known of the Buddhist schools in the Western world.

VAJRAYANA

Vajrayana Buddhism (Sanskrit: "Vehicle of the Diamond [or Thunderbolt]"), also called Tantric Buddhism, was an important development within Buddhism in India and neighbouring countries. Vajrayana, in the history of Buddhism, marks the transition from Mahayana speculative thought to the enactment of Buddhist ideas in individual life. The term *vajra* (Sanskrit: "diamond," or "thunderbolt") is used to signify the absolutely real and indestructible in humans, as opposed to the fictions an individual entertains about himself and his nature; *yana* is the spiritual pursuit of the ultimately valuable and indestructible.

Other names for this form of Buddhism are Mantrayana ("Vehicle of the Mantra"), which refers to the use of the mantra to prevent the mind from going astray into the world of its fictions and their attendant verbiage and to remain aware of reality as such; and Guhyamantrayana, in which the word *guhya* ("hidden") refers not to concealment but to the intangibility of the process of becoming aware of reality.

Philosophically speaking, Vajrayana embodies ideas of both the Yogacara discipline, which emphasizes the ultimacy of mind, and the Madhyamika philosophy, which undermines any attempt to posit a relativistic principle as the ultimate. Dealing with inner experiences, the Vajrayana texts use a highly symbolic

FALUN GONG

The controversial Chinese spiritual movement called Falun Gong (Falungong, Falundafa) was founded by Li Hongzhi in 1992. Its name means "the Practice of the Wheel of Dharma," and its adherents exercise ritually to obtain mental and spiritual renewal. The teachings of Falun Gong draw from the Asian religious traditions of Buddhism, Daoism, Confucianism, and Chinese folklore as well as those of Western New Age movements. The movement's sudden emergence in the 1990s was a great concern to the Chinese government, which viewed Falun Gong as a cult.

The origins of the movement are found both in long-standing Chinese practices and in recent events. Qi Gong (Chinese: "Energy Working"), the use of meditation techniques and physical exercise to achieve both good health and peace of mind, has a long history in Chinese culture and religion; however, practitioners in modern China present these techniques as purely secular in an effort to escape official restrictions against independent religious activity. Nevertheless, in the late 20th century new masters appeared who taught forms of Qi Gong more clearly rooted in religion. The most influential of these masters, Li Hongzhi (born in 1951, according to followers, or in 1952, according to critics, who contend that Li "adjusted" his birthdate to lend it Buddhist spiritual significance), worked in law enforcement and corporate security before becoming the full-time spiritual leader of Falun Gong in 1992.

While in traditional Chinese Buddhism falun *means the "wheel of law" or "wheel of dharma," Li used the word to indicate the centre of spiritual energy, which he located in the lower abdomen and believed could be awakened through a set of exercises called Xiu Lian ("Cultivating and Practicing"). Unlike other Qi Gong groups, Falun Gong insists that its founder is the only authoritative source for determining the correct exercises and that a spiritual discipline, the "cultivation of the Xinxing" ("Mind-Nature"), is essential to the success of the exercises. On a more esoteric level, Li also taught that demonic space aliens seek to destroy humanity and, since their arrival in 1900, have manipulated scientists and world leaders. Critics of the movement not only ridicule such claims but regard its reliance on Xiu Lian as an alternative to official medicine as hazardous to the members' health. Indeed, the Chinese government claims that 1,400 Falun Gong devotees have died as a result of this alleged rejection of modern medicine.*

After gathering a large following in China (100 million, according to Falun Gong, or between 2 and 3 million, according to the Chinese government), Li took his movement abroad in the mid-1990s, settling permanently in New York City in 1998. The next year, a massive campaign was launched by the medical establishment (including both practitioners and academics) and the Chinese government to denounce Falun Gong as a xiejiao ("teaching of falsehood," or "cult"). Unlike other Chinese organizations, Falun Gong responded strongly, staging an unauthorized demonstration of more than 10,000 followers in Beijing on April 25, 1999, which prompted an even greater government response. In October the enforcement of a new anticult law led to the arrest of 100 Falun Gong leaders (joining 1,000 members who had been arrested earlier). Public trials began in November and continued into the 21st century, with many defendants receiving prison sentences of up to 12 years. While the Chinese government gained the cooperation of some Western "anticult" groups in its domestic and international campaign to expose Falun Gong as a "cult," it was also criticized by human rights organizations who denounced inter alia the suspicious deaths, allegedly by accident, of some Falun Gong members detained in Chinese jails.

The government's actions were rooted in concerns about the recent revival of independent religious activities in China and fears of the revolutionary nature of religious movements in Chinese history (e.g, the Taiping Rebellion).

language that aims at helping the followers of its disciplines to evoke within themselves experiences considered to be the most valuable available to man. Vajrayana thus attempts to recapture the Enlightenment experience of the Gautama Buddha.

In the Tantric view, Enlightenment arises from the realization that seemingly opposite principles are in truth one. The passive concepts *Sunyata* ("voidness") and *prajña* ("wisdom"), for example, must be resolved with the active *karuna* ("compassion") and *upaya* ("means"). This fundamental polarity and its resolution are often expressed through symbols of sexuality.

The historical origin of Vajrayana is unclear, except that it coincided with the spread of the mentalistic schools of Buddhism. It flourished from the 6th to the 11th century and exerted a lasting influence on the neighbouring countries of India. The rich visual arts of Vajrayana reach their culmination in the sacred mandala, a representation of the universe used as an aid for meditation.

POPULAR RELIGIOUS PRACTICES

Like other great religions, Buddhism has generated a wide range of popular practices. Among these, two simple practices are deeply rooted in the experience of the earliest Buddhist community and have remained basic to all Buddhist traditions.

The first is the veneration of the Buddha or other buddhas, bodhisattvas, or saints, which involves showing respect, meditating on the qualities of the Buddha, or giving gifts. Such gifts are often given to the relics of the Buddha, to images made to represent him, and to other traces of his presence, such as places where his footprint can supposedly be seen. After the Buddha's death the first foci for this sort of veneration seem to have been his relics and the stupas that held them. By the beginning of the Common Era, anthropomorphic images of the Buddha were being produced, and they took their place alongside relics and stupas as focal points for venerating him. Still later, in the context of the Mahayana and Vajrayana traditions, the veneration of other buddhas and bodhisattvas came to supplement or replace the veneration of the Buddha Gautama. In the course of Buddhist history, the forms have become diverse, but the practice of honouring and even worshiping the Buddha or Buddha figure has remained a central component in all Buddhist traditions.

The second basic practice is the exchange that takes place between monks and laypersons. Like the Buddha himself, the monks embody or represent the higher levels of spiritual achievement, which they make available in various ways to the laity. The laity improve their soteriological condition by giving the monks material gifts that function as sacrificial offerings. Although the exchange is structured differently in each Buddhist tradition, it has remained until recently a component in virtually all forms of Buddhist community life.

Both of these practices appear independently within the tradition. The veneration of the Buddha or Buddha figure is a common ritual often practiced independently of other rituals. Both of these practices, however, are embedded in one way or another in virtually all other Buddhist rituals, including calendric rituals, pilgrimage rituals, rites of passage, and protective rites.

CALENDRIC RITES AND PILGRIMAGE

The Buddhist calendar contains a number of holy days, anniversaries, and festivals, each dedicated to the observance of certain rites and the performance of particular rituals. Already within the first two centuries of the Buddha's death, pilgrimage had become an important component in the life of the Buddhist community. It retains that significance to this day.

ANNIVERSARIES

The three major events of the Buddha's life—his birth, enlightenment, and entrance into final nirvana—are commemorated in all Buddhist countries but not everywhere on the same day. In Theravada countries the three events are all observed together on Vesak, the full moon day of the sixth lunar month (Vesakha), which usually occurs in May. In Japan and other Mahayana countries, however, the three anniversaries of the Buddha are observed on separate days (in some countries the birth date is April 8, the enlightenment date is December 8, and the death date is February 15). Festival days honouring other buddhas and bodhisattvas of the Mahayana and Vajrayana traditions are also observed, and considerable emphasis is placed on anniversaries connected with the patriarchs of certain schools. Padmasambhava's anniversary, for example, is especially observed by the Rnying-ma-pa sect in Tibet, and the birthday of Nichiren is celebrated by his followers in Japan.

ALL SOULS FESTIVAL

The importance of the virtues of filial piety and the reverence of ancestors in China and Japan have established

Ullambana, or All Souls Day, as one of the major Buddhist festivals in those countries. In China worshipers in Buddhist temples make *fachuan* ("boats of the law") out of paper, some very large, which are then burned in the evening. The purpose of the celebration is twofold: to remember the dead and to free those who are suffering as *pretas*, or hell beings, so that they may ascend to heaven. Under the guidance of Buddhist temples, societies (*hui, Youlanhui*) are formed to carry out the necessary ceremonies—lanterns are lit, monks are invited to recite sacred verses, and offerings of fruit are made. An 8th-century Indian monk, Amoghavajra, is said to have introduced the ceremony into China, from where it was transmitted to Japan. During the Japanese festival of Bon, two altars are constructed, one to make offerings to the spirits of dead ancestors and the other to make offerings to the souls of those dead who have no peace. *Odorinembutsu* (the chanting of invocations accompanied by dancing and singing) and invocations to Amida are features of the Bon celebrations.

NEW YEAR'S AND HARVEST FESTIVALS

New Year's festivals demonstrate Buddhism's ability to co-opt preexisting local traditions. On the occasion of the New Year, images of the Buddha in some countries are taken in procession through the streets. Worshipers visit Buddhist sanctuaries and circumambulate a stupa or a sacred image, and monks are given food and other gifts.

One of the most remarkable examples of the absorption of a local New Year's celebration in Buddhist practice was the Smonlam festival in Tibet, celebrated on a large scale in Lhasa until the beginning of Chinese communist rule in 1959. The festival was instituted in 1408 by Tsong-kha-pa, the founder of the Dge-lugs-pa sect, who transformed an old custom into a Buddhist festivity. Smonlam took place at the beginning of the winter thaw, when caravans began to set out once again and the hunting season was resumed. The observances included exorcistic ceremonies performed privately within each family to remove evil forces lying in wait for individuals as well as for the community as a whole. They also included propitiatory rites performed to ward off evil such as droughts, epidemics, or hail during the coming year. During the more public propitiatory rites, the *sangha* cooperated with the laity by invoking the merciful forces that watch over good order, and processions, fireworks, and various amusements created an atmosphere of hopefulness. Through the collaboration of the monastic community and the laity, a general reserve of good karma was accumulated to see everyone through the dangerous moment of passage from the old year to the new.

Harvest festivals also provide Buddhism an opportunity to adopt local customs and adapt them to the Buddhist calendar. The harvest festival celebrated in the Tibetan villages during the eighth lunar month was quite different from the New Year ceremonies. Most commonly, offerings of thanks were made to local deities in rites that were only externally Buddhist. The same interplay between Buddhism and folk tradition is observable elsewhere. An integral part of the harvest celebrations in many Buddhist countries is the sacred performance of an episode in the life of a buddha or a bodhisattva. In Tibet, for instance, troupes of actors specialize in performances of Buddhist legends.

BUDDHIST PILGRIMAGE

Throughout early Buddhist history there were at least four major pilgrimage centres—the place of the Buddha's birth at Lumbini, the place of his enlightenment at Bodh Gaya, the Deer Park in Varanasi (Benares), where he supposedly preached his first sermon, and the village of Kusinara, which was recognized as the place of his Parinirvana (final nirvana or final death).

During the post-Asokan period, four other sites in northeastern India became preeminent pilgrimage sites. In addition to these eight primary sites in the Buddhist "homeland," major pilgrimage centres have emerged in every region or country where Buddhism has been established. Many local temples have their own festivals associated with a relic enshrined there or an event in the life of a sacred figure. Some of these, such as the display of the tooth relic at Kandy, Sri Lanka, are occasions for great celebrations attracting many pilgrims. In many Buddhist countries famous mountains have become sacred sites that draw pilgrims from both near and far. In China, for example, four such mountain sites are especially important: Emei, Wutai, Putuo, and Jiuhua. Each is devoted to a different bodhisattva whose temples and monasteries are located on the mountainside. In many Buddhist regions there are pilgrimages that include stops at a whole series of sacred places. One of the most interesting of these is the Shikoku pilgrimage in Japan, which involves visits to 88 temples located along a route that extends for more than 1,130 km (700 miles).

Buddhist pilgrimages, like those in other religions, are undertaken for a wide range of reasons. For some Buddhists pilgrimage is a discipline that fosters spiritual development; for others it is the fulfillment of a vow made, for example, to facilitate recovery from an illness; and for others it is simply an occasion for travel and enjoyment. Whatever its motivations, pilgrimage remains one of the most important Buddhist practices.

RITES OF PASSAGE AND PROTECTIVE RITES

Buddhists practice three major types of rites: initiation rites, funeral rites, and protective rites.

INITIATION RITES

Admission to the *sangha* involves two distinct acts: *pabbajja* (lower ordination), which consists of renunciation of secular life and acceptance of monastic life as a novice, and *upasampada* (higher ordination), official consecration as a monk. The evolution of the procedure is not entirely clear; in early times the two acts probably occurred at the same time. Subsequently, the *Vinaya* established that *upasampada*, or full acceptance into the monastic community, should not occur before the age of 20, which, if the *pabbajja* ceremony took place as early as the age of 8, would mean after 12 years of training. Ordination could not occur without the permission of the aspirant's parents. The initial Pali formula was "Ehi bhikkhu," "Come, O monk!"

In Mahayana Buddhism new rituals were added to the ceremony of ordination prescribed by the Pali *Vinaya*. The declaration of the Triple Refuge is as central an assertion as ever, but special emphasis is placed on the candidate's intention to achieve enlightenment and his undertaking of the vow to become a bodhisattva. Five monks are required for the ordination: the head monk, one who guards the ceremony, a master of secrets (the esoteric teachings, such as mantras), and two assisting officiants.

The esoteric content of Vajrayana tradition requires a more complex consecration ceremony. Along with other ordination rites, preparatory study, and training in yoga, the Tantric neophyte receives *abhiseka* (Sanskrit: "sprinkling" of water). This initiation takes several forms, each of which has its own corresponding *vidya* (Sanskrit: "wisdom"), rituals, and esoteric formulas and is associated with one of the five Celestial or Dhyani Buddhas. The initiate meditates on the *vajra* (Sanskrit: "thunderbolt") as a symbol of Vajrasattva Buddha (the Adamantine Being), on the bell as a symbol of the void, and on the mudra (ritual gesture) as "seal." The intent of the initiation ceremony is to produce an experience that anticipates the moment of death. The candidate emerges reborn as a new being, a state marked by his receipt of a new name.

FUNERAL RITES

The origin of Buddhist funeral observances can be traced back to Indian customs. The cremation of the body of the Buddha and the subsequent distribution of his ashes are told in the *Mahaparinibbana Sutta* ("Sutta on the Great Final Deliverance"). Early Chinese travelers such as Faxian described cremations of venerable monks. After cremation the ashes and bones of the monk were collected and a stupa built over them. That this custom was widely observed is evident from the large number of stupas found near monasteries.

With less pomp, cremation is also used for ordinary monks and laymen, though not universally. In Sri Lanka, for example, burial is also common, and in Tibet, because of the scarcity of wood, cremation is rare. The bodies of great lamas, such as the Dalai and Panchen lamas, are placed in rich stupas in attitudes of meditation, while lay corpses are exposed in remote places to be devoured by vultures and wild animals.

BARDO THÖDOL

Also called the Tibetan Book of the Dead, Bardo Thödol *is a Tibetan Buddhist funerary text that is recited to ease the consciousness of a recently deceased person through death and assist it into a favourable rebirth. Its Tibetan name means "Liberation in the Intermediate State Through Hearing."*

A central tenet of all schools of Buddhism is that attachment to and craving for worldly things spurs suffering and unease (dukkha), which influence actions whose accumulated effects, or karma, bind individuals to the process of death and rebirth (samsara). Those who have attained enlightenment (bodhi) are thereby released from this process, attaining liberation (moksha). Those who remain unenlightened are drawn by karma, whether good or bad, into a new life in one of six modes of existence: as a sufferer in hell (enduring horrible torture), as a wandering ghost (driven by insatiable craving), as an animal (ruled by instinct), as a demigod (lustful for power), as a human being (balanced in instinct and reason), or as a god (deluded by a long life into believing in one's own immortality).

The Vajrayana (Tantric) Buddhism that emerged in Central Asia and particularly in Tibet developed the concept of the bardos, *the intermediate or transitional states that mark an individual's life from birth to death and rebirth. The period between death and rebirth lasts 49 days and involves three* bardos. *The first is the moment of death itself. The consciousness of the newly deceased becomes aware of and accepts the fact that it has recently died, and it reflects upon its past life. In the second* bardo, *it encounters frightening apparitions. Without an understanding that these apparitions are unreal, the consciousness becomes confused and, depending upon its karma, may be drawn into a rebirth that impedes its liberation. The third* bardo *is the transition into a new body.*

While in the bardo *between life and death, the consciousness of the deceased can still apprehend words and prayers spoken on its behalf, which can help it to navigate through its confusion and be reborn into a new existence that offers a greater chance of attaining enlightenment. Reciting of the* Bardo Thödol, *usually performed by a lama (religious teacher), begins shortly before death (if possible) and continues throughout the 49-day period leading to rebirth.*

Although tradition attributes the Bardo Thödol *to Padmasambhava, the Indian Tantric guru (spiritual guide) who is credited with introducing Buddhism to Tibet in the 7th century, the book was likely composed in the 14th century. Since the early 20th century it has been translated into English and other Western languages many times. The first English-language translation was made by Walter Evans-Wentz (1927), who titled the work* The Tibetan Book of the Dead *because of certain similarities he claimed to detect between it and the Egyptian Book of the Dead—for example, the existence of stages through which the deceased must travel before rebirth.*

Buddhists generally agree that the thoughts held by a person at the moment of death are of essential significance. For this reason sacred texts are sometimes read to the dying person to prepare the mind for the moment of death; similarly, sacred texts may be read to the newly dead, since the conscious principle is thought to remain in the body for about three days following death. In Tibetan, Mongolian, and Chinese lamaseries, a lama sometimes recites the famous *Bardo Thödol*.

PROTECTIVE RITES

From a very early period in its development, Buddhism has included within its repertoire of religious practices specific rituals that are intended to protect against various kinds of danger and to exorcise evil influences.

In the Mahayana and Esoteric traditions, the role taken by protective and exorcistic rituals is great. For example, *dharanis* (short statements of doctrine that supposedly encapsulate its power) and mantras (a further reduction of the *dharani*, often to a single word) were widely used for this purpose. Protective and exorcistic rituals that used such *dharanis* and mantras were extremely important in the process through which the populations of Tibet and East Asia were converted to Buddhism. They have remained an integral part of the Buddhist traditions in these areas, reaching what was perhaps their fullest development in Tibet.

CHAPTER 7

CHINESE ART

In this chapter the term "Chinese art" is used to refer to the painting, calligraphy, architecture, pottery, sculpture, bronzes, jade carving, and other fine or decorative art forms produced in China over the centuries.

ART AS A REFLECTION OF CHINESE CLASS STRUCTURE

One of the outstanding characteristics of Chinese art is the extent to which it reflects the class structure that has existed at different times in Chinese history. Up to the Warring States period (475–221 BCE), the arts were produced by anonymous craftsmen for the royal and feudal courts. It is believed that during the Shang and early Zhou periods the production of ritual bronzes was exclusively regulated under the authority of the court, which could grant or withhold authorization for production by regional workshops among the various states or others who paid fealty to the court. Under the careful regulation of court patrons in the Shang and Zhou periods, design features were shared among specialists working in the various media and were remarkably uniform from bronzes to lacquerwares to textiles.

During the Warring States period and the Han dynasty (206 BCE–220 CE), the growth of a landowning and merchant class brought new patrons. After the Han there began

to emerge the concept of cultural prac-tice as the product of the leisure of the educated gentry, many of whom were amateur practitioners of the arts of poetry, music, calligraphy, and, eventu-ally, painting. At this time a distinction began to arise between the lower-class professional and the elite amateur art-ist; this distinction would have a great influence on the character of Chinese art in later times. Gradually one tradi-tion became identified with the artists and craftsmen who worked for the court or sold their work for profit. The schol-arly amateurs looked upon such people with some contempt, and the visual arts of the literati became a separate tradi-tion that was increasingly refined and rarefied to the point that, from the Song dynasty (960–1279) onward, an assumed awkwardness (*zhuo*) or understatement (*pingdan*) in technique was admired as a mark of the amateur and gentleman. As a medium of highly individual expression, painting and calligraphy also became important media of exchange in a social economy where the giving of gifts was central to the building of an interper-sonal network. Like skill in letters, poetry, or music, skill and expressive quality in the practice of calligraphy and painting helped establish one's status in a society of learned individuals.

One effect of the revolutions of the 20th century was the breaking down of the class barriers between amateur and professional. During the Cultural Revo-lution of 1966–76, literati art and artists were denigrated and an emphasis was placed on anonymous, proletarian-made art like that of the Tang dynasty (618–907) and earlier.

LINEARITY

Since the 3rd century CE, calligraphy, or writing as a fine art, has been considered supreme among the visual arts in China. Not only does it require immense skill and fine judgment, but it is regarded as uniquely revealing of the character and breadth of cultivation of the writer. Since the time when inscribed oracle bones and tortoise shells (China's oldest extant writing) were used for divination in the Shang dynasty (c. 1600–1046 BCE), callig-raphy has been associated with spiritual communication and has been viewed in terms of the writer's own spiritual attun-ement. It is believed that the appreciation and production of calligraphy requires lofty personal qualities and unusual aes-thetic sensitivity. The comprehension of its finer points is thought to require expe-rience and sensibility of a high order.

The Chinese painter uses essentially the same materials as the calligrapher—brush, ink, and silk or paper—and the Chinese judge his work by the same criteria they use for the calligrapher, basi-cally the vitality and expressiveness of the brush stroke itself and the harmoni-ous rhythm of the whole composition. Painting in China is, therefore, essentially a linear art. The painters of most peri-ods were not concerned with striving for originality or conveying a sense of reality and three-dimensional mass through aids such as shading and perspective; rather, they focused on using silk or paper to transmit, through the rhythmic movement of the brush stroke, an awareness of the inner life of things.

The aesthetics of line in calligraphy and painting have had a significant influence on the other arts in China. In the motifs that adorn the ritual bronzes, in the flow of the drapery over the surface of Buddhist sculpture, and in the decoration of lacquerware, pottery, and cloisonné enamel (wares decorated with enamel of different colours separated by strips of metal), it is the rhythmic movement of the line, following the natural movement of the artist's or craftsman's hand, that to a large extent determines the form and gives to Chinese art as a whole its remarkable harmony and unity of style.

CHARACTERISTIC THEMES AND SYMBOLS

In early times Chinese art often served as a means to submit to the will of heaven through ritual and sacrifice. Archaic bronze vessels were made for sacrifices to heaven and to the spirits of clan ancestors, who were believed to influence the living for good if the rites were properly and regularly performed.

Chinese society, basically agricultural, has always laid great stress on understanding the pattern of nature and living in accordance with it. The world of nature was seen as the visible manifestation of the workings of a higher power through the generative interaction of the yin-yang (female-male) dualism. As it developed, the purpose of Chinese art turned from propitiation and sacrifice to the expression of human understanding of these forces, in the form of painting of landscapes, bamboo, birds, and flowers. This might be called the metaphysical, Daoist aspect of Chinese painting.

Particularly in early times, art also had social and moral functions. The earliest wall paintings referred to in ancient texts depicted benevolent emperors, sages, virtuous ministers, loyal generals, and their evil opposites as examples and warnings to the living. Portrait painting also had this moral function, depicting not the features of the subject so much as his or her character and role in society. Court painters were called upon to depict auspicious and memorable events. This was the ethical, Confucian function of painting. High religious art as such is foreign to China. Popular folk religion was seldom an inspiration to great works of art, and Buddhism, which indeed produced many masterpieces of a special kind, was a foreign import.

Human relationships have always been of supreme importance in China, and a common theme of figure painting is that of gentlemen enjoying scholarly pursuits together or of the poignant partings and infrequent reunions that were the lot of officials whose appointments took them across the country.

Among the typical themes of traditional Chinese art there is no place for war, violence, the nude, death, or martyrdom. Nor is inanimate matter ever painted for art's sake alone: the very rocks and streams are felt to be alive, visible manifestations of the invisible forces of the universe. For the most part, no theme would be accepted in traditional Chinese art that was not inspiring, noble (either elevating or admonitory), refreshing to the spirit, or at least charming. Nor is there any place in most of the Chinese artistic tradition for an art of pure form divorced from content: it is not enough for the form to be beautiful if the subject matter is unedifying. In the broadest sense, therefore, in a culture steeped in the rhetoric of metaphor and allegory and forever turning to nature as a source of reference, all traditional Chinese art is symbolic, for everything that is painted reflects some aspect of a totality of which the painter is intuitively aware. At the same time, Chinese art is full of symbols of a more specific kind, some with various possible meanings. Bamboo suggests the spirit of the scholar, which can be bent by circumstance but never broken, and jade symbolizes purity and indestructibility. The dragon, in remote antiquity perhaps an alligator or rain deity, is the benevolent but potentially dangerous symbol of the emperor; the crane symbolizes long life; and paired mandarin ducks symbolize wedded fidelity. Popular among the many symbols drawn from the plant world are the orchid, a Confucian symbol of purity

and loyalty; the winter plum, which blossoms even in the late winter's snow and stands for irrepressible purity, in either a revolutionary political or a spiritual sense; and the gnarled pine tree, which may represent either survival in a harsh political environment or the unconquerable spirit of old age.

Critical to all artistic considerations was the belief that the energy and rhythm generated in artistic practice allied the practitioner with the ultimate source of that energy, drawn forth from earthly and heavenly sources and from the sacred Dao itself. Calligraphy and painting, especially, had the capacity to rejuvenate the artist or to damage him spiritually, according to the rightness of his practice and the character of the man. As such, art was viewed in these terms (and so, too, was the viewing of art), taking the artist as much into account as the artistic subject, with regard to erudition, moral character, and harmonic alignment with (or alienation from) the forces of nature.

MAJOR TYPES: CHINESE BRONZES

Bronzes have been cast in China for about 3,700 years. Most bronzes of about 1500–300 BCE, roughly the Bronze Age in China, may be described as ritual vessels intended for the worship of ancestors, who are often named in inscriptions on the bronzes. Many were specially cast to commemorate important events in the lives of their possessors. These ritual vessels of ancient China represent possibly the most remarkable achievement in the whole history of metalcraft before modern times.

SHANG DYNASTY
(*c.* 1600–1046 BCE)

The earliest examples of bronze vessels were unearthed in Erlitou, near the modern city of Luoyang in Henan province, which may or may not represent the earliest named Shang capital, Po, if not a still earlier Xia dynasty site. There a "palace" with pounded-earth foundation, fine jades, simple bronze vessels, and oracle bones were found. At Erligang, in the Zhengzhou area in Henan province, traces have been found of a walled city that may have been the middle Shang capital referred to as Ao.

Yin, the most enduring of Shang capital sites, lasting through the reigns of the last 9 (or 12) Shang kings, was located near the modern city of Anyang, in Henan province. Its discovery in 1899 by paleographers following the tracks of tomb robbers opened the way to verification of traditional accounts of the Shang dynasty and for the first scientific examination of China's early civilization. There, recorded on oracle bones, the written documentation for the first time is rich, archival, and wide-ranging regarding activities of the theocratic Shang government. Excavations conducted near Anyang between 1928 and 1937 provided the initial training ground for modern

Bronze gu *from Anyang, Henan province, China, Shang dynasty (c. 1600–1046 BCE); in the William Rockhill Nelson Gallery and Mary Atkins Museum of Fine Arts, Kansas City, Mo.* The Nelson-Atkins Museum of Art, Kansas City, Missouri

Chinese archaeology and continued periodically after 1949.

No fewer than 14 royal tombs have been unearthed near Anyang, culminating in the 1976 excavation of the first major tomb to have survived intact—that of Fu Hao, who is believed to have been a consort of the Shang king Wuding and a noted military leader. The Fu Hao tomb contained more than 440 bronze vessels and 590 jade objects among its numerous exquisite works. Remains of Bronze Age settlements of the Shang period have also been found over a large area of northern and central China.

More than any other factor, it was the unearthing of magnificent bronze vessels at Anyang that demonstrated the power and wealth of the Shang rulers. The vessels were used in divinatory ceremonies for sacrificial offerings of meat, wine, and grain, primarily to the spirits of clan ancestors, especially those of the ruler and his family. They were probably kept in the ancestral hall of the clan, and, in some cases, they were buried with their owner.

Surprisingly, perhaps, the bronze vessels were not discussed in Shang oracle bone inscriptions. But by late Shang times they themselves sometimes came to bear short, cast, dedicatory inscriptions providing the name of the vessel type, the patron, and the ancestor to whom the vessel was dedicated. What may be a clan name is also often included, enclosed within an inscribed notched square of uncertain meaning but now called a *yaxing*. The common addition by early Zhou times (1046–256 BCE) of the phrase "May sons and grandsons forever treasure and use it" provides evidence that most vessels were made originally for use in temple sacrifices rather than for burial, but other vessels, poorly cast and inscribed with posthumous ancestral names of the newly deceased, were clearly intended for the tomb.

The right to cast or possess these vessels was probably confined to the royal house itself originally but later was bestowed upon local governors set up by the ruler; still later, in the Zhou dynasty, the right was claimed by rulers of the feudal states and indeed by anyone who was rich and powerful enough to cast his own vessels.

The vessel types are known today either by names given them in Shang or Zhou times that can be identified in contemporary inscriptions, such as the *li*, *ding*, and *xian* (*yan*), or by names such as *you*, *jia*, and *gong* that were given to them by later Chinese scholars and antiquarians. The vessels may be grouped according to their presumed function in sacrificial rites. For cooking food, the main types are the *li*, a round-bodied vessel with a trilobed base extending into three hollow legs; its cousins the *ding*, a hemispheric vessel on three solid legs, and the *fangding*, a square vessel standing on four legs; and the *xian*, or *yan*, a steamer consisting of a bowl placed above a *li* tripod, with a perforated grate between the two. For offering food, the principal vessel was the *gui*, a bowl placed on a ring-shaped foot, like a modern-day wok.

Bronze pan, *late Warring States, c. 3rd century BCE; in the Avery Brundage Collection of the Asian Art Museum of San Francisco.* Courtesy of the Asian Art Museum of San Francisco, The Center of Asian Art and Culture, The Avery Brundage Collection

The word *zun* embraces wine containers of a variety of shapes. Among vessels for heating or offering wine are the *you*, a covered bucket with a swing handle; the *jia*, a round tripod or square quadruped with a handle on the side and raised posts with caps rising from its rim; the related *jue*, a smaller beaker on three legs, with an extended pouring spout in front, a pointed tail in the rear, a side handle, and posts with caps; the *he*, distinguished by its cylindrical pouring spout; the *gong*, resembling a covered gravy boat; and the elegant trumpet-mouthed *gu*. Vessels for ablutions include the *pan*, a large, shallow bowl. The shapes of the round-bodied vessels were often derived from earlier pottery forms; the square-section vessels,

with flat sides generally richly decorated, are thought to derive from boxes, baskets, or containers of carved wood or bone. Other objects connected with the rites were bronze drums and bells. Weapons and fittings for chariots, harness, and other utilitarian purposes also were made of bronze.

Bronze vessels were cast not by the lost-wax process (using a wax mold), as formerly supposed, but in sectional molds, quantities of which have been found at Shang sites. In this complex process, which reflects the Chinese early mastery of the ceramic medium, a clay model of the body is built around a solid core representing the vessel's interior; clay molding is used to encase the model, then sliced into sections and removed; the model is eliminated; the mold pieces are reconstructed around the core, using metal spacers to separate mold and core; and molten bronze is poured into the hollow space. Legs, handles, and appended sculpture are often cast separately and later integrated in a lock-on pour. Surface decoration may be added to the model surface before the mold is applied, requiring a double transfer from clay to clay to metal, or added in reverse to the mold surface after its removal from the model, with an incised design on the mold yielding a raised design on the metal surface. Ritual vessels range from about 15 cm (6 inches) to more than 130 cm (50 inches) in height with weights up to 875 kg (1,925 pounds). The intricacy and sharpness of the decoration shows that by the end of the 2nd millennium BCE the art of bronze casting in China was the most advanced in the world.

While many Shang ritual bronzes are plain or only partly ornamented, others are richly decorated with a variety of geometric and zoomorphic motifs, and a small number take the form of a bird or animal. The dominating motif is the *taotie*, seen either as two stylized creatures juxtaposed face-to-face or as a single creature with its body splayed out on both sides of a masklike head. The term *taotie* first appeared in the late Zhou and is perhaps related to eclipse mythology and the idea of renewal. Song dynasty antiquarians offered the unlikely interpretation that it represented a warning against gluttony. Alternative modern suggestions are that it was a fertility symbol like the later Chinese dragon, bestowing longevity on the ruling clan; that it was a fierce spirit which protected the rites and the participants from harm; that it embodied a variety of creatures related to the ceremonial sacrifices; that it was totemic or related to shamanic empowerment; or that its dual structure represented the inseparable forces of creation and destruction. Other creatures on the bronzes are the *gui* (each like half of the doubled *taotie*), tiger, cicada, snake, owl, ram, and ox. In later times the tiger represented nature's power, the cicada and snake symbolized regeneration, the owl was a carrier of the soul, and the ram and ox were chief animals of ancestral sacrifices. It is not known whether these meanings were attached to the creatures on Shang bronzes, for no Shang writing addresses the issue, but it seems likely that they had a more than purely decorative purpose. There is no suggested environmental setting for these creatures. The human figure appears only rarely in Shang bronzes, usually in the grasp of these powerful zoomorphic creatures.

The art of the Shang bronzes began as technically simple, albeit sometimes quite elegant, thinly cast vessels that were clearly ceramic prototypes. It reached a climax of sculpturesque monumentality at the end of the dynasty, reflecting a long period of peace and stability at Anyang. In the early 1950s the scholar Max Loehr identified five phases or styles in the evolution of Shang bronze surface decor and casting techniques. The thin-walled vessels of Style I typically carry a narrow register of zoomorphic motifs that are more abstract in appearance than motifs of later times; the motifs are composed of thin, raised lines created by incision on the production molds. Style II zoomorphic forms are composed of broad, flat bands in narrow horizontal registers, incised on the model, often on a raised band of ceramic appliqué. In Style III, dense curvilinear designs derived from those of the previous phase begin to cover much of the surface of an increasingly thick-walled vessel, and the zoomorph becomes increasingly difficult to discern. The main zoomorphic motifs of Style IV, although flush to the surface of the vessel (exclusive of appended heads, handles, and fully sculptural attachments), become clearly distinguishable as set against a dense spiral background known as "thunder pattern" (*leiwen*); in this phase, with similar spirals placed sparsely over the zoomorph, which itself is constructed from the same linear vocabulary, an intricate decorative system of interactive forms, rich in philosophical implications, begins to reach maturity. In Style V the main motifs are set forth in increasingly bold plastic relief through the use of ceramic appliqué upon the model. The Style I bodily form clearly reveals conceptualization derived from ceramics, while Style V vessels fully utilize the sculpturesque possibilities of the molded-bronze technology. Styles I and II appear at Zhengzhou; Style III appears at both Zhengzhou and early Anyang; and Styles IV and V are found in the Anyang period only. Pre-Style I vessels, ceramic in form, thin-walled, and with little or no surface decor, have been found at Erlitou near Luoyang, demonstrating early Shang or even Xia origins.

ZHOU DYNASTY (1046–256 BCE)

The ritual bronzes of the early Western Zhou (Xizhou) continued the late Anyang tradition; many were made by the same craftsmen and by their descendants. Even in the predynastic Zhou period, however, new creatures had appeared on the bronzes, notably a flamboyant long-tailed bird that may have had totemic meaning for the Zhou rulers, and flanges had begun to be large and spiky. By the end of the 9th century, moreover, certain Shang shapes such as the *jue*, *gu*, and *gong* were no longer being made, and the *taotie* and other Shang zoomorphs had been broken up and then dissolved into volutes or undulating meander patterns encircling the entire vessel, scales, and fluting, with little apparent symbolic intent.

From the outset of Zhou rule, vessels increasingly came to serve as vehicles for inscriptions that were cast to record events and report them to ancestral spirits. An outstanding example, excavated near Xi'an in 1976, was dedicated by a Zhou official who apparently had divined the date for the successful assault upon the Shang and later used his reward money to have the bronze vessel cast. By late Zhou times a long inscription might have well over 400 characters.

Vessel shapes, meanwhile, had become aggressive or heavy and sagging, and the quality of the casting was seldom as high as in the late Shang. These changes, completed by the 8th century BCE, mark the middle Zhou phase of bronze design.

The bronzes of the Eastern Zhou (Dongzhou) period, after 771 BCE, show signs of a gradual renaissance in the craft and much regional variation, which appears ever more complex as more Eastern Zhou sites are unearthed. Often adorned with boldly modeled handles in the form of animal heads, 8th- and 7th-century bronzes are crude and vigorous in shape. Typical vessels of this phase have been found in a cemetery of the small feudal state of Guo in Henan province. Vessels from Xinzheng in Henan (8th–6th century BCE) reveal a further change to more elegant forms, often decorated with an allover pattern of tightly interlaced serpents; the vessel may be set about with tigers and dragons modeled in the round and topped with a flaring, petaled lid. The aesthetic tendency toward elaboration was given further stimulus by the introduction of the lost-wax method of production (by the late 7th century BCE), leading quickly to zealous experiments in openwork design that are impressive technically though often heavy in appearance and gaudy in effect. The style of bronzes found at Liyu in Shanxi (c. 6th–5th century BCE) is much simpler, more compact, and unified; the interlaced and spiral decoration is flush with the surface. Thereafter, until the end of the dynasty, the bronze style became

increasingly refined: the decoration was confined within a simpler contour, and the interlacing of the Xinzheng style gave way to the fine, hooked "comma pattern" of the vessels of the 5th and 4th centuries BCE. By this time, bronze decor had come under the influence of textile patterns and technique, particularly embroidery, as well as of lacquer decor, suggesting the bronze medium's decline from primacy. Bronzes decorated in this

Chinese bronze zhong, *late Zhou dynasty (1046–256 BCE); in the Freer Gallery of Art, Washington, D.C. Height 67 cm. Courtesy of the Smithsonian Institution, Freer Gallery of Art, Washington, D.C.*

manner have been found chiefly in the Huai River valley.

Bronze bells are another form from this period. Perhaps the oldest class is a small clappered bell called *ling*, but the best known is certainly the *zhong*, a suspended, clapperless bell. *Zhong* were cast in sets of eight or more to form a musical scale, and they were probably played in the company of string and wind instruments. The section is a flattened ellipse, and on each side of the body appear 18 blunt spikes, or basses, arranged in three double rows of three. These often show marks of filing, and it has been suggested that they were devices whereby the bell could be tuned to the requisite pitch by removing small quantities of the metal. The oldest specimen recovered in a closed excavation is one from Pudu Cun, dating from the 9th century BCE. A fine example is an orchestral set of 64 bells, probably produced in Chu and unearthed in 1978 from a royal tomb of the Zeng state, at Leigudun near Sui Xian in Hubei province. The bells were mounted on wooden racks supported by bronze human figurines. They are graded in size (from about 20 to 150 cm [8 to 60 inches] in height) and tone (covering five octaves), and each is capable of producing two unrelated tones according to where it is struck. Gold-inlaid inscriptions on each bell present valuable information regarding early musical terms and performance, while a 65th bell is dedicated by inscription from the king of Chu to Marquis Yi of Zeng (Zenghou Yi), the deceased, and bears a date equivalent to 433 BCE.

In vessels from the rich finds at Jincun near Luoyang, all excrescences are shorn away; the shapes have a classic purity and restraint, and the decoration consists of geometric patterns of diagonal bands and volutes. The taste of the new leisured class is shown in objects that were not merely useful but finely fashioned and beautiful in themselves: ritual and domestic vessels, weapons, chariot and furniture fittings, ceremonial staff ends, bracelets, and the backs of mirrors. Monster masks attaching ring handles are reminiscent of the Shang *taotie*, the first sign of a deliberate archaism that would from time to time throughout history give a special flavour to Chinese decorative art.

The wealth and sophistication of late Zhou culture is apparent in examples of exquisite craftsmanship, while the culture's increasing commercial interaction and artistic fascination with the tribal peoples to their north is apparent in new techniques, such as cast openwork, and many of the works executed with inlays of gold, silver, jade, glass, and semiprecious stones. Bronze garment hooks worn at the shoulder were often fashioned in the form of animals, reflecting the artistic style of China's nomadic neighbours, who through the Eastern Zhou and Han dynasties exerted pressure on its northern frontiers and who both influenced and were influenced by Chinese culture in this period. Scattered finds, chiefly in the Ordos (Mu Us) Desert, show that the arts of these huntsmen and herdsmen were related to those of the steppe peoples of

Central Asia and, remotely, to those of the Luristan (Lorestān) region of Persia. Bronze objects consist chiefly of animal-headed daggers and knives; cheekpieces, jingles, and other harness fittings; ornaments; and plaques of pierced relief work generally depicting with somewhat barbarous vigour an animal combat, a theme remote from the experience of the settled farming communities of northern China.

Bronze mirrors were used in ancient China not only for toiletry but also as funerary objects, in accordance with the belief that a mirror was itself a source of light and could illuminate the eternal darkness of the tomb. A mirror also was thought of as a symbolic aid to self-knowledge. Ancient Chinese mirrors were generally bronze disks polished on the face and decorated on the back, with a central loop handle or pierced boss to hold a tassel. The early ones were small and worn at the girdle; later they became larger and were often set on a stand. A bronze disk found in a tomb at Anyang may have been a mirror. There is less doubt about the small disks from an 8th-century-BCE tomb at Shangcunling in Henan province, believed to be the earliest mirrors yet found in China. Mirrors, however, were not widely used until the 4th and 3rd centuries BCE. Shouzhou, in the state of Chu, was a centre for the manufacture of late Zhou mirrors, the designs on which consist chiefly of zigzag lozenges, quatrefoil petals, scallops, a hooked symbol resembling the character for "mountain" (*shan*), and sometimes animal figures superimposed

on a dense allover pattern of hooks and volutes. These mirrors are often thin, and the execution is refined and elegant. Mirrors from Henan (Luoyang) city are closer in style to the inlaid bronzes. The decoration, often dragons and intricately interwoven zoomorphs whose tails turn into volutes, stands out boldly against a fine geometric background that suggests a textile pattern.

QIN (221–207 BCE) AND HAN DYNASTIES (206 BCE–220 CE)

Already by late Zhou times, the more expensive medium of lacquer was often used in place of bronze. Nevertheless, some bronze vessels were still made for sacrificial rites, and other bronze objects, such as lamps and incense burners, also were made for household use. The "hill censer" (*boshan xianglu*) was designed as a miniature, three-dimensional mountain of the immortals, usually replete with scenes of mythic combat between man and beasts, suggesting the powerful forces of nature that only the Daoist adept could tame. Sacred vapours emanating from materials burned within were released through perforations in the lid (hidden behind the mountain peaks). Cosmic waters were depicted lapping at the base of the hills, conveying the sense of an island, and the whole was set on a narrow stem that thrust the mountain upward as if it were an axis of the universe. Such censers might have been used in ceremonial exorcisms, in funerary rites associated with the ascent of the soul, or in other varieties of Daoist religious practice.

Some Han mirrors have astronomical or astrological patterns. The most elaborate, particularly popular during the Xin dynasty (9–25 CE), bears the so-called TLV pattern. (The TLV pattern is so called because it resembles those roman letters.) These angular shapes, ranged around the main band of decoration between a central square zone and the outer border band, are believed to be linked to a cosmological, chess-like game called *liubo*; the decoration also may include creatures symbolic of the four directions, immortals, and other mythical beings popular in Daoist folklore. Often the mirrors carry inscriptions, varying from a simple expression of good luck to a long dedication giving the name of the maker and referring to the Shangfang, the imperial office in charge of imperial workshops. In the Eastern Han the Daoist elements dominated mirror design, which often includes the legendary Queen Mother of the West, Xiwangmu, and her royal eastern counterpart, Dongwanggong. The coming of Buddhism at the end of the Han dynasty caused a decline in the use of cosmological mirrors. Mirror making, however, was revived in the Tang dynasty (618–907).

MAJOR TYPES: CHINESE POTTERY

Objects made in China of clay and hardened by heat—earthenware, stoneware, and porcelain—are pottery or ceramics.

Nowhere in the world has pottery assumed such importance as in China, and the influence of Chinese porcelain on later European pottery was profound.

STYLISTIC AND HISTORICAL DEVELOPMENT

The earliest evidence for art in any form in ancient China consists of crude cord-marked pottery and artifacts decorated with geometric designs found in Mesolithic sites in northern China and in the Guangdong-Guangxi regions. The dating for prehistoric culture in China is still very uncertain, but this material is probably at least 7,000 or 8,000 years old.

THE FORMATIVE PERIOD (TO *C*. 1600 BCE)

The art of the Neolithic Period represents a considerable advance. The Yangshao (Painted Pottery) culture, named after the first Neolithic site discovered (in 1920), had its centre around the eastern bend of the Huang He (Yellow River), and it is now known to have extended across northern China and up into Gansu province. Yangshao pottery consists chiefly of full-bodied funerary storage jars made by the coiling, or ring, method. They are decorated, generally on the upper half only, with a rich variety of geometric designs, whorls, volutes (spirals), and sawtooth patterns executed in black and red pigment with sweeping, rhythmic brushwork that foreshadows the free brush painting of historical periods.

Some of the pottery from the village site of Banpo (*c.* 4500 BCE), discovered in 1953 near Xi'an in Shaanxi, have schematized fish, bird, deer, and plant designs, which are related thematically to hunting and gathering, and what may be a human face or mask. Dating for the dominant phase of the Yangshao culture may be put roughly between 5000 and 3000 BCE. Over this span of two millennia the Yangshao culture progressed generally westward along the Huang He and Wei River valleys from sites in central China, such as Banpo, to sites farther west, such as Miaodigou, Majiayao, Banshan, and Machang. The art produced at these villages exhibits a clear and logical stylistic evolution, leading from representational designs to linear abstraction (the latter with occasional symbolic references).

The last major phase of the Neolithic Period is represented by the Longshan culture, distinguished particularly by the black pottery of its later stages (*c.* 2200–1700 BCE). Longshan is named after the site of its discovery in 1928, in Shandong province, although evidence increasingly suggests origins to the south along the China coast, in Jiangsu province. Its remains are widely distributed, in some sites lying directly over a Painted Pottery stratum, indicating that the Longshan culture replaced the Yangshao. In other areas there is evidence of a mixed culture, including elements of both Yangshao and Longshan, that occurred between these stages. This mixed culture is called "Longshanoid" or, after one of the sites in Hubei, Qijiaping. By contrast with the Yangshao, the fully developed Longshan pottery is wheel-made and especially thinly potted. The finest specimens have a dark gray or black body burnished to a hard, smooth surface that is occasionally incised but never painted, giving it a metallic appearance. The occasional use of open-worked design and the simulation of lugs and folded plating all suggest the highly skilled imitation of contemporary valuable copper wares (no longer extant); the existence of such copper wares heralded the transition from a lithic to a metallic culture. At this point, the superior calibre of Chinese ceramics was first attained.

In Yangshao pottery, emphasis was on funerary wares. The delicate potting

Painted Pottery funerary urn, Neolithic Banshan phase, c. 3000 BCE, from Yangshao, Henan province, China; in the Museum of Far Eastern Antiquities, Stockholm. Height 33.5 cm. Ostasiatiska Museet, Stockholm

of the Longshan ware and the prevalence of offering stands and goblets suggest that these vessels were made not for burial but for sacrificial rites connected with the worship of ancestral spirits. Ritual vessels, oracle bones (used by shamans in divination), ceremonial jade objects and ornaments, and architecture (pounded-earth foundations, protective city walls, rectilinear organization) reflect an advanced material culture on the threshold of the Bronze Age. This culture continued in outlying areas long after the coming of bronze technology to the central Henan–Shaanxi–southern Shanxi region.

SHANG DYNASTY (C. 1600–1046 BCE)

The Shang dynasty saw several important advances in pottery technology, including the development of a hard-bodied, high-fire stoneware and pottery glazes. A small quantity of stoneware is covered with a thin, hard, yellowish green glaze applied in liquid form to the vessel. Shang potters also developed a fine soft-bodied white ware, employing kaolin (later used in porcelain); this ware was probably for ceremonial use and was decorated with motifs similar to those on the ritual bronzes. The only known complete specimen of a fine white stoneware dating from about 1400 BCE is decorated with chevrons (linked V-shapes) and a key-fret pattern, the shoulder motifs being reminiscent of those seen on contemporary bronze vessels. Much cruder imitations of bronze vessels also occur in the ubiquitous gray pottery of the Shang dynasty.

ZHOU DYNASTY (1046–256 BCE)

Early Western Zhou pottery, like the bronzes, continued the Shang tradition at a somewhat lower technical level, and the soft white Shang pottery disappeared. Stemmed offering dishes, *dou*, were made in a hard stoneware dipped or brushed over with a glaze ranging from gray to brownish green. The fact that some of the richest finds of high-fired glazed wares have been made not in Henan but at Yiqi in Anhui shows that the centre of advance in pottery technology was beginning to move, with the growth of population, to the lower Huai and Yangtze (Chang) valleys. Crude attempts also were made to give pottery the appearance of bejeweled metal by covering *dou* stands with lacquer inlaid with shell disks.

In the second half of the dynasty the range of pottery types and techniques was greatly extended. A low-fired pottery was produced in Henan primarily for burial. Some of it is white, and some is covered with slip, or liquid clay, and painted, reviving an ancient tradition of northern China. A soft-bodied, black, burnished ware, sometimes decorated with scrolls and geometric motifs scratched through the polished surface, has been found at Huixian. In the period of the Warring States, a soft earthenware covered with green lead glaze was made in northern China for burial. In the lower Yangtze valley an almost porcelaneous stoneware developed, covered with a thin feldspathic glaze, the ancestor of the celadon glaze of the Tang dynasty (618–907 CE) and later. Another technique, which appears in the glazed wares of Zhejiang and Jiangsu and was to persist in the southern pottery tradition for many centuries, was the stamping of regular, repeated motifs over the surface of the vessel before firing.

HAN DYNASTY (206 BCE–220 CE)

The first pottery to survive in appreciable quantities belongs to the Han dynasty; most of it has been excavated from graves. Perhaps the commonest form is the *hu*, a baluster-shaped vase copied from bronze vessels of the same name and sometimes decorated with relief ornament in friezes taken directly from a bronze original. The hill jar, which has a cover molded to represent the Daoist "Isles of the Blest," is another fairly frequent form, and many models of servants, domestic animals, buildings, wellheads, dovecotes, and the like also have been discovered in graves.

Han glazed wares are chiefly of two types. Northern China saw the invention, presumably for funerary purposes only, of a low-fired lead glaze, tinted bottle-green with copper oxide, that degenerates through burial to an attractive silvery iridescence. High-fired stoneware with a thin brownish to olive glaze was still being made in Henan, but the main centre of production was already shifting to the Zhejiang region, formerly known as Yue. Yue ware kilns of the Eastern Han, located at Deqing in northern Zhejiang, produced a hard stoneware, often imitating the shapes of bronze vessels and decorated with impressed, bronzelike designs under a thin olive glaze. Other important provincial centres for pottery production in the Han dynasty were Changsha (in Hunan province) and Chengdu and Chongqing (in Sichuan province).

Yue *yao* ("Yue ware") was first made at Yuezhou (present Yuyao), Zhejiang province, during the Han dynasty, although all surviving specimens are later, most belonging to the Six Dynasties (220–589 CE). They have a stoneware body and an olive or brownish green glaze and belong to the family of celadons, a term that looms large in any discussion of early Chinese wares. It is applied to glazes ranging from the olive of Yue to the deep green of later varieties. These colours were the result of a wash of slip containing a high proportion of iron that was put over the body before glazing. The iron interacted with the glaze during firing and coloured it.

THREE KINGDOMS (220–280 CE) AND SIX DYNASTIES (220–589 CE)

The increase in population in the lower Yangtze valley was a great stimulus to the pottery industry in the Six Dynasties. Kilns in Zhejiang (the old kingdom of Yue) were producing a stoneware with an olive brown or greenish glaze. Examples of Yue ware—jars, ewers, pitchers, and other grave goods—have been found in 3rd- and 4th-century tombs in the

Nanjing region. They were made chiefly at Shaoxing, at Shanglin Lake, and at Deqing, north of Hangzhou, which also produced a stoneware with a glossy black glaze. During the Six Dynasties potters freed themselves from the influence of bronze design and produced shapes more characteristic of pottery.

While most of the Zhejiang wares are plain or simply decorated, "northern celadon," produced in Hebei and Henan in the 6th century, is exotic in style, reflecting the taste of Turkish rulers and other cultural contacts with western Asia. Heavy funerary jars are adorned with acanthus and lotus leaves, and flowers and round decorative plaques are molded or applied to the surface in imitation of Sāsānian repoussé metalwork. Tomb figurines of this period are often made of dark gray earthenware and unglazed, though sometimes they are painted.

SUI (581–618) AND TANG (618–907) DYNASTIES

After the comparative sterility of the Six Dynasties, this was a great period in the development of Chinese pottery. Although a white porcelain perfected early in the 7th century is called Xing yao (Xing "ware") because of a reference to the white porcelain of Xingzhou in the 9th-century essay "Cha Jing" ("Tea Classic") by Lu Yu, as yet no kilns have been found there. Kilns near Dingzhou in Hebei, however, were at this time already producing a fine white porcelain, which was the ancestor of the famous

Ding ware of the Northern Song. In the late 7th and the 8th century, ceramists in northern China, working primarily at kilns at Tongchuan near Chang'an and at Gongxian in Henan province, also developed "three-colour" (sancai) pottery wares and figurines that were slipped and covered with a low-fired lead glaze tinted with copper or ferrous oxide in green, yellow, brown, and sometimes blue; the bright colours were allowed to mix or run naturally over the robust contour of these vessels, which are among the finest in the history of Chinese pottery. Northern Chinese kilns in Shaanxi also produced a stoneware with a rich black glaze, and a type of celadon was made north of Xi'an, in Shaanxi. The northern Chinese potters borrowed shapes and motifs from western Asia even more freely than had their 6th-century predecessors: foreign shapes included the amphora, bird-headed ewer, and rhyton (a drinking vessel formed to look like an animal's head). Foreign motifs included hunting reliefs, floral medallions, boys with garlands or swags of vines, and Buddhist symbols adapted and applied with characteristic Tang confidence. Some forms were also borrowed from metalwork or glassware.

Tomb figurines were produced in such enormous quantities that attempts were made through sumptuary laws to limit their number and size; such efforts met with little success. The figurines were made, generally in molds, of earthenware covered with slip and painted or glazed or both. Among the human figures are servants and actors, female dancers, and musicians of exquisite grace. The 7th-century figurines are slender and high-waisted, while those of the 8th century are increasingly rotund and round-faced, reflecting a change in fashion. There are also many figurines of Central Asian grooms and Semitic merchants with caricatured features such as deep-set eyes and jutting noses. Of the camels and horses, the most remarkable are glazed camels bearing on their backs a group of four or five singers and musicians. After the middle of the 8th century, there was a sharp decline both in the quantity and in the quality of tomb wares and figurines in northern China.

The great southward movement of population in the Tang dynasty stimulated the development of many new kilns. Celadons were now made in Jionglai (Sichuan), Changsha (Hunan), and several areas of Guangdong and Fujian. A kiln producing whitewares was active at Jizhou in Jiangxi, and at Jingdezhen in the same province two kilns were producing celadons and whitewares. From these humble beginnings, Jingdezhen was destined to become, in the Ming (1368–1644) and Qing (1644–1911/12) dynasties, the largest pottery factory in the world. In Lu Yu's essay the "Cha Jing," the celadons of Yuezhou in Zhejiang are ranked for their jadelike quality first among the wares suitable for tea drinking, followed by the silvery Xing ware. Yue celadons from kilns at Yuyao and a number of other sites in Zhejiang were also exported, and quantities of fine Yue ware have been found at

Al-Fusṭāṭ in Egypt and at Sāmarrā' in Iraq, the luxurious summer residence of the 'Abbāsid caliphs—notably al-Mu'taṣim (son of Hārūn al-Rashīd)—between 836 and 883. Tang wares, consisting chiefly of celadons from southern Chinese kilns, have also been found in Indonesia and the Philippines, marking the beginning of a vast export trade in Chinese pottery that has continued almost without interruption into modern times.

Perhaps the most important single development was the use of coloured glazes—as monochromes or splashed and dappled. The Tang wares commonest in Western collections are those with either monochrome or dappled glazes covering a highly absorbent, buff, earthenware body. The dappled glazes were usually applied with a sponge, and they include blue, dark blue, green, yellow, orange, straw, and brown colours. These glazes normally exhibit a fine crackle and often fall short of the base in an uneven wavy line, the unglazed surface area varying from about one-third to two-thirds of the vessel.

Dappled glazes are also found on the magnificent series of tomb figures with which this period is particularly associated. Similar figures were made in unglazed earthenware and were sometimes decorated with cold pigment. Although the unglazed specimen or those covered only with the straw-coloured glaze are occasionally modeled superbly, many are crude and apparently made for the tombs of the less affluent and influential. Most of the glazed figures are much better in quality and occasionally reach a large size; figures of the Bactrian camel, for instance, are particularly impressive, some being nearly three feet high. The Bactrian pony, introduced into China about 138 BCE, is to be found in many spirited poses. This fashion for tomb figures fell into disuse at the beginning of the Song dynasty (960–1279 CE) but was revived for a short while during the Ming period (1368–1644), when Tang influence is noticeable.

Marbled wares are seen occasionally. The effect was achieved either by combing slips of contrasting colours (i.e., mingling the slips after they had been put on the pot, by means of a comb) or by mingling differently coloured clays. Another type of Tang ware (probably from Henan) had a stoneware body with a dark brown glaze streaked by pale blue. Most vessels stand on a flat base; although later Tang wares sometimes were given a foot ring, for the most part this can be regarded as evidence in favour of a Song dating.

FIVE DYNASTIES (907–960) AND TEN KINGDOMS (902–978)

The confused state of northern China under the Five Dynasties was not conducive to development of the pottery industry, and some types, such as the Tang three-colour wares, went out of production completely. White porcelain and black glazed stonewares, however, continued into the Song dynasty. In contrast, the flourishing southern courts and

the massive increase in the population of southeastern China were a great stimulus to the craft. A large complex of kilns that had been established at Yuyao, around Shanglin Lake in Zhejiang, which lay in the territory of the kingdom of Wuyue, sent its finest celadons to the court of Li Houzhu (Li Yu) until his realm fell to the Song in 978; after that they were sent as tribute to the Song court at Bianjing. The finest pieces, with decoration carved in the clay body under a very pale olive-green glaze, were called *biseyao* ("secret," or "reserve, colour ware") by 10th-century writers. It is not known whether this referred to a secret process or to the fact that the ware was reserved for the court.

SONG (960–1279), LIAO (907–1125), AND JIN (1115–1234) DYNASTIES

Of the dynasties listed, the Song dynasty marked a high point in the history of Chinese pottery, when technical mastery, refinement of feeling, and a natural spontaneity of technique were more perfectly balanced than at any other time in Chinese history. Unlike the sometimes lifeless perfection that marks the palace wares of the Qing dynasty, the beauty of Song wares is derived from the simplicity of the shapes and purity of glaze tone and colour. In Song wares the touch of the potter's hand can still be perceived, and glazes have a depth and warmth that was later lost when a higher level of manufacturing skill was attained.

SONG DYNASTY

It is convenient to group Song wares geographically: the chief northern wares are Ding, Ru, Jun, northern celadon, Cizhou, and brown and black glazed wares; those of southern China include Jingdezhen whiteware (*yingqing*, or *qingbai*), Jizhou wares, celadons, and blackwares of Fujian. (Other varieties from local kilns will be mentioned later.) This relatively simple approach, in some cases allotting one ware to one kiln, has been greatly complicated by discoveries made first by Japanese and then by Chinese archaeologists during and since World War II. Many new kiln sites have been located, and it is now known that one kiln often produced several different wares and that decorated stonewares named from the principal factory at Cizhou in southern Hebei were made in many kilns across the breadth of northern China.

White porcelain made at Jiancicun in south-central Hebei was already being produced for the northern courts in the Five Dynasties (907–960) and continued as an imperial ware to the beginning of the 12th century. Very finely potted and sometimes decorated with freely incised plants, fish, and birds under the glaze or later with mold-made designs in relief, this Ding ware is directly descended from the northern whitewares of the Tang dynasty. Supposedly because of Huizong's dissatisfaction with Ding ware, it was replaced in the late Northern Song by another official ware known as Ru, the rarest and most highly prized of all Chinese ceramics (until the mid-1980s, only some 60 examples were known). Representing Huizong's celebrated aestheticism, the low-fired Ru stoneware is distinguished by a seemingly soft, milky glaze of pale blue or grayish green with hair-thin crackle. The glaze covers a pale gray or buff body that is usually simple in shape yet highly sophisticated and exquisitely tasteful in effect. Ru ware was produced for only a few years before Huizong's sudden demise. The Ru kilns defied identification until 1986, when they, along with the remains of a workshop, were located at Qingliangsi, more than 160 km (100 miles) southwest of the capital. Another 37 intact examples were soon afterward excavated there. Typical of other kilns, the Ru kilns varied their productions, turning out Cizhou stoneware and Yaozhou-type celadons like those discovered at Yaoan, north of Xi'an.

A sturdy stoneware covered with a thick lavender-blue glaze was made at Junzhou in Henan. This Jun ware is sometimes marked with splashes of purple or crimson produced by copper oxide. On the finest Jun wares, which are close to Ru in quality, these splashes are used with restraint, but on later Jun-type wares manufactured at Jingdezhen and near Guangzhou (Canton) too much purple often gives vessels or flowerpots a mottled, lurid hue that Ming connoisseurs were wont to label "mule's liver" or "horse's lung."

Somewhat related to Jun wares are sturdily potted jars, vases, and bowls with lustrous black or brown glazes. Those that are decorated with flowers and leaves painted in an oxidized rust brown constitute an enormous family of Cizhou wares made for domestic and funerary use in numerous northern China kilns, and they are still being produced in some factories today. Cizhou techniques of decoration included free brush painting under the

Cizhou vase decorated with a dragon, probably from Juluxian, Hebei province, stoneware with white and engraved black slip, early 12th century, Northern Song or Jin dynasty; in the Nelson-Atkins Museum of Art, Kansas City, Missouri, U.S. The Nelson-Atkins Museum of Art, Kansas City, Missouri; purchase: Nelson Trust (36-116)

glaze, carving or scratching (sgraffito work) through one slip to another of a different colour, and painting over the glaze in low-fired colours. The earliest known example of overglaze painting in the history of Chinese pottery bears a date equivalent to 1201. The technique was more widely used for the decoration of Cizhou wares in the 14th century. In both the variety and the vigour of their forms and decoration, Cizhou stonewares present a strong contrast to the restraint and exquisite taste of the courtly wares. Chinese connoisseurs and imperial collectors considered them beneath their notice, and it has taken the interest of Western collectors and the concern for the arts of the masses shown in China since 1949 to elevate them to the honoured place they deserve.

LATE SONG, LIAO, AND JIN DYNASTIES

The pottery produced in northeastern China (Manchuria) under Liao occupation continued the tradition of Tang whiteware and three-coloured ware, with some influence from the Ding and Cizhou wares of Northern Song. Five kilns that produced pottery for the Liao and Jin courts have been located. In addition to imitations of Tang and Song wares, Liao potters produced their own unique shapes, which included long-necked vases, cockscomb vessels, ewers with phoenix-headed mouths, and flattened flasks made in imitation of animal-hide bags for liquor or milk carried at the saddle. These were then slipped and covered with a low-fired brown or rich green glaze or a beautiful white glaze almost as fine as that of Ding ware. In general much less finely potted than Song wares, those of the Liao have the interest and charm of a vital provincial tradition.

After the Song capital was reestablished at Hangzhou, the finest wares obtainable were once more supplied to the court. These southern Guan wares were made for a short time in kilns close to the palace under the direction of the Office of Works. Later the kilns were established near Jiaotan, the altar for sacrifices to heaven and earth, outside the south gate of the city. Jiaotan Guan ware had a dark, opaque body and a beautiful bluish gray layered glaze. A deliberately formed crackle, caused by the shrinking of the glaze as the vessel cooled after firing, is the only ornament on this exquisite ware.

The southern Guan was the finest of a huge family of celadons produced in an increasing number of kilns in southeastern China. Longquan in southern Zhejiang made a fine celadon with bluish green glaze, the best of which was almost certainly supplied to the court and may hence be classed as Guan. A variant with strongly marked crackle became known as Ge ware in deference to the tradition that it was made by the elder brother (*ge*) of the director of the Longquan factory. Among the wide range of shapes made in Song celadon are those derived from forms of archaic bronzes, such as *li*, *ding*, and *zun*, testifying to the increasingly antiquarian taste of court and gentry.

Meanwhile, a small factory at Jingdezhen in Jiangxi was growing to meet the vast increase in the population of southern China. In the Song its most characteristic ware was a fine, white, sugary porcelain covered with a transparent, slightly bluish glaze; the ware has been known since Song times as *qingbai* ("bluish white"), but modern Chinese dealers call it *yingqing* ("shadowy blue"). *Yingqing* ware is very thinly potted, the decoration carved in the clay body or applied in raised slip or beading under the glaze. Song *yingqing* wares are the predecessors of a vast output of fine, white Jingdezhen porcelain that was to dominate the Chinese pottery industry during the Yuan, Ming, and Qing dynasties. Other whitewares were made at Yonghe near Ji'an in Jiangxi. These Ji'an, or Kian, wares appear to be imitations of Ding, and there may be truth in the tradition that the kilns were set up by refugees from the north. The Yonghe kilns were unable to compete with Jingdezhen, however, and had ceased production by the end of the Song.

Kilns in the wooded hills around Jianyang in northern Fujian produced almost nothing but heavily potted stoneware tea bowls covered with a thick black glaze. The finest and rarest of these Jian ware bowls have streaky "hare's fur" or iridescent "oil spot" effects that were much prized by Japanese tea masters, who called this ware *temmoku* after Tianmu, the sacred Buddhist mountain in Zhejiang province that was near the port from

Tea bowl, Jian-type stoneware with oil-spot effect (yohen temmoku) *from Fujian province, 12th–13th century, Southern Song dynasty; in the Seikado Bunko Art Museum, Tokyo.* © The Seikado Bunko Art Museum

which the ware was shipped to Japan. Yonghe kilns also turned out a coarse variety of *temmoku* and experimented with novel decorative effects produced by laying floral paper cuts or skeleton leaves under the glaze before firing.

This greatly simplified account of Song wares cannot include the many provincial kilns that flourished in almost every province of China. Most marked was the growth of the industry in the south (modern Guangdong and Fujian), where kilns turned out variants of celadon and *qingbai* both for local consumption and for barter in China's rapidly increasing trade with Indonesia and the Philippines. Huge quantities of these southern Chinese wares have been found in burial sites in the Philippines and often provide archaeologists with the surest way of dating the remains.

YUAN DYNASTY (1206–1368)

While the Mongol occupation destroyed much, it also shook China free from the static traditions and techniques of the late Southern Song and made possible many innovations, both in painting and in the decorative arts. The north was not progressive, and the main centre of pottery activity shifted permanently to the south. The northern traditions of Jun and Cizhou ware continued through the Jin and Yuan, bolder but coarser than before. New shapes included a heavy, wide-mouthed jar, sometimes with decoration boldly carved through a black or brown slip or painted in two or three colours. These new techniques and the overglaze painting already developed in the Jin dynasty prepared the way for the three- and five-colour wares of the Ming.

While no Yuan celadon has the perfection of colour of Song Guan and Longchuan wares, being more olive green in tone, the quality is high. And the variety of decorative techniques used is far wider than that of the Song. These include raised relief designs molded under the glaze, fish and dragons raised "in the biscuit" (that is, unglazed) in relief, and iron-brown spots that the Japanese call *tobi seiji* ("flying celadon"). Vases and dishes were now sturdily potted in porcelain, often mold-made, and of considerable size.

Factories at Jingdezhen were expanding rapidly. While their products included celadon, their chief output, as before, was white porcelain, including richly modeled figurines of Guanyin and other Buddhist deities. *Qingbai* was now decorated with floral motifs and beading in raised relief or incised under the glaze, the most elaborate pieces combining flowers and vines in appliqué relief with openwork panels. A stronger, less sugar-white porcelain with molded or incised decoration was produced; called *shufu* ware, it sometimes bore the characters *shufu*, meaning "central government palace," for the ware was often ordered by imperial officials.

The earliest evidence of the use of cobalt blue, probably imported from the Middle East, is seen in its application as an underglaze pigment on fragments dating to the late 8th or early 9th century that were unearthed at Yangzhou in 1983. The occasional use of underglazed cobalt continued in the Northern Song. It was not until the Yuan dynasty, however, that underglazed blue decoration began a rapid rise in popularity. It was applied on fine white porcelains of the *shufu* type and combined with Islamic decorative taste. These blue-and-white wares soon became the most popular of all Chinese ceramics, both at home and abroad. A pair of richly ornate temple vases dated 1351 (in the Percival David Foundation in London) are proof that the technique had been fully mastered by that time. The finest Jingdezhen examples were reserved for the court, but coarse varieties were made in southern China for trade with Southeast Asia or for export to the Middle East.

Experiments also were made with painting in underglaze copper red, but it was difficult to control and soon abandoned. Both the shapes and decoration of Yuan blue-and-white have a characteristic boldness. The motifs are richly varied, sometimes crowded and unrestrained, but at their best they have great splendour and vitality. Favourite motifs include the lotus, vines, and dragons that had already appeared on the *shufu* wares, creatures such as the *qilin* ("unicorn") and *longma* ("dragon-horse"), and fish and Daoist figures. Also popular for a while were scenes from historical dramas and romances written by unemployed Confucian scholars.

MING DYNASTY (1368–1644)

While northern traditions of Cizhou and Jun ware continued to decline, pottery production in the south expanded. It was chiefly centred on Jingdezhen, an ideal site because of the abundance of minerals used for porcelain manufacture—kaolin (china clay) and petuntse (china stone)—ample wood fuel, and good communications by water. Most of the celadon, however, was still produced in Zhejiang, notably at Longchuan and Chuzhou, whose Ming products are more heavily potted than those of the Song and Yuan and are decorated with incised and molded designs under a sea-green glaze. Celadon dishes,

some of large size, were an important item in China's trade with the Middle East, whose rulers, it was said, believed that the glaze would crack or change colour if poison touched it.

At Jingdezhen the relatively coarse-bodied *shufu* ware was developed into a hard white porcelain that no longer reveals the touch of the potter's hand. The practically invisible designs sometimes carved in the translucent body are known as *anhua* ("secret decoration"). In the Yongle period (1402–24) the practice began of putting the reign mark on the base. This was first applied to the finest white porcelain and to monochrome ware decorated with copper red under a transparent glaze. As aforementioned, a white porcelain with ivory glaze was also made at Dehua in Fujian.

In the early decades of the Ming, the repertoire of designs on Yuan blue-and-white was continued and refined. At first, this ware evidently was considered too vulgar for court use, and none bears the imperial reign mark until the Xuande period (1425–35). By this time the often crowded Yuan patterns had given way chiefly to dragons or floral motifs of great clarity and grace, vigorously applied in a thick, deep-blue pigment to dishes, vases, stem cups, and flattened pilgrim jars. Sometimes a richer effect was achieved by painting dragons in underglaze red on a blue ground or vice versa. In the Chenghua period (1464–87), the blue-and-white designs became somewhat tenuous and overrefined, and the characteristic wares made for the Zhengde emperor (1505–21) and his Muslim eunuchs often bear Arabic inscriptions. In the Jiajing (1521–67) and Wanli (1572–1620) periods, the imperial kilns were badly mismanaged, and their products were often of poor quality. Private factories, however, turned out lively wares until the end of the dynasty.

Overglaze painting was applied with delicate care in the Chenghua period, chiefly in the decoration of small wine cups with chicken motifs, much admired by Chinese connoisseurs. These "chicken cups" were already being copied later in the 16th century and again, very expertly, in the 18th. Overglaze painting soon became popular; it was applied in the 16th century in stronger colours brilliantly contrasted against a dead-white background. These vigorous *wucai* ("five-colour") wares, which utilized a wide palette, were especially free and bold in the Jiajing and Wanli periods. Crude but lively imitations of these and of the blue-and-white of Jingdezhen were made in kilns in southern China partly for the Southeast Asian market and are known as "Swatow ware," named after one of the export sites. Among the most impressive of Ming pottery types are the *sancai* ("three-colour") wares, chiefly vases and jars decorated with floral motifs in turquoise, purple, yellow, and deep violet blue, the colours separated by raised lines in imitation of the metal strips used in cloisonné work. This robust ware was made in several centres, the best of it between 1450 and 1550.

Beginning in the early 16th century, a new ceramic tradition emerged in the town of Yixing, on the western side of Lake Tai, catering to the tea taste of scholars in the nearby Suzhou area. Individually made, sometimes to order, rather than mass-produced, Yixing wares were often signed or even poetically inscribed by highly reputable master craftsmen, such as Shi Dabin of the Wanli era and Chen Mingyuan of the Qing dynasty Kangxi

Flask decorated with a dragon and wave scrolls in underglaze blue, Ming dynasty, 14th century; in the Victoria and Albert Museum, London. Height 36.8 cm. Courtesy of the Victoria and Albert Museum, London

Dome-shaped Yixing ware teapot with a six-lobed body, signed Gongchun, dated 1513, Ming dynasty; in the Hong Kong Museum of Art. Height 9.9 cm. Reproduction by permission of the Urban Council Hong Kong from the Hong Kong Museum of Art

period. The wares were usually unglazed and derived their striking colours—brown, beige, reddish purple, yellow, black, and blue—after firing from the distinctive clays of the region and were known as "purple-sand" teapots. Pieces alternated between two body types: complex floral shapes and exquisitely simple geometric designs. Produced in relatively small quantities and treasured by Chinese collectors, these vessels attracted little attention outside China until the late 20th century.

QING DYNASTY (1644–1911/12)

The pottery industry suffered severely in the chaotic middle decades of the 17th century, of which the typical products were "transitional wares," chiefly blue-and-white. The imperial kilns at Jingdezhen were destroyed and were not fully reestablished until 1682, when the Kangxi emperor appointed Cang Yingxuan as director. Under his control, imperial porcelain reached a level of excellence it had not seen for well over a century.

Eggshell porcelain bowl, a copy of a Yongle period bowl, Qing dynasty, Kangxi reign (1661–1722); in the Victoria and Albert Museum, London. Courtesy of the Victoria and Albert Museum, London

The finest pieces include small monochromes, which recaptured the perfection of form and glaze of classic Song wares.

New colours and glaze effects were introduced, such as eel-skin yellow, snakeskin green, turquoise blue, and an exquisite soft red glaze shading to green (known as "peach bloom") that was used for small vessels made for the scholar's desk. Also perfected was *langyao* ("sang-de-boeuf," or oxblood, ware), which was covered with a rich copper-red glaze. Kangxi period blue-and-white is particularly noted for a new precision in the drawing and the use of cobalt washes of vivid intensity.

Five-colour (*wucai*) overglaze painted wares of the Kangxi period became known in Europe as famille verte from the predominant green colour in their floral decoration. These wares also included expert imitations of the overglaze painting of the Chenghua emperor's reign. Another variety has floral decoration painted directly on the biscuit (unglazed pottery body) against a rich black background (famille noire). Toward the end of the Kangxi reign, a rose-pink made

continued with scarcely diminishing delicacy through the Qianlong period. Meanwhile, the skill of the Jingdezhen potters was being increasingly challenged by the demand at court for imitations in porcelain of archaic bronzes, gold, and jade and for such objects as musical instruments and perforated and revolving boxes, which were highly unsuited to manufacture in porcelain. Although fine porcelain was made from time to

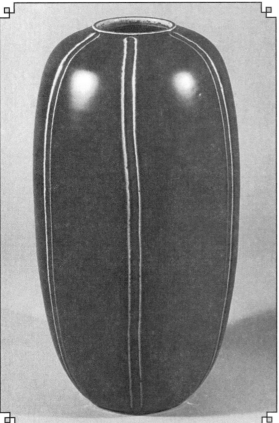

Vase with flambé *glaze (yao bian) of reduced copper, Qing dynasty, reign of the Qianlong emperor, 1736–96; in the Victoria and Albert Museum, London. Height 32.4 cm.* Courtesy of the Victoria and Albert Museum, London; photograph, A.C. Cooper Ltd.

Famille rose *porcelain vase of* yangcai *ware, Qing dynasty, Yongzheng reign (1722–35); in the Victoria and Albert Museum, London.* Courtesy of the Victoria and Albert Museum, London

from gold chloride was introduced from Europe. It was used with other colours in the decoration of porcelain (famille rose) and in cloisonné and overglaze painting.

Famille rose porcelain reached a climax of perfection at Jingdezhen under the direction of Nian Xiyao (1726–36) and

time in the 19th century, notably in the Daoguang and Guangxu reigns, the quality as a whole greatly declined.

MAJOR TYPES: CHINESE PAINTING

The development of painting within the 18 historical provinces—bounded by the Plateau of Tibet on the west, the Gobi Desert to the north, and Myanmar (Burma), Laos, and Vietnam to the southwest—is the subject of this chapter.

The first communities that can be identified culturally as Chinese were settled chiefly in the basin of the Huang He (Yellow River). Gradually they spread out, influencing other tribal cultures, until, by the Han dynasty (206 BCE–220 CE), most of China proper was dominated by the culture that had been formed in the cradle of northern Chinese civilization. Over this area there slowly spread a common written language, a common belief in the power of heaven and the ancestral spirits to influence the living, and a common emphasis on the importance of ceremony and sacrifice to achieve harmony among heaven, nature, and humankind. These beliefs were to have a great influence on the character of Chinese painting, and indeed all the arts of China.

Chinese civilization is by no means the oldest in the world: those of Mesopotamia and Egypt are far older. But, while the early Western cultures died, became stagnant, or were transformed to the point of breaking all continuity, that of China has grown continuously from prehistoric settlements into the great civilization of today.

The Chinese themselves were among the most historically conscious of all the major civilizations and were intensely aware of the strength and continuity of their cultural tradition. They viewed history as a cycle of decline and renewal associated with the succession of ruling dynasties. Both the political fragmentation and social and economic chaos of decline and the vigour of dynastic rejuvenation could stimulate and colour important artistic developments. Thus, it is quite legitimate to think of the history of Chinese painting primarily in terms of the styles of successive dynasties, as the Chinese themselves do.

ZHOU DYNASTY (1046–256 BCE)

The arts of the Zhou dynasty, the longest dynasty in Chinese history, reflect the profound changes that transformed Chinese society during this period of nearly 800 years. The first Zhou rulers virtually took over the Shang culture; indeed, the earliest bronze vessels bearing Zhou inscriptions might, from their style, have been made in the Shang dynasty. The Zhou kings parceled out their expanding territory among feudal lords, each of whom was free to make ritual objects for his own court use. As the feudal states rose in power and independence, so did the central Zhou itself shrink, to be further weakened by the eastward shift of the capital from sites in the Wei River valley near modern-day Xi'an to Luoyang in 771

BCE. Thereafter, as the Zhou empire was broken up among rival states, many local styles in the arts developed. The last three centuries of the Zhou dynasty, known as the Warring States period (475–221 BCE), saw a flowering of the arts in many areas. The breakdown of the feudal hegemony, the growth of trade between the states, and the rise of a rich landowning and merchant class all brought into existence new patrons and new attitudes that had a great influence on the arts and crafts.

Practically nothing survives of Zhou painting, although from literary evidence it seems that the art developed considerably, particularly during the period of the Warring States. Palaces and ancestral halls were decorated with wall paintings. Late Zhou texts tell of a craftsman working for the Zhougong (duke of Zhou) who covered the stock of a whip with minute paintings of dragons, snakes, horses, chariots, and "all the ten thousand things" and of another painter who told the king of Qi that spirits and ghosts were easier to draw than dogs and horses, whose precise appearance is known to all. The rhetorical questions or riddles in the *Tianwen* ("Questions to Heaven"), attributed to the poet Chu Yuan, are traditionally thought to have been inspired by wall paintings.

The most significant development of the late Zhou, one among the most revolutionary of all moments in Chinese art, was the emergence of a representational art form, a departure from the ritualized depiction of fanciful and usually isolated creatures of the Shang and early to middle Zhou that is evident in the bronzes of this period. In decorating ceremonial objects, artists began to depict the ceremonies themselves, such as ancestral offerings in temple settings, as well as ritual archery contests (important in the recruitment and promotion of officials), agriculture and sericulture (the raising of silkworms for the production of raw silk), hunting, and the waging of war—all activities vital to a well-ordered state. Such representations were cast with gold or silver inlay or engraved onto the sides of bronze vessels, most notably the *hu*, where all these themes might be combined on a single vessel. This conceptual transformation began by the late 6th century BCE, at about the same time Confucius and other philosophers initiated humane speculation on the nature of statecraft and social welfare.

The early representation of landscape, indicated only crudely on bronzes, appears in more sophisticated fashion on embroidered textiles of the 4th–3rd centuries BCE from south-central Chinese sites such as Mashan, near Jiangling in the state of Chu (modern Hubei province). There, as in the Han dynasty art that followed, landscape is suggested by rhythmic lines, which serve as mountain contours to organize spatially a variety of wild animals in front and back and which, while structurally simple, convey in linear fashion a sophisticated concept of mountain landscape as fluid, dynamic, and spiritual.

Further indications of the subject matter of Dong (Eastern) Zhou pictorial art are given by objects in lacquer, chiefly from the state of Chu and from

Sichuan, on which hunting scenes, chariots and horsemen, and fantastic winged creatures drawn from folklore were painted in a simple but lively style natural to the fluid character of the medium. Large painted lacquer coffins with such creatures depicted were present in the 5th-century-BCE royal tomb of Marquis Yi of Zeng. The labour required for these coffins is suggested by the set of nested coffins from the Han dynasty found at Mawangdui (two bearing exquisite landscape designs, described below), which are said to represent one million man-hours. A painted lacquer storage box from the Zeng tomb bears the earliest

Drawing of ancestral offering scenes (ritual archery, sericulture, hunting, and warfare) cast on a ceremonial bronze hu, *6th–5th century BCE, Zhou dynasty; in the Palace Museum, Beijing.* Wang Lu/ChinaStock Photo Library

depiction of two of the Chinese directional animals (formerly thought to date from the later Han), together with the names of the 28 stars used in Chinese astrology (previously believed to have been introduced at a later time from Iran or India).

Some of these motifs and, perhaps, the early treatment of landscape itself may derive in both theme and style from foreign sources, particularly China's northern nomadic neighbours. Those scenes concerned with ceremonial archery and ritual offerings in architectural settings, sericulture, warfare, and domestic hunting, however, seem to be essentially Chinese. These renditions generally occur with figures in two-dimensional silhouette spread evenly over most of the available pictorial surface. By the very late Zhou, however, occasional examples—such as the depiction of a mounted warrior contending with a tiger, executed in inlaid gold and silver on a bronze mirror from Jincun (c. 3rd century BCE, Hosokawa collection, Tokyo)—suggest the emerging ability of artists to conceive of two-dimensional images in terms of implied bulk and spatial context.

The few surviving Zhou period paintings on silk—from about the 3rd century BCE, the oldest in all East Asia—were produced in the state of Chu and unearthed from tombs near Changsha. One depicts a woman, perhaps a shaman or possibly the deceased, with a dragon and phoenix; one depicts a gentleman conveyed in what appears to be a dragon-shaped boat; and a third, reported to be from the same tomb as the latter, is a kind of religious almanac (the earliest known example of Chinese writing on silk) decorated around its border with depictions of deities and sacred plants.

QIN (221–207 BCE) AND HAN (206 BCE–220 CE) DYNASTIES

In 221 BCE the ruler of the feudal Qin state united all of China under himself as Qin Shihuangdi ("First Sovereign Emperor of Qin") and laid the foundation for the long stability and prosperity of the succeeding Han dynasty. His material accomplishments were the product of rare organizational genius, including centralizing the Chinese state and legal system, unifying the Chinese writing script and its system of weights and measures, and consolidating many of the walls of northern China into an architectural network of beacon towers able to spot any suspicious military movement and relay messages across the territory in a single day. However, his means were brutal and exhausted the people, and the dynasty failed to survive his early death.

The Xi (Western) Han (206 BCE–25 CE), with its capital at Chang'an (near modern Xi'an), reached a climax of expansive power under Wudi (ruled 141/140–87/86 BCE), who established colonies in Korea and Indochina and sent expeditions into Central Asia, which made Chinese arts and crafts known abroad and opened up China itself to foreign ideas and artistic influences. After the period of the usurping Xin dynasty

(9 to 25 CE), the Dong (Eastern) Han (25–220 CE), with its capital at Luoyang, recovered something of the dynasty's former prosperity but was increasingly beset by natural disasters and rebellions that eventually brought about its downfall. The art of the Han dynasty is remarkable for its variety and vigour, which resulted from its foreign contacts, from the contemporary sense of being a united nation within which many local traditions flourished, and from the patronage of a powerful court and the new, wealthy landowning and official classes.

Literature and poetry indicate that the walls of palaces, mansions, and ancestral halls were plastered and painted. Themes included figure subjects, portraits, and scenes from history that had an ethical or didactic purpose. Equally popular were themes taken from folk and nature cults that expressed the beliefs of popular Daoism. The names of the painters are generally not known. Artists were ranked according to their education and ability from the humble craftsmen-painters (*huagong*) up to the painters-in-attendance (*daizhao*), who had high official status and were close to the throne. This bureaucratic system lasted into the Qing dynasty (1644–1911/12).

In addition to wall paintings, artists painted on standing screens, used as room dividers and set behind important personages, and on long rolls of silk. Paper was invented in the Han dynasty, but it is doubtful whether it was much used for painting before the 3rd or 4th century CE.

Surviving Han paintings include chiefly tomb paintings and painted objects in clay and lacquer, although incised and inlaid bronze, stamped and molded tomb tiles, and textile designs provide further indications of the painting styles of the time. The most important painted tombs have been found at Luoyang, where some are decorated with the oldest surviving historical narratives (1st century BCE); at Wangdu in Hebei (Dong Han), where they are adorned with figures of civil and military officials; and at Liaoyang in Liaoning, where the themes include a feasting scene, musicians, jugglers, chariots, and horsemen. The Liaoyang paintings are in a crude but lively style, with a feeling of space and strong lateral movement. On the celebrated bricks taken from a tomb shrine of the Dong Han (now in the Museum of Fine Arts, Boston), elegant and individualized gentlemen engaged in animated conversation are rendered with a sensitive freedom of movement.

Funerary slabs also reflect the variety of Han pictorial art. The most famous are those from tomb shrines of the Wu family at Jiaxiang in Shandong, dated between about 147 and 168 CE. The subjects range from the attempted assassination of the first Qin emperor to feasting and mythological themes. Although they are depicted chiefly in silhouette with little interior drawing, the effect is lively and dramatic. These well-known works have been generally taken as representative of Han painting style since their discovery in 1786. They are now understood, however, to be very conservative in style, even archaic, perhaps with the intent of advertising the sponsoring family's chaste attachment to the pure and simple virtues of past times. A far earlier painting, a funerary banner from about 168 BCE, excavated in 1972 at Mawangdui, reveals how much more sophisticated early Han and even late Zhou painting must have been. Painted with bright, evenly applied mineral pigments and fine, elegant brush lines on silk, the banner represents a kind of cosmic array, with separate scenes of a funerary ceremony, the underworld, and the ascent of the deceased (the Lady Dai mentioned above) to a heavenly setting filled with mythic figures. It contains stylistic features not previously seen before the 4th century CE, creating spatial illusion through foreshortening, overlapping, and placement upon an implied ground plane, as well as suggesting certain lighting effects through contrasting and modulated colours.

Han landscape painting is well represented by the lacquer coffins of Lady Dai at Mawangdui, two of which are painted with scenes of mountains, clouds, and a variety of full-bodied human and animal figures. Two approaches are used: one, more architectonic, uses overlapping pyramidal patterns that derive from the bronze decor

Landscape scene from a bronze fitting of a chariot canopy from Dingxian, Hebei province, drawing, c. 2nd–1st century BCE, Western Han dynasty; in the Hebei Provincial Museum, Wuhan, China. Zhang Ping/ChinaStock Photo Library

of the late Zhou period (1046–255 BCE); the other continues the dynamic linear convention already noted on the embroidered textiles from Jiangling, in the Warring States period (475–221 BCE), as well as on late Zhou painted lacquers, on inlaid bronze tubes used as canopy fittings for chariots, and on woven silks found at Noin Ula, in Mongolia. Elsewhere, in the late Han, a new feeling for pictorial space in a more open outdoor setting appeared on molded bricks decorating tombs near Chengdu; these portrayed hunting and harvesting, the local salt-mining industry, and other subjects.

THREE KINGDOMS (220–280) AND SIX DYNASTIES (220–589)

For 60 years after the fall of Han, China was divided between three native dynasties: the Wei in the north, Wu in the southeast, and Shuhan in the west. It was briefly reunited under the Xi (Western) Jin; but in 311 Luoyang and in 316 Chang'an fell to the invading Xiongnu, and before long the whole of northern China was occupied by barbarian tribes who set up one petty kingdom after another until, in 439, a Turkish tribe, the Tuoba, brought the region under their rule as the Bei (Northern) Wei dynasty. They established a capital at Pingcheng (modern Datong) in Shanxi that they populated through the forced immigration of tens of thousands of Chinese. The Chinese they recruited into their service influenced the Tuoba until they became completely Sinicized. In 495 the

Wei moved their capital to Luoyang in the heartland of ancient Chinese civilization, where they lost what little Turkish identity they still possessed. They were succeeded in 535 by other petty barbarian dynasties who held the north until the reunification of China in 581.

The barbarians adopted Buddhism as a matter of state policy, for Buddhism was an international religion with a concept of kingship that helped them to equate their earthly power with their spiritual authority and thus to legitimize their control over the Chinese. Moreover, in the devastated land that was northern China in the 4th and 5th centuries, when the Confucian system was in ruins and Daoism a refuge for the few, the Buddhist doctrine of salvation through faith and good works acted as a powerful consoling and uniting force, much like the role the Christian church played in the Middle Ages in Europe. Therefore, when the Bei Wei embarked on great projects of temple building and the carving of colossal images, the people supported them, and Buddhist art flourished in the north.

The Six Dynasties of South China, which ruled from Nanjing, were slower to respond to the Buddhist message, partly because they were less accessible to the missionaries entering China from Central Asia and partly because Confucianism and Daoism had been kept alive among the refugees from the north. Buddhist missionaries and art came to Nanjing by way of Indochina, but this cultural traffic did not become important before the 4th century. Although the rulers (with few exceptions) were weak, corrupt, or cruel and the court a maze of intrigue, it was chiefly in Nanjing that the great poets, calligraphers, painters, and critics flourished, and they in turn greatly influenced the arts of the occupied north.

The breakdown of the Confucian system after the Han dynasty (206 BCE–220 CE) was reflected in painting and painting theory: increasingly, Daoist and Buddhist themes and theoretical reasons for painting were emphasized. This period saw the first activity by the courtier class, who painted as amateurs and who were far better remembered in the written record of the art than were their professional, artisan-class counterparts. Among the first named painting masters, Cao Buxing and Dai Kui painted chiefly Buddhist and Daoist subjects. Dai Kui was noted as a poet, painter, and musician and was one of the first to establish the tradition of scholarly amateur painting (*wenrenhua*). He was also the leading sculptor of his day, almost the only instance in Chinese history of a gentleman who engaged in this craft.

The greatest painter at the southern court in this period was Gu Kaizhi, an amateur painter from a family of distinguished Dong (Eastern) Wei dynasty scholar-officials in Nanjing and an eccentric member of a Daoist sect. One of the most famous of his works (which survives in a Tang dynasty copy in the British Museum) illustrates a 3rd-century didactic text *Nüshizhen* ("Admonitions of the Court Instructress"), by Zhang Hua. In this hand scroll, narrative illustration is bound strictly to the text (as if used as a mnemonic device): the advice to imperial concubines to bear sons to the emperor, for instance, is accompanied by a delightful family group. The figures are slender and fairylike, and the line is fine and flows rhythmically. The roots of this elegant southern style, which then epitomized the highest Nanjing court standard, can be traced back to Changsha in the late Zhou (1046–256 BCE)–early Han period, and it was later adopted as court style by the Bei Wei rulers (e.g., at Longmen) when they moved south to Luoyang in 495. Gu Kaizhi also was noted as a portraitist, and, among Buddhist subjects, his rendering of the sage Vimalakirti became a model for later painters.

The south saw few major painters in the 5th century, but the settled reign of Wudi in the 6th produced a number of notable figures, among them Zhang Sengyao, who was commissioned by the pious emperor to decorate the walls of Buddhist temples in Nanjing. All his work is lost, but his style, from early accounts and later copies, seems to have combined realism with a new freedom in the use of the brush, employing dots and dashing strokes very different from the fine precision of Gu Kaizhi. He also painted "flowers in relief" on the temple walls, which were much admired. Whether the effect of relief was produced by chiaroscuro or by the thickness of the pigment itself is not known.

Painters in northern China were chiefly occupied in Buddhist fresco painting (painting on a freshly plastered wall).

Bodhisattva, detail of a painted mural, mid-5th century, Bei (Northern) Wei dynasty, in cave 272, Dunhuang, Gansu province, China. Chen Zhi'an/ChinaStock Photo Library

While all the temples of the period have been destroyed, a quantity of wall painting survives at Dunhuang in northwestern Gansu in the Caves of the Thousand Buddhas, Qianfodong, where there are nearly 500 cave shrines and niches dating from the 5th century onward. There are also wall paintings in the caves of Maijishan and Bingling Temple. Early Dunhuang paintings chiefly depict incidents in the life of the Buddha, the *Jatakas* (stories of his previous incarnations), and such simple themes as the perils from which Avalokiteshvara (Chinese Guanyin) saves the faithful. In style they show a blend of Central Asian and Chinese techniques that reflects the mixed population of northern China at this time.

Painters practicing foreign techniques were active at the northern courts in the 6th century. Cao Zhongda painted, according to an early text, "after the manner of foreign countries" and was noted for closely clinging drapery that made his figures look as though they had been drenched in water. At the end of the 6th century, a painter from Khotan (Hotan), Weichi Bozhina, was active at the Sui court. A descendant of his, Weichi Yiseng, painted frescoes in the temples of Chang'an using a thick impasto (a thick application of pigment) and a brush line that was "tight and strong like bending iron or coiling wire." Those foreign techniques caused much comment among the Chinese but seem to have been confined to Buddhist painting and were eventually abandoned.

The beginning of aesthetic theory in China was another product of the spirit of inquiry and introspection that characterized these restless years. About 300 CE a long, passionate poem, *Wen Fu* ("Rhymeprose on Literature"), was composed by Lu Ji on the subject of artistic creation. Also from this period, the *Wenxin Diaolong* ("Literary Mind and Carving of Dragons") by Liu Xie has long remained China's premier treatise on aesthetics. It offers insightful consideration of a wide range of chosen topics, beginning with a discussion of *wen*, or nature's underlying pattern. Set forth as central to the mastery of artistic expression are the control of "wind" (*feng*, emotional vitality) and "bone" (*gu*, structural organization).

In the Nan (Southern) Liang dynasty critical works were written on literature and calligraphy; and, about the mid-6th century, the painter Xie He compiled the earliest work on art theory that has survived in China, the *Guhuapinlu* ("Classified Record of Painters of Former Times"). In this work he grades 27 painters in three classes, prefacing his list with a short statement of six aesthetic principles by which painting should be judged. These are *qiyun shengdong* ("spirit resonance, life-motion"), an enigmatic and much debated phrase that means that the painter should endow his work with life and movement through harmony with the spirit of nature; *gufa yongbi* ("structural method in use of the brush"), referring to the structural power and tension of the brushstroke in both painting and calligraphy, through which the vital spirit is expressed; *yingwu xianxing* ("fidelity to the object in portraying forms"); *suilei fucai* ("conforming to kind in applying colours"); *jingying weizhi* ("planning and design in placing and positioning"); and *chuanyi moxie* ("transmission of ancient models by copying"). The last principle seems to refer to the copying of ancient paintings both for technical training and as a means of preserving them and hence the tradition itself. Of the six principles, the first two are fundamental, for, unless the conventional forms are brought to life by the vitality of the brushwork, the painting has no real merit, however carefully it is executed; the latter principles imply that truth to nature and tradition also must be obtained for the first two to be achieved. The six principles of Xie He have become the cornerstone of Chinese aesthetic theory down through the centuries.

The integration of spirituality and naturalism is similarly found in the short, profoundly Daoist text of the early 5th century, *Huashanshuixu* ("Preface on Landscape Painting," China's first essay on the topic), attributed to Zong Bing. Zong suggests that if well-painted—that is, if both visually accurate and aesthetically compelling—a landscape painting can truly substitute for real nature, for, even though miniaturized, it can attract vital energy (*qi*) from the spirit-filled void (*dao*) just as its real, material counterpart does. This interplay between macrocosm and microcosm became a constant foundation of Chinese spiritual thought and aesthetics.

SUI (581–618) AND TANG (618–907) DYNASTIES

The founding of the Sui dynasty reunited China after more than 300 years of fragmentation. The second Sui emperor engaged in unsuccessful wars and vast public works, such as the Grand Canal linking the north and south, that exhausted the people and caused them to revolt. The succeeding Tang dynasty built a more enduring state on the foundations the Sui rulers had laid, and the first 130 years of the Tang was one of the most prosperous and brilliant periods in the history of Chinese civilization. The empire at the time extended so far across Central Asia that for a while Bukhara and Samarkand (now in Uzbekistan) were under Chinese control, the Central Asian kingdoms paid China tribute, and Chinese cultural influence reached Korea and Japan. Chang'an became the greatest city in the world; its streets were filled with foreigners, and foreign religions—including Zoroastrianism, Buddhism, Manichaeism, Nestorianism, Christianity, Judaism, and Islam—flourished. This confident cosmopolitanism is reflected in all the arts of this period.

The splendour of the dynasty reached its peak between 712 and 756 under Xuanzong (Minghuang), but before the end of his reign a disastrous defeat caused Central Asia to enter the control of the advancing Arabs, and the rebellion of General An Lushan in 755 almost brought down the dynasty. Although the Tang survived another 150 years, its great days were over, and, as the empire shrank and the economic crisis deepened, the government and people turned against foreigners and foreign religions. In 845 all foreign religions were briefly but disastrously proscribed; temples and monasteries were destroyed or turned to secular use, and Buddhist bronze images were melted down. Today the finest Buddhist art and architecture in the Tang style is to be found not in China but in the 8th-century temples at Nara in Japan. While the ancient heartland of Chinese civilization in the Henan-Shaanxi area sank in political and economic importance, the southeast became ever more densely populated and prosperous, and in the last century of the Tang it was once again the cultural centre of China, as it had been in the Six Dynasties (220–589).

The patronage of the Sui and Tang courts attracted painters from all over the empire. Yan Liben, who rose to high office as an administrator, finally becoming a minister of state, was also a noted 7th-century figure painter. His duties included painting historical scrolls, notable events past and present, and portraits, including those of foreigners and strange creatures brought to court as tribute, to the delight of his patron, Taizong. Yan Liben painted in a conservative style with a delicate, scarcely modulated line. Part of a scroll depicting 13 emperors from Han to Sui (in the Museum of Fine Arts, Boston) is attributed to him. His brother Yan Lide was also a painter. Features of their style may possibly be preserved in wall paintings in recently discovered 7th- and early

8th-century tombs in northern China, notably that of Princess Yongtai (reburied 706) near Xi'an.

The royal tombs near Xi'an (706) show the emergence of a more liberated tradition in brushwork that came to the fore in mid- to late 8th-century painting, as it did in the calligraphy of Zhang Xu, Yan Zhenqing, and other master writers. The greatest brush master of Tang painting was the 8th-century artist Wu Daoxuan, also called Wu Daozi, who not only enjoyed a career at court but had sufficient creative energy to execute, according to Tang records, some 300 wall paintings in the temples of Luoyang and Chang'an. His brushwork, in contrast to that of Yan Liben, was full of such sweeping power that crowds would gather to watch him as he worked. He painted chiefly in ink, leaving the colouring to his assistants, and he was famous for the three-dimensional, sculptural effect he achieved with the ink line alone. His work (e.g., a mural at the Datong Hall of the imperial palace, representing almost 300 miles [500 km] of Sichuan's Jialing River, produced in a single day without preliminary sketches) survives only through descriptions and very unreliable copies. Wu Daozi had a profound influence, particularly on figure painting, in the Tang and Song dynasties. His style may be reflected in some of the 8th-century caves at Dunhuang, although the meticulous handling of the great paradise compositions in the caves increasingly came to approximate the high standards of Chinese court artists and suggests the

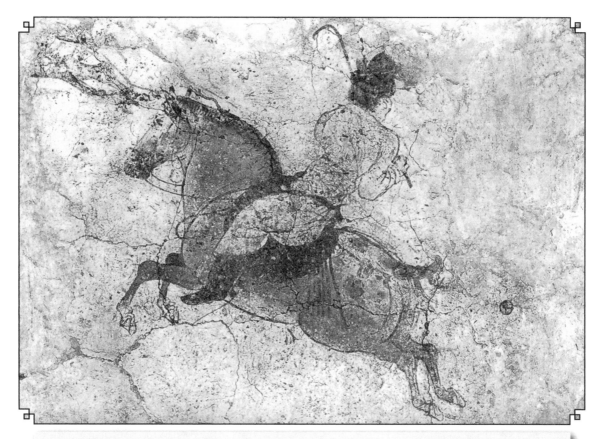

Polo player, detail of a mural from the tomb of Li Xian (the crown prince Zhanghuai), near Xianyang, Shaanxi province, 706 CE, Tang dynasty; in the Shaanxi Provincial Museum, Xi'an, China. Wang Lu/ChinaStock Photo Library

inspiration of earlier and more conservative Buddhist painters, who included Zheng Fazhi and Dong Boren. This more restrained style can also be seen in the Japanese temple murals at Hōryū Temple near Nara, executed about 670–710 in the Chinese "international" manner.

Figure painters who depicted court life in a careful manner derived from Yan Liben rather than from Wu Daozi included Zhang Xuan and Zhou Fang. The former's *Ladies Preparing Silk* survives in a Song dynasty copy (in the Museum of Fine Arts, Boston), while later versions of several compositions attributed to Zhou Fang exist. Eighth-century royal tomb murals and Dunhuang Buddhist paintings demonstrate the early appearance and widespread appeal of styles that these court artists helped later to canonize, with individual figures (especially women) of monumental, sculpturesque proportion arranged upon a blank background with classic simplicity and balance.

Horses played an important role in Tang military expansion and in the life of the court; riding was a popular recreation, and even the court ladies played polo. Horses also had become a popular subject for painting, and one of the emperor Xuanzong's favourite court artists was the horse painter Han Gan. A damaged and much restored 8th-century painting of the emperor's favourite charger, *Zhaoyebai* (*Shining White in the Night*, in the Metropolitan Museum of Art, New York City), attributed to Han Gan, gives a hint of that artist's vital talent. The other great horse-painting master was the army general Cao Ba, said by the poet Du Fu to have captured better the inner character of his subjects and not just the flesh. Most later horse painters claimed to follow Han Gan or Cao Ba, but the actual stylistic contrast between them was already reported in Bei (Northern) Song times as no longer distinguishable and today is hardly understood.

The more than three centuries of the Sui and Tang were a period of progress and change in landscape painting. The early 7th- and 8th-century masters Zhan Ziqian, Li Sixun, and the latter's son Li Zhaodao developed a style of landscape painting known as *qinglübai* ("green, blue, white") or *jinbi shanshui* ("gold-blue-green landscape"), in which mineral colours were applied to a composition carefully executed in fine line to produce a richly coloured effect. Probably related to Central Asian painting styles of the Six Dynasties period and associated with the jeweled-paradise landscapes of the Daoist immortals, this "blue-and-green" type readily appealed to the Tang court's taste for international exotica, religious fantasy, and boldly decorative art. A painting in this technique, known as *Minghuang's Journey to Shu* (that is, to Sichuan; in the National Palace Museum, Taipei, Taiwan), reflects what is considered to be the style of Li Zhaodao, although it is probably a later copy. This style gradually crystallized as a courtly and professional tradition, in contrast to the more informal calligraphic ink painting of the literati.

The generally accepted founder of the school of scholarly landscape painting (*wenrenhua*) is Wang Wei, an 8th-century scholar and poet who divided his time between the court at Chang'an, where he held official posts, and his country estate of Wang Chuan, of which he painted a panoramic composition preserved in later copies and engraved on stone. Among his Buddhist paintings, the most famous was a rendering of the Indian sage Vimalakirti, who became, as it were, the "patron saint" of Chinese Buddhist intellectuals. Wang Wei sometimes painted landscapes in colour, but his later reputation was based on the belief that he was the first to paint landscape in monochrome ink. He was said to have obtained a subtle atmosphere by "breaking the ink" (*pomo*) into varied tones. The belief in his founding role, fostered by later critics, became the cornerstone of the philosophy of the *wenrenhua*, which held that a man could not be a great painter unless he was also a scholar and a gentleman.

More adventurous in technique was the somewhat eccentric late 8th-century painter Zhang Zao, who produced dramatic tonal and textural contrasts, as when he painted simultaneously, with one brush in each hand, two branches of a tree, one moist and flourishing, the other desiccated and dead. This new freedom with the brush was carried to extremes by such painters of the middle to late Tang as Wang Xia (Wang Mo) and Gu Kuang, southern Chinese Daoists who "splashed ink" (also transliterated as *pomo* but written with different characters than "broken ink") onto the silk in a manner suggestive of 20th-century "Action painters" such as Jackson Pollock. The intention of these ink-splashers was philosophical and religious as well as artistic: it was written at the time that their spontaneous process was designed to imitate the divine process of creation. Their semifinished products, in which the artistic process was fully revealed and the subject matter had to be discerned by the viewer, suggested a Daoist philosophical skepticism. These techniques marked the emergence of a trend toward eccentricity in brushwork that had free rein in periods of political and social chaos. They were subsequently employed by painters of the southern "Sudden" school of Chan (Zen) Buddhism, which held that enlightenment was a spontaneous, irrational experience that could be suggested in painting only by a comparable spontaneity in the brushwork. Chan painting flourished particularly in Chengdu, the capital of the petty state of Shu, to which many artists went as refugees from the chaotic north in the last years before the Tang dynasty fell. Among them was Guanxiu, an eccentric who painted Buddhist saints with a weird air and exaggerated features that had a strong appeal to members of the Chan sect. The element of the deliberately grotesque in Guanxiu's art was further developed during the Five Dynasties and Ten Kingdoms period by Shi Ke, who was active in Chengdu in the mid-10th century. In his paintings, chiefly of Buddhist and Daoist subjects, he set out in the Chan manner to shock the viewer by distortion and roughness of execution.

FIVE DYNASTIES (907–960) AND TEN KINGDOMS (902–978)

At the fall of the Tang, northern China, ruled by five short-lived dynasties, plunged into a state of political and social chaos. The corrupt northern courts offered little support to the arts, although Buddhism continued to flourish until persecution in 955 destroyed much of what had been created in the 110 years since the previous anti-Buddhist campaign. The 10 independent kingdoms that ruled various parts of southern China, though no more enduring, offered more enlightened patronage. At first the Qian (Former) Shu (with its capital at Chengdu) and then, for a longer period, the kingdoms of the Nan (Southern) Tang (with the capital at Nanjing) and Wuyue (with its capital at Hangzhou) were centres of comparative peace and prosperity. Li Houzhu (Li Yu), the last ruler of the Nan Tang, was a poet and liberal patron at whose court the arts flourished more brilliantly than at any time since the mid-8th century. Not only were the southern courts at Chengdu and Nanjing leading patrons of the arts, but they also began formalizing court sponsorship of painting by organizing a centralized atelier with an academic component and by granting painters an elevated bureaucratic stature—policies that would be followed or modified by subsequent dynasties.

LANDSCAPE PAINTING

In northern China only a handful of painters were working. The greatest of them, Jing Hao, who was active from about 910 to 950, spent much of his life as a recluse in the Taihang Mountains of Shanxi. No authentic work of his survives, but it seems from texts and later copies that he created a new style of landscape painting. Boldly conceived and executed chiefly in ink with firmness and concentration, his precipitous crags, cleft with gullies and rushing streams, rise up in rank to the top of the picture. For 150 years before his time, the centre of landscape painting activity had been in the southeast. Jing Hao's importance therefore lies in the fact that he both revived the northern spirit and created a type of painting that became the model for his follower Guan Tong and for the classic northern masters of the early Song period (960–1279), Li Cheng and Fan Kuan. An essay on landscape painting, *Bifaji* ("Notes on

Travelers Among Mountains and Streams, *ink and slight colour on silk hanging scroll by Fan Kuan, c. 960–c. 1030, Bei (Northern) Song dynasty; in the National Palace Museum, Taipei, Taiwan.* National Palace Museum, Taipei, Taiwan

Brushwork"), attributed to Jing Hao, sets out the philosophy of this school of landscape painting, one that was consistent with newly emergent Neo-Confucian ideals. Painting was to be judged both by its visual truthfulness to nature and by its expressive impact. The artist must possess creative intuition and a reverence for natural subject matter, tempered by rigorous empirical observation and personal self-discipline. Consistent with this, in all the major schools of Song landscape painting that followed, artists would render with remarkable accuracy their own regional geography, letting it serve as a basis for their styles, their emotional moods, and their personal visions.

In contrast to the stark drama of this northern style, landscapes associated with the name of Dong Yuan, who held a sinecure post at the court of Li Houzhu in Nanjing, are broad and almost impressionistic in treatment. The coarse brushstrokes (known as "hemp-fibre" texture strokes), dotted accents ("moss dots"), and wet ink washes of his monochrome style, said to be derived from Wang Wei, suggest the rounded, tree-clad hills and moist atmosphere of the Jiangnan ("South of the Yangtze River") region. The contrast between the firm brushwork and dramatic compositions of such northern painters as Jing Hao and his followers and the more relaxed and spontaneous manner of Dong Yuan and his follower Juran laid the foundation for two distinct traditions in Chinese landscape painting that have continued up to modern times. The style developed by Dong Yuan and Juran became dominant in the Ming (1368–1644) and Qing (1644–1911/12) periods, preferred by amateur artists because of its easy reduction to a calligraphic mode, its calm and understated compositional nature, and its regional affiliation.

While the few figure painters in northern China, such as Hu Huai, characteristically recorded hunting scenes, the southerners, notably Gu Hongzhong and Zhou Wenju, depicted the voluptuous, sensual court life under Li Houzhu. A remarkable copy of an original work by Gu Hongzhong depicts the scandalous revelries of the minister Han Xizai. Zhou Wenju was famous for his pictures of court ladies and musical entertainments, executed with a fine line and soft, glowing colour in the tradition of Zhang Xuan and Zhou Fang.

FLOWER PAINTING

Flower painting, previously associated chiefly with Buddhist art, came into its own as a separate branch of painting in the Five Dynasties. At Chengdu, the master Huang Quan brought to maturity the technique of *mogu hua* ("boneless painting"), in which he applied light colours with delicate skill, hiding the intentionally pale underdrawing and seeming thereby to dispense with the usually dominant element of a strong brush outline. His great rival, Xu Xi, working for Li Houzhu in Nanjing, first drew his flowers in ink in a bold, free manner suggestive of the draft script, *caoshu*, adding a little colour afterward. Both men established standards

that were followed for centuries afterward. Because of its reliance on technical skill, Huang Quan's naturalistic style (also referred to as *xiesheng*, or "lifelike painting") was mainly adopted by professional painters, while the scholars admired the calligraphic freedom of Xu Xi's style (referred to as *xieyi*, or "painting the idea").

Both men were also noted painters of bamboo, an object that had symbolic associations for the scholar-gentleman and at the same time posed a technical challenge in the handling of the brush. After the founding of the Song, *xiesheng* artists from Sichuan, including Huang Quan and his sons Huang Jucai and Huang Jubao, traveled to the new court at Bianjing (Kaifeng), where they established a tradition that dominated the Bei Song period. Xu Xi found greater favour during the Yuan (1206–1368), Ming, and Qing periods.

SONG (960–1279), LIAO (907–1125), AND JIN (1115–1234) DYNASTIES

Although reunited and ably ruled for well over a century by the first five Song emperors, China failed to recover the northern provinces from the barbarian tribes. A Khitan tribe, calling their dynasty Liao, held all of northeastern China until 1125, while the Xi (Western) Xia held the

A Pheasant and Sparrows Among Rocks and Shrubs, ink and colours on silk hanging scroll attributed to Huang Jucai, 10th century, Bei (Northern) Song dynasty; in the National Palace Museum, Taipei, Taiwan. National Palace Museum, Taipei, Taiwan

northwest, cutting off Chinese contact with western and Central Asia. From the new capital, Bianjing, the Song rulers pursued a pacific policy, buying off the Khitan and showing unprecedented toleration at home. While it brought Chinese scholarship, arts, and letters to a new peak of achievement, this policy left the northern frontiers unguarded. When in 1114 the Juchen Tatars in the far northwest revolted against the Khitan, the Chinese army helped the rebels destroy their old enemy. The Juchen then turned on the Song: they invaded China, besieged the capital in 1126, and took as prisoner the emperor Qinzong, the emperor emeritus Huizong (who had recently abdicated), and the imperial court. They then established their own dynasty, the Jin, with their capital at the city later to be called Beijing. The remnants of the Song court fled to the south in 1127 and, after several years of wandering, established their "temporary" capital at the beautiful city of Hangzhou. The Nan Song (Southern Song) never seriously tried to recover the north but enjoyed the beauty and prosperity of their new home, while the arts continued to flourish in an atmosphere of humanity and tolerance until the Mongols entered China in the 13th century and swept all before them. In 1234 they destroyed the Juchen Tatars, and, although the Chinese armies resisted valiantly, Hangzhou fell in 1276. Three years later a loyal Song minister drowned himself and the young emperor.

The Bei (Northern) Song was a period of reconstruction and consolidation. Bianjing was a city of palaces, temples, and tall pagodas; Buddhism flourished, and monasteries and temples once again multiplied. The Song emperors attracted around them the greatest literary and artistic talent of the empire, and something of this high culture was carried on by their successors of Liao and Jin. The atmosphere at the Nan Song court in Hangzhou, perhaps even more refined and civilized, was clouded by the loss of the north, and the temptation to enjoy the delights of Hangzhou and neglect their armies on the frontier turned men in on themselves. Power and confidence no longer characterized Nan Song art; instead it was imbued with an exquisite sensibility and a romanticism that is sometimes poignant, given the disaster that befell China in the 13th century.

Song interest in history and a revival of the classics were matched by a new concern with the tangible remains of China's past. This was the age of the beginning of archaeology and of the first great collectors and connoisseurs. One of the most enthusiastic of these was the Bei Song emperor Huizong (1100–1125/26), whose passion for the arts blinded him to the perils that threatened his country. Huizong's sophisticated antiquarianism reflects an attitude that became an increasingly important factor in Chinese art. He collected and cataloged pre-Qin bronzes and jades while the palace studios turned out close replicas and archaic emulations of both media. Building his royal garden, the Genyue, was said to have nearly bankrupted the state, as gigantic garden stones hauled up by boat from the south closed down the Grand Canal for long periods. He was also the most distinguished of all imperial painting collectors, and the catalog of his collection (the *Xuanhe Huapu*, encompassing 6,396 paintings by 231 painters) remains a valuable document for the study of early Chinese painting. (Part of the collection passed into the hands of the Jin conquerors, and the remainder was scattered at the fall of Bianjing.) Huizong also elevated to new heights the recent process of bureaucratizing court painting, with entrance examinations modeled on civil service norms, with ranks and promotions like those of scholar-officials, and with regularized instruction sometimes offered by the emperor himself as chief academician. The favours granted throughout the Song to lower-class artisans at court incurred the ire of aristocratic courtiers and provided stimulus for the rise of the amateur painting movement among these scholar-officials (*shidafu hua*), which ultimately became the literati painting mode (*wenrenhua*) that dominated most of Yuan (1206–1368), Ming (1368–1644), and Qing (1644–1911/12) history.

Settled conditions and a tolerant atmosphere helped to make the Bei Song a period of great achievement in landscape painting. Li Cheng, a follower of Jing Hao who lived a few years into the Song, was a scholar who defined the soft, billowing earthen formations of the northeastern Chinese terrain with "cloud-like" texture, interior layers of graded ink wash bounded by firmly brushed, scallop-edged contours. He is remembered especially for winter landscapes and for simple compositions in which he set a pair of tall, rugged, aging evergreens against a low, level view of desiccated landscape. As with Jing Hao and Guan Tong, probably none of his original work survives, but aspects of his style have been perpetuated in thousands of other artists' works.

An even more formidable figure was the early 11th-century painter Fan Kuan, who began by following Li Cheng's style but turned to studying nature directly and finally followed only his own inclinations. He lived as a recluse in the mountains of Shaanxi, and a Song writer said that "his manners and appearance were stern and old-fashioned; he had a great love of wine and was devoted to the Dao." A tall landscape scroll, *Travelers Among Mountains and Streams* (National Palace Museum, Taipei, Taiwan), bearing his hidden signature, depicts peasants and pack mules emerging from thick woodland at the foot of a towering cliff that dwarfs them to insignificance. The composition is monumental, the detail is realistic, and the brushwork, featuring a stippling style known as "raindrop" strokes, is powerful and close-textured. While the details of the work are based on closely observed geographic reality (perhaps some specific site such as Mount Heng), a profoundly idealistic conception is revealed in the highly rational structure of the painting, which conforms closely to aspects of Daoist cosmology and numerology.

Other northern masters of the 11th century who helped to establish the great classical tradition were Xu Daoning, Gao Kegong, and Yan Wengui. The second half of the century was dominated by Guo Xi, who became an instructor in the painting division of the Imperial Hanlin Academy. His style combined the technique of Li Cheng with the monumentality of Fan Kuan, and he made some advances, particularly in the relief that he attained by shading with ink washes ("cloudlike" texture), a spectacular example of which is his *Early Spring* (1072; National Palace Museum, Taipei, Taiwan). He was a great decorator and liked to work on such large surfaces as plaster walls and standing screens. His observations on landscape painting were collected and published by his son Gao Si under the title *Linquan Gaozhi* ("Lofty Record of Forests and Streams"). In addition to giving ideas for paintings and notes on the rules of the art, in this work he stresses that the enjoyment of landscape painting can function as a substitute for wandering in the mountains, an indulgence for which the conscientious Confucian scholar-official was too busy.

While the monumental realistic tradition was reaching its climax, quite another approach to painting was being expressed by a group of intellectuals that included the poet-statesman-artist Su Shi (Su Dongpo), the landscape painter Mi Fu, the bamboo painter Wen Tong, the plum painter and priest Zhongren Huaguang, and the figure and horse painter Li Gonglin. Su and Mi, together with their friend Huang Tingjian, were also the foremost calligraphers of the dynasty, all three developing the tradition established by Zhang Xu, Yan Zhenqing, and Huaisu in the mid-8th century. The aim of these artists was not to depict nature realistically—that could be left to the professionals—but to express themselves, to "satisfy the heart." They spoke of merely "borrowing" the literal shapes and forms of things as a vehicle through which they could "lodge" their thoughts and feelings. In this amateur painting mode of the scholar-official (*shidafu hua*, later called *wenrenhua*), skill was suspect because it was the attribute of the professional and court painter. The scholars valued spontaneity above all, even making a virtue of awkwardness as a sign of the painter's sincerity.

Mi Fu, an influential and demanding connoisseur, was the first major advocate and follower of Dong Yuan's boneless style, reducing it to mere ink dots (Mi *dian*, or "Mi dots"). This new technique influenced many painters, including Mi Fu's son Mi Youren, who combined it with a subdued form of ink splashing. Wen Tong and Su Dongpo were both devoted to bamboo painting, an exacting

Early Spring, *detail of a hanging scroll, ink and slight colour on silk, by Guo Xi, 1072, Northern Song dynasty; in the National Palace Museum, Taipei, Taiwan.* National Palace Museum, Taipei, Taiwan

art form very close in technique to calligraphy. Su Dongpo wrote poems on Wen Tong's paintings, thus helping to establish the unity of the three arts of poetry, painting, and calligraphy that became a hallmark of the *wenrenhua*. When Su Dongpo painted landscapes, Li Gonglin sometimes executed the figures. Li was a master of *baimiao* ("plain line") painting, without colour, shading, or wash. He brought a scholar's refinement of taste to a tradition theretofore dominated by Wu Daozi's dramatic style.

The northern emperors were enthusiastic patrons of the arts. Huizong, perhaps the most knowledgeable of all Chinese emperors about the arts, was himself an accomplished calligrapher (he developed a unique and extremely elegant style known as "slender gold") and a painter chiefly of birds and flowers in the realistic tradition stretching back to Huang Quan and developed by subsequent court artists such as Cui Bai of the late 11th century. While meticulous in detail, his works were subjective in mood, following poetic themes that were calligraphically inscribed on the painting. A fine example of the kind of painting attributed to him is the minutely observed and carefully painted *Five-Coloured Parakeet on Blossoming Apricot Tree* (Museum of Fine Arts, Boston). He demanded the same qualities in the work of his court painters and would add his cipher to pictures of which he approved. It is consequently very difficult to distinguish the work of the emperor from that of his favoured court artists.

Among the distinguished academicians at Huizong's court were Zhang Zeduan, whose extraordinarily realistic *Qingming Festival* scroll (Palace Museum, Beijing) preserves a wealth of social and architectural information in compellingly artistic form, and Li Tang, who fled to the south in 1127 and supervised the reestablishment of the northern artistic tradition at the new court in Hangzhou. Although Guo Xi's style remained popular in the north after the Jin occupation, Li Tang's mature style came to dominate in the south. Li was a master in the Fan Kuan tradition, but he gradually reduced Fan's monumentality into more refined and delicate compositions and transformed Fan's small "raindrop" texture into a broader "ax-cut" texture stroke that subsequently remained a hallmark of most Chinese court academy landscape painting.

In the first two generations of the Nan Song, however, historical figure painting regained its earlier dominance at court. Gaozong and Xiaozong, respectively the son and grandson of the imprisoned Huizong, sought to legitimize their necessary but technically unlawful assumption of power by supporting works illustrating the ancient classics and traditional virtues. Such works, by artists including Li Tang and Ma Hezhi, often include lengthy inscriptions purportedly executed by the emperors themselves. They represent the finest survival today of the ancient court tradition of propagandistic historical narrative painting in a Confucian political mode.

Subsequently, in the late 12th and early 13th centuries, the primacy of landscape painting was reasserted. The tradition of Li Tang was turned in an increasingly romantic and dreamlike direction, however, by the great masters Ma Yuan, his son Ma Lin, Xia Gui, and Liu Songnian, all of whom served with distinction in the painting division of the imperial Hanlin Academy. These artists used the Li Tang technique, only more freely, developing the so-called "large ax-cut" texture stroke. Their compositions are often "one-cornered," depicting a foreground promontory with a fashionably rusticated building and a few stylish figures separated from the silhouettes of distant peaks by a vast and aesthetically poignant expanse of misty emptiness—a view these painters must have seen any summer evening as they gazed across Hangzhou's West Lake. The Ma family's works achieved a philosophically inspired sense of quietude, while Xia Gui's manner was strikingly dramatic in brushwork and composition. The Ma-Xia school, as it came to be called, was greatly admired in Japan during the Muromachi and Azuchi-Momoyama periods, and its impact can still be found today in Japanese gardening traditions.

Toward the end of this period, Chan (Zen) Buddhist painting experienced a brief but remarkable florescence, stimulated by scholars abandoning the decaying political environment of the Nan Song court for the monastic life practiced in the hill temples across the lake from Hangzhou. The court painter Liang Kai had been awarded the highest order, the Golden Girdle, between 1201 and 1204, but he put it aside, quit the court, and became a Chan recluse. What is thought to be his earlier work has the professional skill expected of a colleague of Ma Yuan, but his later paintings became freer and more spontaneous.

The greatest of the Chan painters was Muqi, or Fachang, who reestablished the Liutong Monastery in the western hills of Hangzhou. The wide range of subjects of his work (which included Buddhist deities, landscapes, birds and animals, and flowers and fruit) and the spontaneity of his style bear witness to the Chan philosophy that the "Buddha essence" is in all things equally and that only a spontaneous style can convey something of the sudden awareness that comes to the Chan adept in his moments of illumination. Perhaps his best-known work is his hastily sketched *Six Persimmons* (preserved and idolized in Japan), while a somewhat more conservative style is seen in his triptych of three hanging scrolls with Guanyin flanked by a crane and gibbons (Daitoku Temple, Kyōto, Japan). Chinese connoisseurs disapproved of the rough brushwork and lack of literary content in Muqi's paintings, and none appear to have survived in China. However, his work, and that of other Chan artists such as Liang Kai and Yujian, was collected and widely copied in Japan, forming the basis of the Japanese *suiboku-ga* (*sumi-e*) tradition.

Chan Buddhism borrowed greatly from Daoism, both in philosophy and in painting manner. One of the last great Song artists was Chen Rong, an

Six Persimmons, *ink on paper hanging scroll attributed to Muqi (active mid-13th century), Nan (Southern) Song dynasty; in the Daitoku Temple, Kyōto, Japan. Width 36.2 cm.* Daitoku-ji, Kyoto; photograph, Zen Cultural Laboratory

YUAN DYNASTY (1206–1368)

Although the Mongol conquest made China part of an empire that stretched from Korea to Hungary and opened its doors to foreign contacts as never before, this short-lived dynasty was oppressive and corrupt. Its later decades were marked by social and administrative chaos in which the arts received little official encouragement. The Mongols distrusted the Chinese intelligentsia, relying primarily on Central Asians for government administrative functions. Nevertheless, some influential Chinese writers recognized that the Mongols brought a sense of martial discipline that was lacking in the Song (960–1279), and after 1286 an increasing number of Chinese scholars were persuaded to enter government service, undoubtedly hoping to influence their rulers to adopt a more benign policy toward the Chinese people.

One school that flourished under Yuan official patronage was that of Buddhist and Daoist painting; important wall paintings were executed at the Yongle Temple in Shanxi (now restored and moved to Ruicheng). A number of royal patrons, including Kublai, the emperors Buyantu and Tog-temür, and Kublai's great-granddaughter Sengge, built an imperial collection of important early works and also sponsored paintings that emphasized such themes as architecture and horses. Still, their activities were not a match for Song royal patronage, and it was in this period that the amateur art of painters of the scholar class (in the

official, poet, and Daoist who specialized in painting the dragon, a symbol both of the emperor and of the mysterious all-pervading force of the Dao. Chen Rong's paintings show these fabulous creatures emerging from amid rocks and clouds. They were painted in a variety of strange techniques, including rubbing the ink on with a cloth and spattering it, perhaps by blowing ink onto the painting.

tradition of Su Dongpo and his late Bei Song colleagues) first came to dominate Chinese painting standards.

The restriction of the scholars' opportunities at court and the choice of many of them to withdraw into seclusion rather than serve the Mongols created a heightened sense of class identity and individual purpose, which in turn inspired their art. Eremitic rather than courtly values now shaped the art of painting as never before, and a stylistic gulf sprang up between literati painters and court professionals that was not bridged until the 18th century. Whereas most painting had previously displayed technical refinement and had conservatively transmitted the heritage of the immediate past, gradually evolving through modest individual departures, the literati thenceforth typically based their styles on a wide-ranging knowledge of distant stylistic precedents, selectively chosen and radically transformed by means of expressive calligraphic brushwork. Style and subject were both intended to reflect closely the artist's own personality and mood rather than conforming to the wishes of a patron. Typical were the simply brushed orchid paintings of Zheng Sixiao, who painted this traditional symbol of political loyalty without any ground beneath as a comment on the grievous loss of China to foreign domination.

Qian Xuan was among the first to define this new direction. From Wuxing in Zhejiang, he steadfastly declined an invitation to serve at court, as reflected in his painting style and themes. A conservative painter before the Mongol conquest, especially of realistic flowers and birds, he altered his style to incorporate the primitive qualities of ancient painting, favouring the Tang blue-and-green manner in his landscape painting, stiff or peculiarly mannered renditions of vegetation and small animals, and the archaic flavour of clerical script in his brushwork. Calligraphy became a part of his design and frequently confirmed through historical references a link between subject matter and his eremitic choice of lifestyle. Like many Chinese scholars who espoused this amateur ideal, Qian Xuan was obliged by demeaning circumstances to exchange his paintings in return for his family's livelihood.

The most distinguished of the scholar-painters was Zhao Mengfu, a fellow townsman and younger follower of Qian Xuan who became a high official and president of the imperial Hanlin Academy. In his official travels he collected paintings by Bei Song masters that inspired him to revive and reinterpret the classical styles in his own fashion. A notable example is *Autumn Colours in the Qiao and Hua Mountains* (1296; National Palace Museum, Taipei, Taiwan), a nostalgic, deliberately archaistic landscape in the Tang manner. The hand scrolls *Twin Pines and Level View* (Metropolitan Museum of Art, New York City) and *Water Village* (1302; Palace Museum, Beijing) exemplify his reinterpretation of past masters (Li Cheng and Dong Yuan, respectively) and furthered the new direction of scholarly landscape painting by applying the standards and techniques of calligraphy to painting.

The Yuan produced many fine calligraphers, including Zhao Mengfu, who was the most influential, Yang Weizhen, and Zhang Yu. The period was less innovative in calligraphy than in painting, however, and Zhao's primary accomplishment was to sum up and resynthesize the past. His well-studied writing style was praised in his time for its breadth of historical understanding, and his standard script became the national model for book printing, but he was later criticized for a lack of daring or expression of personality, for a brush style too sweet and pleasing.

Other gentlemen-painters who worked at the Yuan court perpetuated more conservative Song styles, often rivaling or even surpassing their Song predecessors in the process. Ren Renfa worked in great detail and was perhaps the last of China's great horse painters; he defended his court service through both the style and theme of his paintings. Li Kan carefully studied the varieties of bamboo during his official travels and wrote a systematic treatise on painting them; he remains unsurpassed as a skilled bamboo painter. Gao Kegong

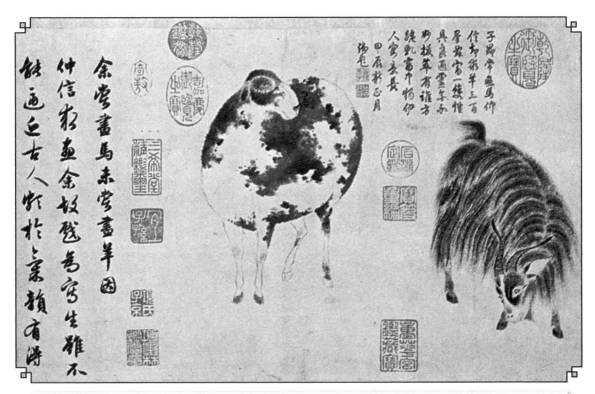

A Sheep and a Goat, *painting in ink by Zhao Mengfu; in the Freer Gallery of Art, Washington, D.C. Courtesy of the Smithsonian Institution, Freer Gallery of Art, Washington, D.C.*

followed Mi Fu and Mi Youren in painting cloudy landscapes that symbolized good government. Wang Mian, who served not the Mongols but anti-Mongol forces at the end of the dynasty, set the highest standard for the painting of plums, a symbol of irrepressible purity and, potentially, of revolutionary zeal.

In retrospect, however, it was the ideals of the retired scholars that had the most lasting effect on later Chinese art. This may be summed up as individuality of expression, brushwork more revealing of the inner spirit of the subject—or of the artist himself—than of outward appearance, and suppression of the realistic and decorative in favour of an intentional plainness, understatement (*pingtan*), and awkwardness (*zhuo*), which marks the integrity of the gentleman suspicious of too much skill. Four masters of the middle and later Yuan, all greatly influenced by Zhao Mengfu, came to be regarded as the foremost exponents of this philosophy of painting in the Yuan period.

Huang Gongwang, a Daoist recluse, was the oldest. His most revered and perhaps only authentic surviving work is the hand scroll *Dwelling in the Fuchun*

Dwelling in the Fuchun Mountains, *detail from a hand scroll, ink on paper by Huang Gongwang, 1350, Yuan dynasty; in the National Palace Museum, Taipei, Taiwan.* National Palace Museum, Taipei, Taiwan

Mountains (National Palace Museum, Taipei, Taiwan), painted with dynamic brushwork during occasional moods of inspiration between 1347 and 1350. Unlike the academicians, Gongwang did not hesitate to go over his brushwork, for expression, not representation, was his aim. The cumulative effect of his masterpiece is obtained not by its fidelity to visible forms but by a profound feeling of oneness with nature that set an ideal standard for later scholarly painting.

This scholarly serenity was also expressed in the landscapes of Wu Zhen, a poor Daoist diviner, poet, and master painter who, like Huang Gongwang, was inspired by Dong Yuan and Juran, whose manner he rendered, in landscapes and bamboo painting alike, with blunt brushwork, minimal motion, and utmost calm. His bamboo paintings are also superb, and, in an album in the National Palace Museum (Taipei), he pays tribute to his Song dynasty predecessors Su Dongpo and Wen Tong.

The third of the Four Masters of the Yuan dynasty was Ni Zan, a prosperous gentleman and bibliophile forced by crippling taxation to give up his estates and become a wanderer. As a landscapist, he eliminated all depictions of human beings. He thus reduced the compositional pattern of Li Cheng (symbolizing lofty gentlemen in isolation from the court) to its simplest terms, achieving, as Wu Zhen had, a sense of austere and monumental calm with the slenderest of means. He used ink, it was said, as sparingly as if it were gold.

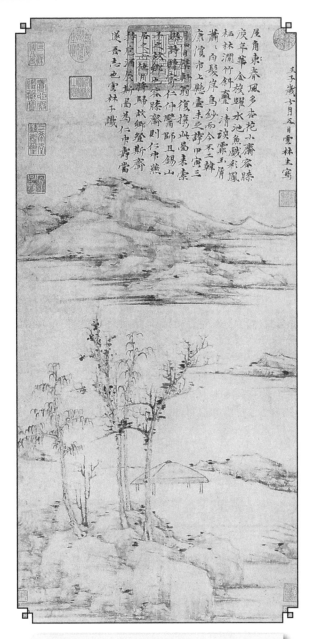

The Rongxi Studio, *ink on paper hanging scroll by Ni Zan, 1372, late Yuan dynasty; in the National Palace Museum, Taipei, Taiwan.* National Palace Museum, Taipei, Taiwan

Quite different was the technique of the fourth Yuan master, Wang Meng, a grandson of Zhao Mengfu. His brushwork was dense and energetic, derived from Dong Yuan but tangled and hoary and thereby imbued with a feeling of great antiquity. He often drew heavily from Guo Xi or from what he perceived as Tang traditions in his landscape compositions, which he filled with scholarly retreats. He sometimes used strong colours as well, which added a degree of visual charm and nostalgia to his painting that was lacking in the other three masters' work.

The combination in the Four Masters of a consistent philosophical and political attitude and a wide range of ink techniques made them models for later scholar-painters, both in their lives and in their art. It is impossible to appreciate the work of the landscape painters of the Ming and Qing (1644–1911/12) dynasties unless one is aware of how acutely conscious they were of their debt to the Yuan masters and how frequently they paid tribute to them both in their style and in their inscriptions. From this point on, indeed, the artist's own inscription, as well as the colophons of admirers and connoisseurs, became an integral part of the total work of art.

MING DYNASTY (1368–1644)

The restoration of a native dynasty made China once again a great power. The Ming dynasty felt a kinship with the heyday of the Tang dynasty (618–907), a connection reflected in the vigour and rich colour of Ming arts and crafts. Early in the 1400s, China again expanded into Central Asia, and maritime expeditions brought Central Asian products around the Indian Ocean to its own shores. Chinese pottery exports also greatly increased. The 15th century was a period of settled prosperity and great achievement in the arts, but the last century of the dynasty was marked by corruption at court and a deep discontent among the scholar-gentry that is reflected in their painting.

The first Ming emperor, Hongwu, was a highly distrustful personality whose vengeful focus fell upon Suzhou, the local base of his chief rival for the throne as well as home to the Yuan period (1206–1368) literati painting movement. So many artists became victim to his recriminations, typically for political rather than artistic reasons, that a novel movement in Chinese painting history was nearly halted. Among those literati painters who lost their lives during this period were Wang Meng, Zhao Yuan, Xu Ben, Chen Ruyan, Zhang Yu, Zhou Wei, and Sheng Zhu. Rejecting the individualist standard of literati painting, early Ming emperors who revived the custom of summoning painters to court sought instead to create a cultural bridge to the last native regimes, the Tang and Song. Although they revived Song professional court styles, they never organized their painters into a central teaching academy and indeed sometimes dealt quite harshly with them. Scholar-painters, increasingly few in number in the early Ming, stayed at home in the south, further widening the gulf between themselves and court artists.

Early Ming court painters such as Xie Huan and Li Zai at first revived the Tang blue-and-green and Bei Song court styles of Guo Xi. Bian Wenjin and his follower Lu Ji carried forward the bird-and-flower painting tradition of Huang Quan, Cui Bai, and the Song emperor Huizong. Gradually, however, the Nan Song styles of the landscape artists Li Tang, Ma Yuan, and Xia Gui came to hold sway, beginning with Dai Jin, who served under the fifth emperor, the Xuande emperor (himself a painter of moderate ability). Nevertheless, Dai Jin, who was opposed in the Beijing capital by jealous court rivals and who found the restrictions there intolerable (as did many others who followed), was affected by the calligraphically inspired scholars' art: his brushwork shows far greater freedom than is found in his Nan Song models.

Like Dai Jin, many professional painters went to Beijing from the old Nan Song capital region around Hangzhou, and they were said to belong to the Zhe school of painting. Many of the so-called Zhe school artists were in fact scholars disgruntled with the autocratic Ming politics and drawn to Daoist eremitic themes and eccentric brushwork. Most dazzling among them, perhaps, was Wu Wei, from Jiangxia in Hubei, whose drunken bouts at court were forgiven out of admiration for his genius with the brush.

Among the few important amateur painters to hold a scholarly position at the early Ming court was Wang Fu, who survived a long period of banishment to the frontier under the first emperor to return as a court calligrapher. He became a key figure in the survival and transmission of Yuan literati style and was the first to single out the masters Huang Gongwang, Wu Zhen, Ni Zan, and Wang Meng as models. Other early Ming scholar-official painters in the Yuan tradition were the bamboo painter Xia Chang and Liu Jue, who retired to Suzhou at the age of 50 after having been president of the Board of Justice. In his landscapes Liu Jue gives to the cool, often austere style of the Yuan masters a looser, more genial character, thus making them more accessible to the large number of amateur gentlemen-painters who flourished in the Jiangnan region—notably those in and around Suzhou, during the settled middle years of the 15th century.

The Wu district of Jiangsu, in which Suzhou lies, gave its name to the Wu school of landscape painting, dominated in the late 15th century by Shen Zhou, a friend and pupil of Liu Jue. Shen Zhou never became an official but instead devoted his life to painting and poetry. He often painted in the manner of the Yuan masters, but his interpretations of Ni Zan and Wu Zhen are more clearly structured and firmer in brushwork. His work is unsurpassed in all Chinese art for its humane feeling; the gentle and unpretentious figures he introduced give his paintings great appeal. Shen Zhou commanded a wide range of styles and techniques, on which he impressed his warm and vigorous personality. He also became the first to establish among the literati painters a flower painting tradition. These works, executed in the "boneless" fashion developed by 10th-century court artists but with the freedom of such late Song Chan painters as Muqi, were followed with greater technical versatility by Chen Shun and Xu Wei in the late Ming and then by Shitao (Daoji) and Zhu Da of the early Qing. Their work, in turn, served as the basis for the revival of flower painting in the late 19th and the 20th century.

Shen Zhou's younger contemporary and friend Wen Zhengming showed an even greater interest in the styles of the past, which he reinterpreted with a refined and scholarly precision. He, too, had many styles and was a distinguished calligrapher. He was an active teacher of painting as well, and among his gifted pupils were his son Wen Jia and his nephew Wen Boren. Their landscapes display a lyrical delicacy in composition, touch, and colour, qualities that in the work of lesser late Ming artists of the Wu school degenerated into a precious and artificial style.

Three early 16th-century professional Suzhou masters, Zhou Chen, Qiu Ying, and Tang Yin, established a somewhat different standard from that of the scholarly Wu group, never renouncing the professional's technical skills yet mastering the literary technique as well. They achieved a wide range, and sometimes a blend, of styles that could hardly be dismissed by scholarly critics and that won great popular acclaim. In fact, Tang Yin, who was not only a student of Zhou Chen but also a brilliant scholar and longtime friend of Wen Zhengming, became mythologized in the centuries that followed.

In the succeeding generations, other painting masters similarly helped confuse the distinction between amateur and professional standards, and, in the early 17th century, a number of these artists also showed the first influence of the European technique that had been brought to China through engravings and then oil paintings by Matteo Ricci and other Jesuit missionaries after 1600. Among these painters were the landscapists Wu Bin from Nanjing, Zhang Hong from Suzhou, and Lan Ying from Qiantang in Zhejiang province. The southern painter Chen Hongshou and the Beijing artist Cui Zizhong initiated the first major revival of figure painting since Song times, possibly as a result of their encounters with Western art. Perspective and shading effects appear among other naturalistic features in the art of this generation, along with a newfound interest in saturated colours and an attraction to formal distortion, which may have derived in part from a fascination with the unfamiliar in Western art. Beyond the revived interest in naturalism, which seems to have inspired in some artists a renewed attention to Five Dynasties (907–960) and Song painting (as the last period in which Chinese artists had displayed knowledge about such matters), there occurred an even more fundamental questioning of contemporary standards. In the work of Chen and Cui, which exhibits all the aforementioned qualities, an almost unprecedented interest in grotesquerie and satire visually enlivens their work, yet it also reflects something of the restless individualism and deep disillusionment that were part of the spirit of this period of national decline. The breakdown of orthodoxy reached an extreme form in Xu Wei. In his explosive paintings, chiefly of flowers, plants, and bamboo, he showed an absolute mastery of brush and ink and a total disregard of tradition.

Standing above all others of this period in terms of historical impact, the theorist, critic, and painter Dong Qichang saw the proliferation of styles as a symptom of the decline in morale of the scholar class as the Ming became increasingly corrupt. His aim to reestablish standards in landscape painting paralleled a movement to restore traditional virtue to government. In his brief but influential essay "Huashuo" ("Comments on Painting"), he set out what he held to be the proper lineage of scholarly painting models, from Wang Wei of the Tang through Dong Yuan and Juran of the Five Dynasties, Su Dongpo and Mi Fu of the Song, Huang Gongwang, Wu Zhen, Ni Zan, and Wang Meng of the Yuan, and Shen Zhou and Wen Zhengming of the Ming. He labeled these artists as "Southern school" in reference to the

Southern school of Chan Buddhism and its philosophy of spontaneous enlightenment, while he rejected such "Northern school" (i.e., gradualist, pedantic) artists as Guo Xi, Ma Yuan, Xia Gui, and Qui Ying. Dong believed that the greatest painters were highly creative individuals who, to be followed effectively, had to be creatively reinterpreted. Appropriately, his own landscape painting was often quite original, sometimes daringly so, even while based on a systematic reduction and synthetic reintegration of past styles. However, having breathed new life into a troubled tradition by looking inward and to the past, his reinterpretations (particularly of the styles of Dong Yuan and Juran) set an ideal beyond which his contemporaries and followers could not go without either a great leap of imagination, a direct return to nature, or a departure from the historical core of Chinese painting standards. Only a few artists, in the early Qing, could achieve this, primarily through the route of artistic imagination; many more throughout the Qing followed Dong too slavishly in theory without attaining new heights or perspectives in actual practice.

One further feature of late Ming art was the popularity of wood-block printing, including the appearance of a sophisticated tradition of polychrome printing, done in imitation of painting. Among the earliest major examples were the collections of ink designs *Fangshi Mopu* of 1588 and *Chengshi Moyuan* of 1606 ("Mr. Fang Yulu's Ink Catalog" and "Mr. Cheng

Dayue's Ink Garden," respectively); both catalogs utilized graphic designs by significant artists to promote the products of Anhui province's foremost manufacturers of ink sticks. The *Shizhuzhai Shuhuapu* ("Ten Bamboo Studio Manual of Painting and Calligraphy"), produced by Hu Zhengyan between 1619 and 1633, set the highest standard for polychrome woodblock printing and helped influence the development of colour printing in Japan. Painters such as Chen Hongshou participated in print production in forms ranging from book illustration to playing cards, while others, including Xiao Yuncong, generated high-quality topographical illustrations. Through such artists, the medium came to influence painting as well as to be influenced by it.

QING DYNASTY (1644–1911/12)

The Manchu conquest did not produce a dislocation of Chinese social and cultural life in the same way the Mongol invasion had done. On the contrary, even before their conquest, the Manchus began imitating Chinese ways, and the Qing rulers, particularly Kangxi (1661–1722) and Qianlong (1735–96), were well-educated men who were eager to enlist the support of Chinese scholars. They were extremely conservative in their political and cultural attitudes; in artistic taste, their native love of extravagance (which the Chinese viewed as barbarous) was tempered, ironically, by an equally strong conservative propensity. The art of the

Qing dynasty, even the painting of many of its finest eccentrics and the design of its best gardens, is similarly characterized both by lavish decoration and ornate effects as well as by superb technique and conservative taste. By the 19th century, however, China's internal weakness and humiliation by the Western powers were reflected in a growing stagnation of the arts.

The dual attraction of the Manchu rulers to unbridled decoration and to orthodox academicism characterized their patronage at court. In regard to the former, they favoured artists such as Yuan Jiang, who, in the reign of Kangxi, combined with great decorative skill the model of Guo Xi and the mannered distortions that had cropped up in the late Ming (1368–1644), partly as a result of Ming artists' exposure to an unfamiliar Western art. More thoroughly Westernized work, highly exotic from the Asian perspective, was produced both by native court artists such as Jiao Bingzhen, who applied Western perspective to his illustrations of the text *Gengzhitu* ("Rice and Silk Culture"), which were reproduced and distributed in the form of wood engravings in 1696, and by the Italian missionary Giuseppe Castiglione. In the mid-18th century Castiglione produced a Sino-European technique that had considerable influence on court artists such as Zuo Yigui, but he was ignored by literati critics. His depictions of Manchu hunts and battles provide a valuable visual record of the times.

On the other hand, Manchu emperors saw to it that conservative works in the scholar-amateur style by Wang Hui, Wang Yuanqi, and other followers of Dong Qichang were also well represented at court, largely putting an end to the conflict at court between professional and amateur styles that had been introduced in the Song (960–1279) and that played a significant role in the Ming. In a sense, the amateur style was crowned victor, but it came at the expense of the amateurism that had defined its purpose, given the prominent role these artists enjoyed at court. This politically effective aspect of Manchu patronage was not necessarily a specifically calculated strategy; rather, it was a natural extension of their concerted attempts to cultivate and recruit the scholar class in order to establish their legitimacy.

The Qianlong emperor was the most energetic of royal art patrons since Huizong of the Song, building an imperial collection of more than 4,000 pre-Qing paintings and calligraphy and cataloging them in successive editions of the *Shiqubaoji*. The shortcomings of his taste, however, were displayed in his preference for recent forgeries rather than the originals in his collection (notably, copies of Huang Gongwang's *Dwelling in the Fuchun Mountains* and of Fan Kuan's *Travelers among Mountains and Streams*) and in his propensity for covering his collected masterpieces with multiple impressions of court seals and calligraphic inscriptions in a mediocre hand.

The conservatism of Qing period painting was exemplified by the Six Masters of the late 17th and the early 18th century, including the so-called "Four Wangs," Wu Li, and Yun Shouping. In the works of most of these artists and of those who followed their lead, composition became routinized, with little in the way of variation or genre detail to appeal to the imagination; fluency of execution in brushwork became the exclusive basis for appreciation. Wang Shimin, who had been a pupil of Dong Qichang, retired to Taicang near modern Shanghai at the fall of the Ming, making it the centre of a school of scholarly landscape painting that included his friend Wang Jian and the younger artist Wang Hui. Wang Hui was a dazzling prodigy whose landscapes included successful forgeries of Bei Song and Yuan masters and who did not hesitate to market the "amateur" practice, both among fellow scholars and at the Manchu court; however, the hardening of his style in his later years foreshadowed the decline of Qing literati painting for lack of flexible innovation. In contrast, Wang Shimin's grandson, Wang Yuanqi, was the only one of these six orthodox masters who fully lived up to Dong Qichang's injunction to transform the styles of past models creatively, as he did in his tour de force *Wang River Villa, After Wang Wei* (Metropolitan Museum of Art, New York City). At court, Wang Yuanqi rose to high office under the Kangxi emperor and served as chief compiler of the

imperial painting and calligraphy catalog, the *Peiwenzhai Shuhuapu.*

Receiving no patronage from the Manchu court and leaving only a minor following before the latter half of the 19th century was a different group of artists, now frequently referred to as "Individualists." Collectively, these artists represent a triumphant, if short-lived, moment in the history of literati painting, triggered in good part by the emotionally cathartic conquest of China by the Manchus. They shared a rejection of Manchu political authority and the choice of an eremitic, often impoverished lifestyle that obliged them to trade their works for their sustenance, in spite of their allegiance to amateur ideals. Stylistically, just like their more orthodox contemporaries, they often revealed the influence of Dong Qichang's systematization of painting method; but, unlike the more conservative masters, they pursued an emotional appeal reflective of their own temperaments. For example, Gong Xian, a Nanjing artist whose budding political career was cut short by the Manchu conquest, used repetitive forms and strong tonal contrasts to convey a pervasive feeling of repressive constraint, lonely isolation, and gloom in his landscapes (most impressive is his *Thousand Peaks*

White Clouds over Xiao and Xiang, hanging scroll after Zhao Mengfu by Wang Jian, one of the Six Masters of the early Qing period, ink and colour on paper, 1668; in the Freer Gallery of Art, Washington, D.C. Courtesy of the Smithsonian Institution, Freer Gallery of Art, Washington, D.C.

River Landscape, *detail of a hand scroll by Fan Qi, one of the Eight Masters of Nanjing, 17th century, Qing dynasty, ink and colour on silk; in the Museum of Asian Art, one of the National Museums of Berlin, Germany.* Courtesy of Staatliche Museen Preussischer Kulturbesitz, Museum für Ostasiatische Kunst, Berlin

and Myriad Ravines in the Rietberg Museum, Zürich, Switzerland; C.A. Drenowatz Collection). He was the most prominent of the artists who came to be known as the Eight Masters of Nanjing. This group was only loosely related stylistically, though contemporary painters from Nanjing did share solidity of form derived from Song prototypes and, possibly, from the influence of Western art.

The landscapes of Kuncan (Shiqi), who became a somewhat misanthropic abbot at a Buddhist monastery near Nanjing, also express a feeling of melancholy. His works were typically inspired by the densely tangled brushwork of Wang Meng of the Yuan (exemplified by his painting *Bao'en Temple*, Sumitomo Collection, Ōiso, Japan).

Another Individualist artist to join the Buddhist ranks was Hongren, exemplar of a style that arose in the Xin'an or Huizhou district of southeastern Anhui province and that drew on the famed landscape of the nearby Huang Mountains. The group of artists now known as the Anhui school (including Ding Yunpeng, Xiao Yuncong, Mei Qing, Zha Shibiao, and Dai Benxiao) mostly pursued an emotional extreme opposite from Gong Xian and Kuncan, a severe coolness based on the sparse, dry linear style of the Yuan artist Ni Zan. However individualistic, virtually all these artists reveal the influence of Dong Qichang's compositional means. In the 17th century, when the Anhui style became popular among wealthy collectors in the area of present-day Shanghai, propagated in part through wood-block catalogs illustrating Anhui's vaunted ink and painting-paper products, ownership of a Hongren painting became the mark of a knowing connoisseur.

Two artists, both members of the deposed and decimated Ming royal family, stood out among these Individualist masters and left, albeit belatedly recognized, the most enduring legacy of all. Known by a sequence of names, perhaps designed to protect his royal identity, Zhu Da, or Bada Shanren, suffered or at least feigned a period of madness and muteness in the 1680s. He emerged from this with an eccentric style remarkable for its facility with extremes, alternating between a wet-and-wild manner and a dry, withdrawn use of brush and ink. His paintings of glowering birds and fish casting strange and ironic glances, as well as his structurally interwoven studies of rocks and vegetation, are virtually without precedent in composition, although aspects of both the eccentric Xu Wei and Dong Qichang are discernible in his work. His esoteric inscriptions reveal a controlled intent rather than sheer lunacy and suggest a knowledgeable, if hard to unravel, commentary on China's contemporary predicament.

Zhu Da's cousin Daoji was raised in secret in a Chan Buddhist community. He traveled widely as an adult in such varied artistic regions as the Huang Mountains district of Anhui province and Nanjing and finally settled in the newly prosperous city of Yangzhou, where in his later years he publicly acknowledged his royal identity, renounced his Buddhist status, and engaged in professional practices. His work has a freshness inspired not by masters of the past but by an unfettered imagination, with brush techniques that were free and unconventional and a daring use of colour. In his essay "Huayulu" ("Comments on Painting"), he ridiculed traditionalism, writing that his own method was "no method" and insisting that, like nature, creativity with the brush must be spontaneous and seamless, based on the concept of *yihua*, the "unifying line."

Daoji's extreme stand in favour of artistic individuality stands out against the growing scholasticism of Qing painting and was an inspiration to the artists, roughly grouped together as the "Eight Eccentrics" (including Zheng Xie, Hua Yan, Huang Shen, Gao Fenghan, Jin Nong, and Luo Pin), who were patronized by the rich merchants in early 18th-century Yangzhou. The art of Zhu Da and Daoji was not firmly enshrined, however, until the late 19th century, when a new individualist thrust appeared in Shanghai in response to the challenge of Western culture. Their influence on Chinese art since then, especially in the 20th century, was profound.

SINCE 1912

Painting in China, as with all the arts of China since 1912, has reflected the effects of modernization, the impact of Western art, and the political, military, and economic struggles of the period, including the war with Japan (1937–45), the civil war that ended in the establishment in 1949 of the People's Republic of China, and the rapid economic changes of the late 20th and early 21st centuries.

PAINTING AND PRINTMAKING

Shanghai, which had been forcibly opened to the West in 1842 and boasted a newly wealthy clientele, was the logical site for the first modern innovations in Chinese art at the turn of the 20th century. A Shanghai regional style had appeared by the 1850s, led by Ren Xiong, his more popular follower Ren Yi (Ren Bonian), and Ren Yi's follower Wu Changshi. The style drew its inspiration from a series of Individualist artists of the Ming and Qing, including Xu Wei, Chen Shun, Chen Hongshou, Zhu Da, and Daoji. It focused on birds and flowers and figural

Self-portrait on a hanging scroll, ink and colour on paper by Ren Xiong, undated (probably 1855–57); in the Palace Museum, Beijing. 177.4 × 78.5 cm. Hu Chui/ChinaStock Photo Library

themes more than the old landscape tradition did, and it emphasized decorative qualities, exaggerated stylization, and satiric humour rather than refined brushwork and sober classicism. Under Wu Changshi's influence, this style was passed on to Beijing in the early 20th century through the art of Chen Hengke (Chen Shizeng) and Qi Baishi.

The first Chinese artists to respond to international developments in modern art were those who had visited Japan, where the issues of modernization appeared earlier than they did in China. The Japanese blended native and Western traditions in styles such as Nihonga painting and in establishing an institutional basis of support (under the leadership of Okakura Kakuzō, who founded the Tokyo Fine Arts School in 1889). Among the first Chinese artists to bring back Japanese influence were Gao Jianfu, his brother Gao Qifeng, and Chen Shuren. Gao Jianfu studied art for four years in Japan, beginning in 1898; during a second trip there, he met Sun Yat-sen, and subsequently, in Guangzhou (Canton), he participated in the uprisings that paved the way for the fall of imperial rule and the establishment in 1912 of a republic. Inspired by the "New Japanese Style," the Gao brothers and Chen inaugurated a "New National Painting" movement, which in turn gave rise to a Cantonese, or Lingnan, regional style that incorporated Euro-Japanese characteristics. Although the new style did not produce satisfying or lasting solutions, it was a significant harbinger and continued to thrive in Hong Kong, practiced by such artists as Zhao Shao'ang.

The first establishment of Western-style art instruction also dates from this period. A small art department was opened in Nanjing High Normal School in 1906, and the first art academy, later to become the Shanghai Art School, was founded in the year of the revolution, 1911, by the 16-year-old Liu Haisu. In the next decade he would pioneer the first public exhibitions (1913) and the use of live models, first clothed and then nude, in the classroom.

Increasingly, by the mid-1920s, young Chinese artists were attracted not just to Japan but also to Paris and German art centres. A trio of these artists brought back some understanding of the essential contemporary European traditions and movements. Liu Haisu was first attracted to Impressionist art, while Lin Fengmian, who became director of the National Academy of Art in Hangzhou in 1928, was inspired by the experiments in colour and pattern of Henri Matisse and the Fauves. Lin advocated a synthesis combining Western techniques and Chinese expressiveness and left a lasting mark on the modern Chinese use of the brush. Xu Beihong, head of the National Central University's art department in Nanjing, eschewed European Modernist movements in favour of more conservative Parisian academic styles. He developed his facility in drawing and oils, later learning to imitate pencil and chalk with the Chinese brush. The monumental figure paintings he created would serve as a basis for Socialist Realist painters after the communist revolution of 1949.

By the 1930s all these modern trends were clearly developed and institutionalized. Although most of the major artists of the time advocated Modernism, two continued to support more traditional styles: Qi Baishi, who combined Shanghai style with an infusion of folk-derived vitality, and the relatively conservative landscapist Huang Binhong, who demonstrated

that the old tradition could still produce great masters.

Socialism produced a new set of artistic demands that were first met not by painting but by the inexpensive mass medium of wood-block prints, which had been invented in China and first used in the Tang dynasty (618–907) to illustrate Buddhist sutras. Initially stimulated by the satiric leftist writer Lu Xun, printmakers flourished during the 1930s and '40s under the dual influence of European socialist artists like Käthe Kollwitz and

Fleeing Refugees, *ink on paper (woodblock print) by Li Hua, 1944.* © Li Hua/ChinaStock Photo Library

the Chinese folk tradition of New Year's prints and papercuts. Among the most prominent print artists were Li Hua and Gu Yuan, who attained a new standard of political realism in Chinese art.

In 1942, as part of the Chinese Communist Party's first intellectual rectification movement, Mao Zedong delivered two speeches at the Yan'an Forum on Literature and Art that laid out the official party dictates on aesthetics for decades to come—namely, the necessity to popularize styles and subjects in order to reach a mass audience, the need for artists to share in the lives of ordinary people, and the requirement that the party and its goals be treated positively rather than subjected to satiric criticism. "Art for art's sake" was strictly denounced as a bourgeois liberal attempt to escape from the truly political nature of art. Although Mao later defended a place for the artistic study of nude models, a staple of Western naturalism, the tone he set led to severe limitations on the actual practice of this.

The Sino-Japanese War of 1937–45 led many artists of varied persuasions to flee eastern China for the temporary Nationalist capital in Chongqing, Sichuan province. This exodus brought a tremendous mixing of styles and artistic ferment, but the opportunity for innovation that this promised was thwarted by subsequent events. After the 1949 revolution, Communist Party control of the arts was firmly established by the placement of the academies under the jurisdiction of the Ministry of Culture;

by the creation of artists' federations and associations, under the management of the party's Department of Propaganda, which served as an exclusive pathway to participation in exhibitions and other means of advancement; by the establishment of a strict system of control over publications; and by the virtual elimination of the commercial market for contemporary arts.

Throughout the 1950s, as Socialist Realist standards were gradually implemented, oil painting and woodblock printing were favoured and political cartoons and posters were raised to the status of high art. Artists working in the traditional media—with their basis in the Individualist art of the old "feudal" aristocracy—struggled institutionally for survival, eventually succeeding only as a result of the nationalist fervour that accompanied China's ideological break with the Soviet Union late in the decade. The internationalist but relatively conservative Xu Beihong was installed as head of the new Central Academy of Fine Arts in Beijing, but he died in 1953. Other older-generation leaders died shortly afterward (e.g., Qi Baishi and Huang Binhong) or were shunted aside (e.g., Liu Haisu and Lin Fengmian), and a younger generation soon came to the fore, ready to make the necessary compromises with the new regime. The talented landscapist Li Keran, who had studied with Qi Baishi, Lin Fengmian, Huang Binhong, and Xu Beihong, combined their influences with realistic sketching to achieve a new naturalism in the traditional medium. A

Chairman Mao at Jinggang Mountain, *oil on canvas by Luo Gongliu, 1961; in the Museum of Chinese Revolutionary History, Beijing.* Zhao Liye/ChinaStock Photo Library

leading figure painter was Cheng Shifa, a descendant of the Shanghai school who utilized that style in politically polished depictions of China's minority peoples. Many talented artists, including Luo Gongliu and Ai Zhongxin, painted in oils, which, because of their link to the Soviet Union and Soviet art advisers, held a favoured position until the Sino-Soviet split of the late 1950s.

While the early 1960s provided a moment of political relaxation for Chinese artists, the Cultural Revolution of 1966–76 brought unprecedented hardships, ranging from forced labour and severe confinement to death. Destruction of traditional arts was especially rampant in the early years of the movement. Only those arts approved by a military-run apparatus under the sway of Mao's wife, Jiang Qing, could thrive; these followed the party's increasingly strict propagandist dictates and were often created anonymously as collective works. In the early 1970s, when China first reopened Western contacts, Premier Zhou Enlai attempted to restore government patronage for the traditional arts. When Zhou's health declined,

Boat People, *ink and colours on paper hanging scroll by He Huaishuo, 1979; in the Water, Pine, and Stone Retreat Collection, Hong Kong*. The Water, Pine and Stone Retreat Collection, Hong Kong

traditional arts and artists again suffered under Jiang Qing, including being publicly denounced and punished as "black arts" after officials saw exhibitions in Beijing, Shanghai, and Xi'an in 1974.

The passing of Mao and Maoism after 1976 brought a new and sometimes refreshing chapter in the arts under the leadership of Deng Xiaoping. The 1980s were characterized by decreasing government control of the arts and increasingly bold artistic experimentation. Three phenomena in 1979 announced this new era: the appearance of Cubist and other Western styles as well as nude figures (although the government covered the nudes) in the murals publicly commissioned for the new Beijing airport; an influential private arts exhibition by the "Stars" art group at the Beijing Art Gallery; and the rise of a truly realistic oil painting movement, which swept away the artificiality of Socialist Realist propaganda. In the 1980s a resurgence of traditional Chinese painting occurred, featuring the return of formerly disgraced artists, including Li Keran, Cheng Shifa, Shi Lu, and Huang Yongyu, and the emergence of such fresh talents as Wu Guanzhong, Jia Youfu, and Li Huasheng.

After 1985, as an increasingly bold avant-garde movement arose, the once-threatening traditional-style painting came to seem to the government like a safe alternative. In the final months before the June 1989 imposition of martial law in Beijing, an exhibition of nude oil paintings from the Central Academy of Fine Arts at the Chinese National Gallery and an avant-garde exhibition featuring installation art, performance art, and printed scrolls mocking the government both drew record crowds. The latter was closed by police, and both exhibits were eventually denounced as having lowered local morals, supposedly helping to precipitate the tragic events that followed in June 1989. New limitations on artistic production, exhibition, and publication ensued. At the conclusion of these events, a number of leading artists, including Huang Yongyu, fled China, joining others—including Zhang Daqian, He Huaishuo, and Lin Fengmian—who had previously fled or abandoned China to establish centres of Chinese art throughout the world.

PAINTING AT THE TURN OF THE 21ST CENTURY

Many of the artists who remained in China after the events of Tiananmen Square adopted styles influenced by Western Pop art. In one Chinese variation of the style, "Political Pop," artists such as Wang Guangyi and Li Shan juxtaposed Red Guard imagery of workers, peasants, and soldiers with capitalist imagery such as the Coca-Cola logo (a favourite image of American Pop artist Andy Warhol). The image of Mao Zedong was frequently utilized—and ridiculed—in paintings of this style. Other artists used cartoonish portraiture and bright colours (a style reminiscent of American Roy Lichtenstein) in works that explore the banalities of bourgeois life. While such derivations of Pop art often possessed common stylistic elements, they differed in their tendencies either to challenge or to reflect popular culture, politics, and economic realities. Artists representing these movements participated in prestigious international art fairs such as the Venice Biennale.

As the 1990s progressed, the Chinese visual arts developed in an environment increasingly characterized by an open-market economy and a relatively liberal political climate. Artists became freer to express themselves than they had ever been in the history of Chinese art. In this democratic atmosphere, different styles and forms of art coexisted.

Changes in government policy allowed artists to study modern art from the West more extensively than ever before. Many canonical writings on aesthetics and art theory were translated and published in China. Chinese artists also greatly enriched their understanding of Western art once elegant catalogs were imported from overseas and once exhibitions of the work of artists such as the German Expressionist painters, Pablo Picasso, and Robert Rauschenberg traveled to China. Inspired by the "art for art's sake" quality of much of the work they saw, many Chinese artists began to reject the idea—long-standing in China—that art must serve politics and the people. Increasingly, many Chinese artists faithfully imitated Western styles, exploring such styles as Cubism and Abstract Expressionism. While such experiments shook the Chinese art system and laid a foundation for the birth of new forms, many artists made work that was overly derivative of Western styles; by the mid-1990s, such overtly referential work had decreased in popularity.

Realism maintained an important position in China at the end of the 20th century. Most Chinese artists graduated from academies of fine art that rigorously trained them in realist techniques. In the early 1990s, classical Chinese oil painting, as seen in the work of Jing Shangyi, reached a high degree of excellence. Many artists—including those in the fields of oil painting, traditional Chinese painting, printmaking, and sculpture—depicted realistic scenes of daily life in their works, much like the older generations had done. Artists such as Luo Zhongli followed the tenets of traditional Chinese art while also drawing on the methods of international modern art (and sometimes Chinese folk art) in their work. Others used their skills at realism to adopt contemporary Western trends, including Photo-realism and work inspired by Western artists such as Andrew Wyeth and Balthus. Many such interpretations of realism also won international attention and prizes.

By the late 1990s, in addition to continuing traditional forms, Chinese artists renewed the avant-garde experimentation of the mid-1980s and explored performance art, conceptual art, earth art, installation art, and video art, all chief media of the international art scene. As the art world became increasingly global, China thus became a part of it. At the 2000 Shanghai Biennial, theoreticians, critics, and artists discussed the virtues of retaining traditional Chinese forms as well as the importance of learning from foreign styles. These two often conflicting themes continued to define Chinese art into the 21st century.

OTHER VISUAL ARTS: JADE AND LACQUERWORK

Although in China they are considered less important than the arts of painting and calligraphy, jade and lacquerwork occupy a special place in the Chinese arts. Jade is valued more than gold in the West, and, unlike gold, it possesses moral connotations. Many carved-jade objects have been produced in China from the Neolithic Period (c. 3000–2000 BCE) onward. The Chinese have historically regarded carved-jade objects as intrinsically valuable, and they metaphorically equated jade with purity and indestructibility.

MEANING OF JADE

The *Shuowenjiezi* ("Discussions of Writings and Explanations of Character") of Xu Shen defined jade (*yu*) as follows:

> *A stone that is beautiful, it has five virtues. There is warmth in its lustre and brilliance; this is its quality of kindness; its soft interior may be viewed from the outside revealing [the goodness] within; this is its quality of rectitude; its tone is tranquil and high and carries far and wide; this is its quality of wisdom; it may be broken but cannot be twisted; this is its quality of bravery; its sharp edges are not intended for violence; this is its quality of purity.* (Translation adapted from Zheng Dekun)

Because of this and the belief in its indestructibility, jade from early times was lavishly used not only for dress ornaments but also for ritual objects, both Confucian and Daoist, and for the protection of the dead in the tomb.

COMPOSITION OF JADE

The jade stone used since ancient times in China is nephrite, a crystalline calcium magnesium silicate, which in its pure state is white but may be green, cream, yellow, brown, gray, black, or mottled because of the presence of impurities, chiefly iron compounds. The Chinese used the generic term *yu* to cover a variety of related jadelike stones, including nephrite, bowenite (a type of serpentine), and jadeite. In the Neolithic Period, by the mid-4th millennium BCE, jade from Lake Tai (in Jiangsu province) began to be used by southeastern culture groups, while deposits along the Liao River in the northeast (called "Xiuyan jade," probably bowenite) were utilized by the Hongshan culture. In historical times China's chief source of nephrite has been the riverbeds of Yarkand and Hotan in present-day Xinjiang autonomous region in northwestern China, where jade is found in the form of boulders. Since the

18th century, China has received from northern Myanmar (Upper Burma) a brilliant green jadeite (also called *feicui*, or "kingfisher feathers") that is a granular sodium-aluminum silicate harder than but not quite so tough as nephrite. Having a hardness like that of steel or feldspar, jade cannot be carved or cut with metal tools but has to be laboriously drilled, ground, or sawed with an abrasive paste and rotational or repetitive-motion machinery, usually after being reduced to the form of blocks or thin slabs.

HISTORY

The earliest examples of jade from the lower Yangtze River (Chang Jiang) region appear in the latter phases of the Majiabang culture (c. 5100–3900 BCE) and continue into the 4th–3rd millennia BCE in the Songze and Qingliangang cultures of that region. Remarkably sophisticated jade pieces appear after 2500 BCE in the Liangzhu culture of southern Jiangsu and northern Zhejiang provinces (c. 3400–2200 BCE), many with an apparent lack

Ceremonial cong of jade (calcined nephrite), 3rd millennium BCE, Neolithic Liangzhu culture; in the Seattle Art Museum, Seattle, Washington, U.S. The Seattle Art Museum, purchased by the Foster family in memory of Albert O. Foster, photographed by Paul Macapia

of wear and practical usage that suggests a primarily ceremonial function. These include the first examples of the flat, perforated *bi* disk (with a hole in the centre), which became the symbol of heaven in later times, and of the *cong*, a tube with a square exterior and a cylindrical hollow exterior. These two items remained part of the Chinese imperial paraphernalia until the early 20th century. The precise meaning of the *cong*, as well as its possible association with astronomical sighting or geomantic site selection, and its conjunction of yin (square, earth, female) and yang (circular, heaven, male) features remain unclear. Also present at this time, in the Liangzhu culture and, in Shandong province, the Longshan culture, are ceremonial *gui* and *zhang* blades and axes, as well as an increasing variety of ornamental arc-shaped and circular jade pendants, necklaces, and bracelets (often in animal form), together with the significant appearance of mask decoration; all these forms link the Neolithic jades to those of the subsequent Shang period.

SHANG DYNASTY (*c.* 1600–1046 BCE)

In the Shang dynasty and particularly at Anyang, the craft of jade carving made a notable advance. Ceremonial weapons and fittings for bronze weapons were carved from jade; ritual jades included the *bi*, *cong*, and symbols of rank. Plaques and dress ornaments were carved from thin slabs of jade, but there are also small figurines, masks, and birds and animals carved in the round, some of these

perhaps representing the earliest examples of *mingqi* ("spirit vessels"), artistic figures substituted for live victims buried in order to serve the deceased.

ZHOU DYNASTY (1046–256 BCE)

In the Zhou, production of jade *bi*, *cong*, and other Shang ritual forms was continued and their use systematized. Differently shaped sceptres were used for the ranks of the nobility and as authority for mobilizing troops, settling disputes, declaring peace, and so on. At burial, the seven orifices of the body were sealed with jade plugs and plaques. Stylistically, Zhou dynasty jades at first continued Shang traditions, but then, just as the ritual bronzes did, they turned toward looser, less-systematic designs by middle Zhou times, with zoomorphic decor transformed into abstract meander patterns. This breakdown of formal structure continued to the end of the dynasty.

The introduction of iron tools and harder abrasives in the Dong (Eastern) Zhou led to a new freedom in carving in the round. Ornamental jades, chiefly in the form of sword and scabbard fittings, pendants, and adornment for clothing, were fashioned into a great variety of animals and birds, chiefly from flat plaques no more than a few millimetres thick.

SONG DYNASTY (960–1279 CE)

Given the archaizing fashion of the Song, jades of this period are often difficult to detect. Tombs of the Five Dynasties

(907–960) and Song (960–1279) have yielded jades that tend to confirm the view that adaptation of the form of ancient vessels, ritual objects, plaques, belt hooks, and ornaments was particularly common, as well as the view that the styles of the Warring States and Han (206 BCE–220 CE) were much admired. As the technique of jade carving had changed little in the interval, these are hard to distinguish from genuine archaic jades except by a somewhat playful elegance and a tendency to combine shapes and decoration not found together on ancient pieces. Jades in archaic styles thereafter were often inspired by illustrations in catalogs rather than by a study of genuine antiques.

QING DYNASTY (1644–1911/12)

China directly controlled the Central Asian jade-yielding regions of Hotan and

Dragon among clouds, carved jade medallion or button, Qing dynasty, probably late 18th century (reign of Qianlong); in the Victoria and Albert Museum, London. Courtesy of the board of trustees of the Victoria and Albert Museum, London, Wells Legacy

Yarkand between about 1760 and 1820, during which time much fine nephrite was sent to Beijing for carving. Jadeite from Myanmar (Burma) reached the capital from the second quarter of the 18th century, and chromite- or graphite-flecked "spinach jade" from the Baikal region of Siberia was imported in the 19th century. The finest Qing dynasty jade carving is often assigned to the reign of Qianlong, but carved jade is difficult to date, and some high-quality pieces in the Qianlong style have been made since 1950 in the Handicraft Research Institute in Beijing. Typical of what is considered of Qianlong date are vases with lids and chains carved from a single block, vessels in antique bronze shapes with pseudo-archaic decoration, fairy mountains, and brush pots for the scholar's desk.

CHINESE LACQUERWORK

Lacquerwork is a labour-intensive decorative work produced by the application of many coats of lacquer to a core material such as wood, bamboo, or cloth. True lacquerwork is Chinese or Japanese in origin. The technique was copied in Europe, where it was known as "japanning," but European lacquerwork lacks the hardness and brilliance of Asian lacquer. True lacquer is the purified and dehydrated sap of *Rhus vernicifera*, the lac tree, which is native to China and cultivated in Japan. Lacquer becomes extremely hard but not brittle on exposure to air and takes a high polish. Many thin layers are applied, allowed to dry, and smoothed before the surface is ready for decoration by carving, engraving, or inlay.

The Chinese had discovered as early as the Shang dynasty (c. 1600–1046) that the juice of the lac tree, a naturally occurring polymer, could be used for forming hard but lightweight vessels when built up in very thin layers through the repeated dipping of a core of carved wood, bamboo, or cloth. With the addition of pigments, most commonly red and black, less frequently green and yellow, it could also be used for painting and decorating the outer layers of these vessels. Coffins, chariots, furniture, and other objects found in Shang tombs were often lacquered, and lacquer was used to fix inlays of shell and coloured stone.

Being sticky, painted lacquer must be applied slowly with the brush, giving rise to prolonged motions and fluid, often elegantly curvilinear designs. Since lacquer is almost totally impervious to water, vessels and wine cups have been excavated in perfect condition from waterlogged graves of the late 5th-century-BCE Zeng state in Suixian, of the 4th–3rd-century-BCE Chu state in Jiangling (now Shashi), and of the early 2nd-century-BCE Han dynasty in Changsha. Such works ranged from large-scale coffins to bird- or animal-shaped drum stands to such daily utensils as nested toiletry boxes and food-serving implements. By the Warring States period (475–221 BCE), lacquerwork had developed into a major industry; and, being approximately 10 times more costly than their bronze equivalents, lacquer vessels came to rival bronzes as the most esteemed medium for providing offerings in ancestral ceremonies among the wealthy aristocracy.

Objects in lacquer, chiefly from the state of Chu and from Sichuan, depict hunting scenes, chariots and horsemen, and fantastic winged creatures drawn from folklore and painted in a simple but lively style.

The most remarkable excavated tomb of the Han dynasty belonged to the wife of a mid-level aristocrat, one of three family tombs of the governor of Chansha found in Mawangdui, a suburb of that southern city, and dating from 168 BCE or shortly after. Small in scale but richly equipped and perfectly preserved, the wooden tomb consists of several outer compartments for grave goods tightly arranged around a set of four nested lacquered coffins. An outer layer of sticky white kaolin clay prevented moisture from penetrating the tomb, and an inner layer of charcoal fixed all the available oxygen within a day of burial, so the deceased (Xinzhui, or Lady Dai, the governor's wife) was found in a near-perfect state of preservation. Included among the grave goods, which came with a written inventory providing contemporaneous terminology, are the finest caches yet discovered of early Chinese silks (gauzes and damasks, twills and embroideries, including many whole garments) and lacquerwares (including wood-, bamboo-,

and cloth-cored examples), together with a remarkable painted banner that might have been carried by the shaman in the funerary procession.

By the Han dynasty, lacquer production was chiefly carried on at Changsha and in four regional factories in Shu (modern Sichuan) under government control. In addition to the fine lacquerwares excavated from tombs in Changsha, splendid products of the Sichuan workshops, bearing inscriptions dated between 85 BCE and 71 CE, have been found in tombs of Chinese colonists at Lelang (Nangnang) in North Korea, and pieces of Han lacquerware have been found as far afield as northern Mongolia and Afghanistan.

The different stages of Han lacquer manufacture were divided among a number of specialized craftsmen. The *sugong*, for example, prepared the base, which might be of hemp cloth, wood, or bamboo basketwork; after priming, the base was covered with successive layers of lacquer by the *xiugong*. The top layer, applied by the *shanggong*, was polished and so prepared for the painter, *huagong*, who decorated it. Others might inlay the design or engrave through the top coating to another colour beneath it, add gilding, and write or engrave an inscription. A wine cup found at Lelang bears an inscription giving its capacity, the names of the people concerned in its manufacture, a date equivalent to 4 CE, and place of origin, the "Western Factory" in Shu Commandery.

Among the most celebrated examples of Han lacquer painting is a basket found at Lelang (National Museum, Seoul), decorated with 94 small figures of paragons of filial piety, virtuous and wicked rulers, and ancient worthies. Although confined to a narrow band around the inner rim of the basket, these tiny figures are lively and animated, moving easily in the small space. A tray, also found at Lelang and dated correspondingly to 69 CE, bears near the rim a small painting of Xiwangmu, Queen Mother of the West, sitting with an attendant or visitor on her fairy mountain. Here the lacquer is applied much more thinly, and the brushstrokes have an easy fluency.

Detailed accounts of the lacquerware of the Song dynasty (960–1279) come from two Ming dynasty works. They describe a red lacquer made for use in the palace that was carved with landscapes, figures, and birds; vessels painted in five colours, as well as gold and silver; and bowls black outside and carved red inside. No certain Song pieces matching these descriptions have yet been discovered, however, and it is generally thought that carved red lacquer did not develop until the Yuan dynasty. A bowl (in the British Museum) of lacquered wood with a silver lining engraved with panels of birds and flowers is a rare exception to the character of known Song lacquer; excavated bowls, cups, dishes, and boxes of dull red lacquer are sometimes deeply lobed to resemble a lotus flower but are otherwise undecorated.

While lacquer continued to be made in bolder versions of the undecorated Tang and Song shapes, notable advances in the Yuan dynasty included incising and engraving and filling the lines with gold leaf or silver powder. An example of this technique is a sutra box with floral ornament, dated 1315 (in Komyō-bō, Hiroshima, Japan). The most important innovation was the carving of pictorial designs, floral patterns, or dragons through a thick coating of red or, less frequently, black lacquer. A connoisseur's manual, *Geguyaolun* ("Essential Criteria of Antiquities") by Cao Zhao, says that at the end of the Yuan dynasty Zhang Cheng and Yang Mao, pupils of Yang Hui, were noted for this technique. A number of pieces bearing their names exist today. It had been considered that these were later imitations, made chiefly in Japan, and that carving pictorial designs in lacquer was first practiced in the Ming dynasty. But the 1959 discovery near Shanghai, in a tomb dated equivalent to 1351, of a small lacquer box carved with figures in a landscape shows that this technique was already well established in the mid-14th century.

The carved lacquer first developed in the Yuan dynasty continued through the Ming and Qing and was made in many different factories. It reached a high level in carved red lacquer (*tihong*) dishes, trays, covered boxes, and cups of the Yongle and Xuande reigns. Yongle reign marks, scratched on with a sharp point, are not reliable, but some pieces, bearing carved and gold-inlaid marks of the

Xuande emperor, may be of the period. It is often difficult to distinguish genuine Ming lacquer from Korean and Japanese imitations, and reign marks are not in themselves a reliable guide to dating.

Decoration of this early Ming lacquer includes both pictorial designs (landscapes with figures in pavilions are common) and rich dragon, phoenix, and floral motifs, carved deeply in a full, freely flowing and plastic style, often against a yellow background. While this style continued into the 16th century, the Jiajing period also saw the emergence of more realistic and intricate designs that are shallower and more sharply carved, sometimes through as many as nine layers of different colours, on a background consisting of minute brocade (allover floral and figure designs) or diaper (diamond-shaped) patterns. Other techniques that were popular in the middle decades of the Ming include carving through alternate layers of red and black lacquer, known by the Japanese name *guri*; inlaying one colour with another; and outlining the inlay with engraved lines filled with gold lacquer. Painting and inlaying with mother-of-pearl and other materials were also employed.

CHAPTER 8

CHINESE MUSIC

The musical system that developed in China is one of the oldest and most highly developed of all known systems.

Any survey of Chinese music history must be approached with a certain sense of awe—for what can one say about the music of a varied, still active civilization whose archaeological resources go back to 3000 BCE and whose own extensive written documents refer to endless different forms of music in connection with folk festivals and religious events as well as in the courts of hundreds of emperors and princes in dozens of different provinces, dynasties, and periods? If a survey is carried forward from 3000 BCE, it becomes clear that the last little segment of material, from the Song dynasty (960–1279 CE) to today, is equivalent to the entire major history of European music. For all the richness of detail in Chinese sources, it is only for this last segment that there is information about the actual music itself. Yet the historical, cultural, instrumental, and theoretical materials of earlier times are equally informative and fascinating. This mass of information will be organized into four large chronological units: (1) the formative period, from 3000 BCE through the 4th century CE, (2) the international period, from the 4th through the 9th century, (3) the national period, from the 9th through the 19th century, and (4) the "world music" period of the 20th and early 21st centuries.

ANCIENT ARTIFACTS AND WRITINGS

Chinese writings claim that in 2697 BCE the emperor Huangdi sent a scholar, Ling Lun, to the western mountain area to cut bamboo pipes that could emit sounds matching the call of the *fenghuang*, making possible the creation of music properly pitched for harmony between his reign and the universe. Even this charming symbolic birth of music dates far too late to aid in discovering the melodies and instrumental sounds accompanying the rituals and burials that occurred before the first historically verified dynasty, the Shang (*c.* 1600–1046 BCE). The beautiful sounds of music are evanescent, and before the invention of recordings they disappeared at the end of a performance. The remains of China's most ancient music are found only in those few instruments made of sturdy material. Archaeological digs have uncovered globular clay ocarinas (*xun*), tuned stone chimes (*qing*), and bronze bells (*zhong*); and the word *gu*, for drum, is found incised on Shang oracle bones.

The earliest surviving written records are from the next dynasty, the Zhou (1046–256 BCE). Within the famous Five Classics of that period, it is in the *Liji* ("Record of Rites") of the 2nd century BCE that one finds an extensive discussion of music. The *Yijing* ("Classic of Changes") is a diviner's handbook built around geometric patterns, cosmology, and magic

Bianqing, *Chinese stone chimes*. Courtesy of the Chinese Classical Music Association, Taipei, Taiwan

numbers that indirectly may relate to music. The *Chunqiu* ("Spring and Autumn [Annals]"), with its records of major events, and the *Shujing* ("Classic of History"), with its mixture of documents and forgeries, contain many references to the use of music, particularly at court activities. There are occasional comments about the singing of peasant groups, which is an item that is rare even in the early historical materials of Europe. The *Shijing* ("Classic of Poetry") is of equal interest, for it consists of the texts of 305 songs that are dated from the 10th to the 7th centuries BCE. Their great variety of topics (love, ritual, political satire, etc.) reflect a viable vocal musical tradition quite understandable to modern music appreciators. The songs also include references to less durable musical relics such as the flutes, mouth organ (*sheng*), and, apparently, two forms of the zither (the *qin* and the *se*).

AESTHETIC PRINCIPLES AND EXTRAMUSICAL ASSOCIATIONS

Despite the controversial authenticity and dates of ancient Chinese written sources, a combined study of them produces tantalizing images of courtly parties, military parades, and folk festivals; but it does not provide a single note of music. Nevertheless, in keeping with the prehistoric traditions of China, the philosophies of sages, such as Confucius and Mencius, and the endless scientific curiosity of Chinese acousticians furnish a great deal of rather specific music theory as well as varied aesthetic principles. The straightest path to this material is found on the legendary journey, mentioned earlier, of Ling Lun in search of bamboo pipes.

The charm of such a tale tends to cloud several interesting facts it contains. First, it is noteworthy that the goal of the search was to put music in tune with the universe. It is upheld in theory in the "Annotations on Music" ("Yueji") section of the *Liji* with such comments as "Music is the harmony of heaven and earth while rites are the measurement of heaven and earth. Through harmony all things are made known, through measure all things are properly classified. Music comes from heaven, rites are shaped by earthly designs." Such cosmological ideals may be not merely ancient superstitions but actually cogent insights into the cultural function of music in human societies. Confucius, as pictured in *The Analects* written long after his death, had a similar view of music, including a concern for the choice of music and modes proper for the moral well-being of a gentleman. It is an open question as to how much performance practice followed the admonitions and theories of the scholars; but centuries later one finds numerous pictures of the wise man standing before some natural beauties while his servant follows closely behind him carrying his seven-stringed zither (*qin*) for proper use in such a proper setting.

Another point to be noted in the legend of the origin of music is that Ling

Lun went to the western border area of China to find the correct bamboo. It shall be evident as this chapter progresses how often cultures from Central and West Asia or tribal China influenced the growth and change of music in imperial China. Finally, it is significant that, although the emperor in the myth was primarily concerned with locating pipes that would bring his reign into harmony with the universe, the goal was also the creation of precise, standard pitches.

TONAL SYSTEM AND ITS THEORETICAL RATIONALIZATION

Harmonic pitches produced by the division of strings were known in China. They may have been used to tune sets of bells or stone chimes, but the classical writings on music discuss a 12-tone system in relation to the blowing of bamboo pipes (*lü*). The first pipe produces a basic pitch called yellow bell (*huangzhong*). This concept is of special interest because it is the world's oldest information on a tonal system concerned with very specific pitches as well as the intervals between them. The precise number of vibrations per second that created the yellow bell pitch is open to controversy (between middle C-sharp (C#) and the F above) because the location of this pitch could be changed by the work of new astrologers and acousticians on behalf of a new emperor, in order that his kingdom might stay in tune with the universe.

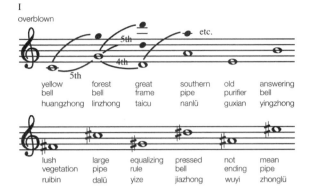

I overblown

| yellow bell huangzhong | forest bell linzhong | great frame taicu | southern pipe nanlü | old purifier guxian | answering bell yingzhong |

| lush vegetation ruibin | large pipe dalü | equalizing rule yize | pressed bell jiazhong | not ending wuyi | mean pipe zhonglü |

(The note C is used in notation I in deference to Western readers; it should not be assumed that a pitch identical to C# was necessarily central to ancient Chinese music.) The choice of the primary pitch in China had extramusical as well as practical applications, for the length of the yellow bell pipe became the standard measure (like a metre); and the number of grains of rice that would fill it were used for a weight measure. Thus, the pipe itself was often the property not of the imperial music department but of the office of weights and measurements.

MATHEMATICAL RELATIONSHIP OF PITCHES

The bamboo *lü* pipe is closed at the bottom by a node in the bamboo, with the result that another pitch a fifth and one octave higher could be produced on it by blowing more strongly (overblowing) as shown in notation I.

This new pitch could be produced an octave lower by constructing a separate pipe two-thirds the size of the first one.

If one then continued to construct pipes alternately four-thirds and two-thirds the length of the previous ones, an entire system of 12 notes could be generated, which is, with the exception of the means of creation, acoustically and proportionately in the same relation as is found in the Greek Pythagorean system. The English versions of the Chinese names for the 12 pitches seem quite fanciful; but they represent theoretically correct pitches, as do terms used in the Western traditional system, such as "C" or "A-flat" ("A♭"). The source of each name in the Chinese system is conjectural; but Chinese classical acousticians, like modern Western scientists, no doubt found value in creating a professional nomenclature that was divorced from everyday speech and potentially descriptive of the nature of the object. For example, the use of bell names may relate to the gradual preference for tuned bells over pipes in the music division of the courts. Names like "old purifier" and "equalizing rule" may refer to the pitch problems of the "Pythagorean comma"—a reference to the cycle of fifths that produces 12 mathematically correct pitches but results in a 13th pitch that does not match the 1st pitch.

A new interpretation of Chinese theory occurred in the late 20th century with the discovery of sets of 4th- and 5th-century tuned bells. Some of the bells produce two pitches and have the pitch names written at the two striking places. This information led to the development of a 12-pitch theory in which 5 pitches are generated in a cycle of fifths, and the 7 remaining pitches are located a major third above or below the first 4. If one starts from the Western C, the tones would appear as seen in notation II.

The actual sounds produced on these ancient bells do not always match the pitch name given, but late 20th-century findings imply that it might have been possible to modulate to new pitch centres and different scales.

SCALES AND MODES

For both Western and Chinese traditions, the 12 pitches are merely a tonal vocabulary from which a specific ordering of a limited number of pitches can be extracted and reproduced on different pitch levels. Such limited structures are called a scale. With a set scale it is possible to emphasize different notes in such a way that they seem to be the pitch centre. Such variations of pitch centre within a scale are called modes. In the Western traditional systems most scales use seven tones that can be transposed and that contain modes. For example, C major (C–D–E–F–G–A–B) can be made a Dorian mode by using D as the pitch centre without changing the pitches used (D–E–F–G–A–B–C), and the whole scale and its modes can be transposed to a higher or lower pitch level (F major, E♭ major, etc.). The Chinese system concentrates in a similar way on a seven-tone scale but with a five-tone core (*wu sheng*) plus two changing (*bian*) tones, as shown in notation III.

The notes of a scale (a set of intervals not tied to specific pitches) are often indicated in Western music with syllables such as "do re mi." The Chinese equivalent terms for notes in their classical scale are given in notation III.

As in the Western system, modes can be constructed in Chinese music, and the scale can be transposed. From these comments it can be seen that the mythical emperor Huangdi seems to have founded a very thorough system indeed. Throughout the Qin (221–207 BCE) and Han (206 BCE–220 CE) dynasties imperial systems were tuned and retuned to meet imperial and heavenly needs. As noted above, theoretical sophistications and experimentations continue on to the present day. How far back they may go in time is unknown, but in the late 20th century there were discovered stone chimes from the 2nd millennium BCE that imply by their tunings that the Chinese classical tone system tradition may actually be as ancient as the legends claim. It is a pity that the music was not equally durable.

EXTRAMUSICAL ASSOCIATIONS

Returning to the extramusical aspects of the Chinese system, one finds that the five fundamental tones are sometimes connected with the five directions or the five elements, while the 12 tones are connected by some writers with the months of the year, hours of the day, or phases of the moon. The 12 tones also can be found placed in two sets of 6 on imperial panpipes (*paixiao*) in keeping with the female-male (yin-yang) principle of Chinese metaphysics. Their placement is based on the generation of the pitches of each pipe by its being either four-thirds larger or two-thirds smaller than the previous one, the smaller ones being female.

CLASSIFICATION OF INSTRUMENTS

The Chinese talent for musical organization was by no means limited to pitches. Another important ancient system called the eight sounds (*ba yin*) was used to classify the many kinds of instruments used in imperial orchestras. This system was based upon the material used in the construction of the instruments, the eight being stone, earth (pottery), bamboo, metal, skin, silk, wood, and gourd. The sonorous stones, ocarinas, and flutes mentioned earlier are examples from the first three categories. The bells are obvious metal examples. Another ancient member of the metal category is a large bronze drum (*tonggu*), which is of special

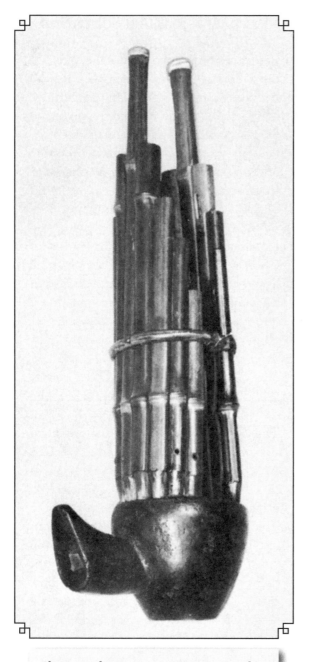

Sheng; *in the Horniman Museum, London.* Courtesy of the Horniman Museum, London; photograph, J.R. Freeman & Co. Ltd.

interest because of the widespread distribution of archaeological examples of it throughout Southeast Asia. Equally intriguing are the designs and sounds of the bronze head of the drum as well as the frequent statues of frogs around the rim of the head. Han dynasty military expeditions to the south report that bronze drums among southern peoples represented the spirit of rain and water and rumbled like bullfrogs. The possession of such bronze drums or, later, gongs was, and still is, prestigious among tribal groups in Southeast Asia.

Stringed instruments of ancient China belong to the silk class because their strings were never gut or metal but twisted silk. Drums are skin instruments, whereas percussive clappers are wood. One of the most enjoyable members of the wooden family is the *yu*, a model of a crouching tiger with a serrated ridge or set of slats along its back that were scratched by a bamboo whisk in a manner recalling the various scratched gourds of Latin American bands. The Chinese category of gourd is reserved for one of the most fascinating of the ancient instruments, the *sheng* mouth organ. Seventeen bamboo pipes are set in a gourd or sometimes in a wooden wind chest. Each pipe has a free metal reed at the end encased in the wind chest. Blowing through a mouth tube into the wind chest and closing a hole in a pipe with a finger will cause the reed to sound, and melodies or chord structures may be played. Many variants of this instrumental principle can be found in Southeast

SHENG

Chinese free reed wind instrument consisting of usually 17 bamboo pipes set in a small wind-chest into which a musician blows through a mouthpiece. Each pipe has a free reed, made of metal (or formerly of bamboo or reed), that vibrates to produce sound when a finger hole on the pipe is covered. The acoustical length of each pipe is determined by a slot in the back of the pipe. The pipes, which are of five different lengths, are arranged in two triangular shapes to symbolize the folded wings of a phoenix bird. In addition to the traditional 13-, 14-, and 17-pipe sets, there are 21- and 24-pipe sets as well as a 36-pipe set based on the chromatic scale, with all 12 semitones. Other modern variants also exist. Images of sheng-like instruments exist from 1100 BCE, and actual instruments survive from the Han dynasty (206 BCE–220 CE).

Several instruments were derived from the sheng, including the Japanese sho and the Korean saenghwang. The Chinese instrument plays melodies with occasional fourth or fifth harmonies (e.g., F or G above C), whereas the Japanese sho normally plays 11-note chords, a tradition that may have emerged from a misinterpretation of ancient court notations. Contemporary Chinese ensembles include the larger sheng, which is capable of playing Western chords. Instruments similar to the sheng are found throughout Southeast Asia, notably the khaen of Laos and parts of Thailand and Vietnam. A sheng taken to Russia in the 1770s helped to stimulate the invention of European instruments using free reeds—including the accordion, concertina, harmonium, and harmonica.

Asia, and it is not possible to know with assurance where this wind instrument first appeared. Western imitations of its sound are found in the reed organ and, later, in the harmonica and the accordion.

HAN DYNASTY: MUSICAL EVENTS AND FOREIGN INFLUENCES

The extensive work in theory and classification in ancient times implies that there must have been an equally large amount of performance practice. Modern information on all these elements of music has suffered because of the destruction of many books and musical instruments under the order of Shihuangdi, emperor of the Qin dynasty. Yet there are several survivals from the Han dynasty that do give some insight into how the musical events took place. In the court and the Confucian temples there were two basic musical divisions: banquet music (*yanyue*) and ritual music (*yayue*). Dances in the Confucian rituals were divided into military (*wuwu*) and civil (*wenwu*) forms. The ensembles of musicians and dancers could be quite large, and ancient listings of their content were often printed in formation patterns in a manner analogous in principle to those of football marching bands in the United States today. Rubbings from Han tomb tiles show more informal and apparently very lively music and dance presentations at social affairs. The early Chinese character for dance (*wu*) implies movement by the body more than by the feet. The folk sources of many of the songs from the *Shijing* and later books show that courtly musical life was not without its gayer and more personal and secular moments. The stringed instruments, notably the seven-stringed *qin* zither, apparently were popular as vehicles for solo music.

The Han dynasty empire expanded and at the same time built walls between its national core and western Asia. But these actions were paralleled by an increasing flow of foreign ideas and materials. Buddhism entered from India to China in the 1st century CE, whereas booty, goods, and ideas came from Central Asian Gandharan, Yuazhi, and Iranian cultures along the various desert trade routes via the cities of Hotan (Khotan) to the south (3rd through 5th century), Kucha (Kuqa) in the centre (4th through 8th century), and Turfan (Turpan) to the north (5th through 9th century). Desert ruins and Buddhist caves from this period and later reveal a host of new musical ensembles and solo instruments. Two stringed instruments of particular interest are the angle harp (*konghu*) and the pear-shaped plucked lute (*pipa*). The harp can be traced back across Central Asia to the ancient bas-reliefs of Assyria. The lute also seems to have West Asian ancestors but is a more "contemporary" instrument. Variants of this instrument have continued to enter or be redesigned in China down to the present day. A delightful symbol of the long-term musical and commercial value of such a plucked lute is found on a 10th-century clay statue of a caravan Bactrian camel with two different styles of *pipa* tied to the saddle post on top of the rest of the cargo.

New percussion instruments are evident in the celestial orchestras seen in Buddhist iconography. One apparent accommodation between old Chinese and West Asian tradition is the *fangxiang*, a set of 16 iron slabs suspended in a wooden frame in the manner of the old sets of tuned stones. Knobless gongs related to the present-day Chinese *luo* seem to have entered the Chinese musical scene before the 6th century from South Asia, while the cymbals (*bo*) may have come earlier from India via Central Asian groups. One of the most sonorous Buddhist additions was a bronze bell in the form of a basin (*qing*) that, when placed rim up on a cushion and struck on the rim, produces a tone of amazing richness and duration. Among the varied new instruments pictured in heavenly ensembles, one can still find occasional "old-time" instruments such as a set of narrow wooden clappers (*chongdu*) tied together on one end like ancient wooden books. The clappers were sounded by compressing them quickly between the hands. Variants of this Zhou dynasty instrument are still heard in Japan and Korea, as well as in China.

Not all the new influences in China came via religious or trade activities. During the Six Dynasties period (220–589 CE) China was rent by internal strife and border wars. The constant confrontations with the Tatars of the north caused an increased interest in the musical signals of the enemy via drums, trumpets, and double reeds. Although related instruments were equally evident to the south and west, there can be little doubt that the creation of cavalry bands with double kettledrums are direct imitations of the musical prowess of the horseback terrorists against whom the walls of China were built. With great effort and much blood, China gradually reunified under the Sui dynasty (581–618), and older courtly music and the latest musical fads were consolidated.

TANG DYNASTY

The few centuries of Tang dynasty existence (618–907) are supersaturated with brilliant imperial growth and cultural flourishing as well as military and natural disasters. Such a rich loam of good and bad nourished one of the most fascinating eras of music history in the world.

THRIVING OF FOREIGN STYLES

The more formal imperial ceremonies revitalized the ancient orchestras of bells, stone chimes, flutes, drums, and zithers, plus large bands of courtly dancers. In reality, imperial power was based perhaps less on the Mandate of Heaven than on the "liberation" of neighbouring countries, a development of more thorough tax systems and more and more trade cities and harbours. Into all these power sources flowed foreign goods and foreign ideas. Persians, Arabs, Indians, and Malayans were found in the foreign quarters of port towns, while every trade caravan brought in masses of new faces and modes of living. Perhaps it is not surprising that an 8th-century poet, Yuan Zhen, should lament about air pollution created by western horsemen, about the ladies who studied western fashions and makeup, and about the entertainers who devoted themselves to only "western" music. (One must remember that the term "western" in Yuan's work refers to the land west of the Great Wall.)

There was hardly a tavern in the capital of Chang'an (now Xi'an, Shaanxi province) that could compete without the aid of a western dancing or singing girl with an accompanying set of foreign musicians. Popular tunes of the period included "South India" and "Watching the Moon in Brahman Land," while beautiful, exotic dancing boys or girls were ever the rage. One set of girls from Sogdiana (centred in modern Uzbekistan) won the support of the emperor Xuanzong (712–756) because they were costumed in crimson robes, green pants, and red deerskin boots and twirled on top of balls. Other girls from the area today called Tashkent inspired a poet of the 9th century, Bai Juyi, with their dance, which began with their emergence from artificial lotuses and ended with the pulling down of their blouses to show their shoulders, a style not unfamiliar to old Western burlesque connoisseurs. A study of the lithe bodies and flying sleeves on Tang clay dancing figurines is an even more compelling proof of the style of the era. In such a context one can understand how eventually an additional character was added sometimes to the word for dance to indicate the movement of the legs as well as of the body.

In addition to all the commercial musical enterprises of the Tang dynasty period, there was another equally extensive system under government supervision. The Tang emperor Xuanzong seemed particularly keen on music and took full advantage of the various musical "tributes" or "captives" sent to him by all the nations of Asia. This plethora of sounds was further enriched by the special area in Chang'an called the Pear Garden (Liyuan), in which hundreds of additional musicians and dancers were trained and in which the emperor himself was most active. Such trainees were often female. They followed in an earlier tradition of court girls (*gongnü*) whose basic duties were to entertain distinguished guests.

The mass of different foreign musical styles in the capital was too much for the government musical bureaucracy. A distinction already had been made between court music (*yayue*) and common music (*suyue*); but Tang nomenclature added a third kind—foreign music (*huyue*). Eventually officials organized imperial music into the 10 kinds of systems (*shibu ji*). Of these categories, one represented

instrumentalists from Samarkand, whereas another group came from farther west in Bukhara (in modern Uzbekistan). Kashgar, at the mountain pass between the east and west, sent yet a different group. Musical ensembles also were presented to the emperor from the eastern Turkistan trade centres of Kucha and Turfan. India and two recently defeated kingdoms of Korea provided still other musicians. Chinese and Kucha music were blended by different musicians. One group was supposed to maintain the old styles of Chinese folk music, and there had to be one special group for the performance of formal Chinese court music. These 10 types by no means completed the picture, for nearly every Asian culture took its chance at musical goodwill in Chang'an. Nothing from farther west appears in Tang China, for culture hardly existed in Europe at that time. Nevertheless, one can sense in Tang musical culture an internationalism not matched until the mass communications of the mid-20th century provided radio and phonograph owners with the delights of a similarly exotic and extensive choice.

COURTLY MUSIC

The only music that can be discussed in a survey of a repertoire so large is the more official courtly music. Ritual presentations are generally divided into two types: so-called standing music, performed without strings and apparently in the courtyard; and sitting music, for a full ensemble played inside a palace. There are lists of the names of some pieces in these categories with their author- ship usually credited to the emperor or empress of the time. For example, "The Battle Line Smashing Song" was said to be by the Tang emperor Taizong (626–649). The accompanying dance is listed for 120 performers with spears and armour. A similarly grandiose piece is "Music of Grand Victory" credited to the next Tang emperor, Gaozong (649–683). Wu Hou (d. 705) is said to have written "The Imperial Birthday Music," in which the dancers form out the characters mean- ing "Long Live the Emperor" in the best modern marching-band tradition. Music inside the palace includes a concert ver- sion of "The Battle Line Smashing Song," with only four dancers, "A Banquet Song," and a piece supposedly composed by the empress Wu Hou in honour of her pet par- rot, who frequently called out "Long Live Her Majesty." Those familiar with music in the courts of Henry VIII and Louis XIV or with the songs always ending in praise of Queen Elizabeth I may recognize the cultural context of such music.

Later-dynasty copies of Tang paint- ings show ladies entertaining the emperor with ensembles of strings, winds, and percussion; and many of the choreographic plans of the larger pieces are also available in books. According to some sources, court orchestra pieces began with a prelude in free rhythm that set the mood and mode of the piece and introduced the instruments. This was followed by a slow section in a steady

beat, and the piece ended in a faster tempo. Documents also tell much about the instrumentation and the colour and design of each costume of the musicians and dancers. No orchestral scores are to be found, however. One solo piece for *qin* survives, and 28 ritual melodies for *pipa* were discovered in the hidden library of the Buddhist caves of Dunhuang (Caves of the Thousand Buddhas), but the grand musical traditions of Tang remain frus- tratingly elusive. Major clues to their actual sounds will be found in marginal survivals of such music. The original tra- ditions waned with the decline of Tang good fortune, and the conflicts of the Five Dynasties and Ten Kingdoms period (907–960) brought the international period to an end.

SONG AND YUAN DYNASTIES

Despite the chaos of kingdoms in the 10th century, or perhaps because of it, cultural traditions solidified, so that by the Song dynasty (960–1279) one can speak of a national rather than an inter- national cultural mood. Many of the short-lived usurpers of regional govern- ments were of "barbarian" (i.e., Turkic) origin, but their general cultural efforts were to appear Chinese rather than to import further foreign fads.

CONSOLIDATION OF EARLIER TRENDS

One significant foreign musical addi- tion of the period was from the northern

Mongols in the form of a two-stringed fiddle, or bowed lute—the "foreign lute" (*huqin*). It became an important feature of the plebian theatre and teahouse world, which grew stronger and larger as more musicians and dancers were dropped from government payrolls. With the establishment of the Song court, Confucian ceremonies and similar "old-fashioned" musical events were revived; but imperial contributions to music of the period were primarily in the creation of gigantic historical or encyclopaedic works. For example, the official *Song shi* (1345; "Song History") contained 496 chapters, of which 17 deal directly with music, and musical events and people appear throughout the entire work. The *Yuhai* encyclopaedia (c. 1267; "Sea of Jade") has 200 chapters, with 10 on music. It is interesting that the *lü* pipes are discussed separately under the topic of measurements. Manuals on how to play the seven-stringed *qin* zither also survive, as well as rare music collections such as *Songs of Whitestone, the Daoist,* based on the poems and songs of Jiang Gui (1155–1221) and first printed in 1202. Many Song poets continued to use the five- and seven-syllable-line *shi* form perfected by Tang writers, which was believed to have been chanted to tunes strictly adhering to the word tones of the Chinese language. The singing girls (*jiguan*) of the teahouses and brothels and the general growth of urban, mercantile life inspired the creation of *ci* poems, which were free of word-tone restrictions,

filled with colloquial phrases, and capable of freewheeling musical settings. A major source for music based on both the old and new forms is found in the rising world of public theatre.

MUSIC THEATRE

Chinese drama can be noted as far back as the Zhou dynasty, but it was really the Tang period Pear Garden school that quite literally set the stage for Chinese opera. Regional music-drama flourished throughout the Song empire, but the two major forms were the southern drama (*nanqu* or *nanxi*) and the northern drama (*zaju* or *beiqu*). The *ci* poetical form was popular in both, although the southern style was held to be softer, with its emphasis on five-tone scales and flute and percussion accompaniments. The northern style is said to have preferred the seven-toned scale, to have used more strings, and in general to have been bolder in spirit. According to period writers, each of the four acts of a northern drama was set in a specific mode in which different tunes were used, interspersed with dialogue. The southern style was more lyrical.

The Mongols under Genghis Khan and later Kublai Khan finally succeeded in invading China, and the foreign Yuan dynasty (1206–1368) was founded. The two styles of drama noted above continued and intermixed under Yuan drama (*Yuanqu*), while the basic poetical form became *sanqu*, popular songs of even freer style. On stage there appeared standard songs for specific situations or emotions that could be used in any opera, thus making it easier to communicate a story to mass audiences who may have spoken in many different dialects. Additional appeals to the general public were made by bringing onto the stage several forms of dancing and acrobatics, events that had been, along with several forms of puppet theatre, such gay parts of Chinese city life during the Song dynasty.

MING AND QING DYNASTIES

Internal Mongol struggles, natural disasters, and peasant revolts permitted the return of Chinese rule and the founding of the Ming dynasty (1368–1644). It in turn gave way to Manchu invasions from the north under which the last dynasty, the Qing (1644–1911/12), was formed. Although there is much history and much blood involved in all such changes, one can view the music of these eras together under their two most active styles—theatre music and instrumental pieces.

FORMS OF THE 16TH–18TH CENTURIES

The flourishing of regional music-drama has continued throughout the centuries from the Song dynasty until the present day. Musically they vary greatly in their instrumentation and particularly in their voice qualities. However, all tend to follow a tradition of using either standard complete pieces (*lianqu*) or stereotyped melodic styles (*banqiang*) in every opera. The complete-piece approach of Yuan drama survives today primarily in a 16th-century form called *kunqu*.

Nurtured in a more aristocratic form of theatre, the music of *kunqu* was less bombastic than that of the popular theatre. The major instruments were the horizontal flute (*dizi*) and the notched vertical flute (*xiao*). The flutes often produce a special mottled tone by the presence of one hole that is covered by thin rice paper that buzzes quietly as one plays. The *sheng* mouth organ and the *pipa* plucked lute could also be found in *kunqu*, along with a single free-reed pipe, *guan*. The term *guan* usually stands for one of several forms of double-reed woodwinds with cylindrical bore and no bell. Survivors of its ancient forms are found in Korean and Japanese court music. Variants of the single-reed *guan* are found throughout Southeast Asia, where it is equally appreciated for its mellow, clarinet-like tone. A plebian instrument found in some *kunqu* is the three-stringed plucked lute (*sanxian*) with a snakeskin soundboard. Plucked with a bone pick, it enjoys great popularity in folk music as well as theatre music, and it developed in two sizes, the shorter one prevalent in the south and the longer one in the north. The shorter form is of particular historical interest, for it was imported into the Ryukyu Islands as the *jamisen* and from there moved to Japan, where it evolved into a samisen.

The vocal style of *kunqu* matched the soft accompaniment and was usually performed by a male singing falsetto. Another style of opera from the same period, *yiyang qiang*, seemed more appealing to the general public and is noteworthy for its use at some point in its development of a chorus (*bangqiang*) as well as of soloists. In addition, passages in colloquial speech were often interpolated between lines of classical poetry in order to explain them. Such lines were often sung. Still another Ming music-drama genre of considerable influence in the myriad regional forms is the clapper opera (*bangzi qiang*). In addition to the rhythmic importance of the clappers, the instrumental accompaniment of this form is noted for its emphasis on strings, the principal form being the moon guitar (*yueqin*), a plucked lute with a large, round wooden body and four strings in double courses. An interesting addition to this instrument is the presence of a thin strip of metal tied at both ends inside the body to give the instrument a richer tone. Among the endless variants of style and accompaniments in Chinese regional opera, one must add the sounds of the extremely large flat gongs heard in the southwest and the *yangqin* (western zither), particularly popular in Cantonese music. The latter is often called a butterfly harp, though it is neither a harp nor a butterfly but a hammered dulcimer derived from a Middle Eastern instrument (*sant̲ūr*) brought into China in the 18th century. Each of the myriad types of regional opera flourishing in China

developed vocal styles and orchestrations that helped make it distinctive. With informed practice, listeners can still distinguish regional vocal styles, which vary from low, sensual sounds to high and nasal falsettos. To understand the enduring appeal of Chinese musical theatre, it is best to turn to the primary music-drama form since the 18th century, *jingxi* or *jingju*.

JINGXI

Credit for the beginning of *jingxi* is given to actors from Anhui appearing in Beijing (then called Peking) in the 1790s. However, *jingxi* really combines elements from many different earlier forms and, like Western grand opera, can be considered to be a 19th-century product. In addition to all the instruments mentioned above, many others may be found.

The most common melodic instrument for opera is some form of fiddle, or bowed lute (*huqin*). It comes in several different forms, such as the *jinghu* and *erhu*. Although the shape of the body may be different, all traditional Chinese fiddles exhibit certain specific structural characteristics. The small body has a skin or wooden soundboard and an open back. The two strings pass over a bridge and then are suspended above a pole to the pegs, which are inserted from the rear of the scroll (not from the sides as on a Western violin). Such a system places one string above the other rather than parallel to it (as on a banjo or a *pipa*). Because of this, the bow passes between the strings, playing one string by pressing down and the other by pulling up. The fingerings of tunes are done by sideways pressure, along the strings; they are too far from the pole for it to serve as a fingerboard, which, because of the vertical stringing, would be a nuisance in any case. It is this unique manner of fiddle construction that helps one determine the source of many of the bowed lutes of Southeast Asia.

Barrel drums with tacked heads (*gu*) and a double reed with a conical bore and bell (*suona*) are used in military scenes, along with cymbals (*bo*) and large flat gongs. The most common percussion instruments are a small flat gong (*luo*), a drum (*bangu*), and clappers (*paiban*). The small gong is some 8 inches (20 cm) in diameter; the face is slightly curved except for a flat centre spot. It is designed in this manner in order that the tone and pitch of the gong will rise quickly each time it is hit. This "sliding" gong effect is characteristic of the Beijing sound. The *bangu* or *danbi gu* is equally unique in construction. The skin is stretched over a set of wooden wedges strapped in a circle with only a small spot in the middle completely hollow. This allows the performer to produce a very dry, sharp sound. Such a tone is practical as well as aesthetic, for the *bangu* player is often the leader of the ensemble, and his signals are essential to the coordination of the performance. The drum player frequently plays the clapper as well, holding the clapper in his left hand while playing the drum with a narrow bamboo stick held in his right hand.

In Chinese music, as in all East Asian music, one must remember that harmony and harmonic progression are not parts of traditional music. The functions of harmony—such as underlining expression, providing sonic contrast, and creating a sense of forward motion—are handled with equal efficiency by rhythm in East Asia, although the methods and sounds are very different. In both traditions, the choices are not arbitrary, and with cultural exposure one comes to recognize the musical intention, even though it is not necessary to know precisely what chord or what rhythm pattern produces an appropriate musical effect. For example, very few listeners to Western music know that a doubly diminished chord (C–E♭–G♭–A) played tremolo means danger, although all would recognize the danger signal by ear. By the same token, a *jingxi* fan hearing the large gong played alone in the rhythm shown in notation IV would know that the situation is a similar moment of confusion but probably would not know that the pattern is named the scattering hammer (*luanjue*). Pattern names are for specialists, but pattern sounds and "meanings" are for attuned listeners. For the moment, attention will be given to the melodic side of *jingxi*.

Like any theatrical music, the tunes of *jingxi* must conform to the text structure and the dramatic situation. In the latter case, one finds that a majority of *jingxi* aria texts are based on series of couplets of 7 or 10 syllables each. Although there may be several verses set in strophic form (i.e., music repeated for each strophe, or stanza), part of the musical tension is maintained by the interjection of comments or short dialogue between the two lines of each verse. These leave the listener waiting for the completion of the line. The tune aids in this forward motion and tension by playing what could be considered an incomplete melodic cadence (point of resolution) at the end of line one, which is brought to a final resolution at the end of the second line. From a dramaturgical standpoint, the arias of *jingxi* can be categorized into different types whose style is recognizable in the same way that one can tell, without language ability, the mood of a love, farewell, or vengeance aria in Italian opera.

Jingxi melodies themselves tend to fall into two prototypes called *xipi* and *erhuang*. Within each of these general types there are several well-known tunes, but the word *prototype* has been used to define them, as each opera and each situation is capable of varying the basic melody greatly. The two basic identifying factors are the mode of the melody and the rhythmic style of the accompanying percussion section. In general, serious and lyrical texts are performed to an *erhuang* melody and *xipi* tunes appear in brighter moments, though in such a large genre there are

many other possibilities. Notation V, below, contains the string introductions to examples in the two basic types. They are transposed to the pitches of notation II (see page 238 for notation II) for the sake of comparison. In actual performance the fiddle may be tuned lower for *erhuang* melodies. How do the tunes differ? Both emphasize the pentatonic core and have a "changing" tone B (its pitch is actually between the Western B and

Bb), but their modes differ. *Xipi* are said to emphasize (in the context of the transposition shown) E and A, and *erhuang* G and C. *Xipi* melodies are often more disjunct. Although both examples are set at a standard tempo (*yuanban*), the *erhuang* is faster and its rhythm denser, as it is a male aria, while the *xipi* is female and slower. Both pieces could be played at a slower (*manban*) or faster (*kuaiban*) tempo, however, or could be accompanied by other special rhythms. Such choices often cause changes in the melody itself. In general, the choice of both tune and rhythm style is guided by the text and the character. In most arias each sentence is separated by an instrumental interlude.

Jingxi is also characterized by colourful costumes and striking character-identifying makeup as well as acrobatic combats and dances. These conventions of Chinese opera are similar to those of 18th-century European traditions, though the sounds are certainly quite different. The need to communicate in music or in theatre requires the repeated use of aural and visual conventions if an audience is to understand and be moved by the event.

An actor performs jingxi. Paula Bronstein/Getty Images

OTHER VOCAL AND INSTRUMENTAL GENRES

The emphasis here has been on opera because it is best known, but there are many other popular forms from the Ming and Qing periods. One is storytelling (*shuoshu*). This tradition, which is as old as humankind and is noted in China's earliest books, continues in China in a purely narrative form, in a sung style, and in a mixture of the two. Until the advent of television and government arts control, there were narrators who recounted traditional stories in nightly or weekly segments. Their idiom was like that of surviving tellers of shorter stories. The text is usually in rhyme and is spoken in rhythm. Chinese storytellers may perform unaccompanied, but generally at least a clapper rhythm is present. One string instrument, such as a three-string *sanxian* or four-string *pipa* lute, is also common. Songs accompanied by a drum (*dagu*) are the best known. The narrator not only relates the story but usually plays the clappers and a drum as well. Since the text is the core of the genre, standard melodies are used. Additional accompaniment may be provided by a string ensemble like that of opera.

Musically, the various shadow- and hand-puppet plays also are similar to the opera tradition except that, as in Southeast Asian puppetry, a manipulator must often be the singer-narrator as well.

These genres, like many regional opera forms, are often performed on temporary street stages and are eclectically creative. Saxophones and other Western instruments may combine with the ubiquitous Chinese fiddles and percussion instruments. Topical popular tunes and well-known Western music can appear among opera melodies as the drama unfolds. Recordings mix with live music so that, for example, a battle scene may be accompanied by Chinese percussion sounds, firecrackers, and a recording of Nikolay Rimsky-Korsakov's "The Flight of the Bumble Bee."

Leaving the many forms of vocal and theatrical music, it is appropriate to turn briefly to the instrumental. The 25-stringed *se* zither, with movable bridges, and the seven-stringed *qin*, with permanent upper and lower bridges (like a piano), were well known for solo music in ancient times. During the last dynasty, collections of *qin* music and instruction books flourished as part of certain Neo-Confucian revivals. Many musical notations were developed, perhaps the most interesting variety for the *qin* being one in which Chinese characters were artificially constructed by combining symbols for the notes with indications of fingering technique, such as upstrokes, downstrokes, or harmonics. Although most of the music was based on vocal pieces or evoked some scene, there were several examples of variation forms that had an important influence on Korean and Japanese forms that followed. The *pipa* likewise developed an extensive repertoire of solo pieces, many of them quite virtuosic and pictorial. For example, anyone hearing a *pipa* battle piece needs to know very little Chinese to recognize the musical interpretations of the action. Since the mid-20th century there has been a considerable revival of solo literature for the *zheng*, a zither with 16 strings and movable bridges whose popularity spreads as far south as Vietnam. The strings are apparently influenced by the Middle Eastern dulcimer mentioned above (*yangqin*), for they are metal.

Chamber music exists in many styles, functions, and locations. Some of it can be considered folk music played by farmers or working people for festivals or private entertainment, as in the American bluegrass tradition. Music of this type can still be heard at weddings or funerals in Chinese communities all over the world. During the Ming and Qing periods, small ensembles of courtiers or professional musicians could be found at palaces, but the major sources for this kind of chamber music were in the world of the musically inclined businessman or trader. Because of this, certain regional forms of chamber music such as Amoy (Xiamen) "southern pipe" and Shantung (Shandong) music survive in such locations as Taiwan, Manila, Singapore, and San Francisco. In this context it is noteworthy that even during Japan's isolation period from the 17th to the 19th century, Chinese vocal and chamber music, known in Japanese as *minshingaku* (Ming and Qing music), was played in Nagasaki, the only open port in Japan. Examples of such dispersed regional music are of great value

in the study of the oral history of Ming and Qing music and of the distribution and development of various musical instruments. Much of the repertoire of such stylistic groups is derived from theatre music, but there are many examples that may imply the sounds of older lost traditions. There are a variety of notation systems, particularly for the solo music. The one most commonly used in tune books of the last dynasties is *gong che*, which indicates notes in a scale as shown in notation VI.

This system is still popularly used, although mainland sources prefer the number system shown in the first line of notation VII.

It is based on the 19th-century French *chevé* system (which used numerals 1–7 for the notes of the scale) and, unlike other Chinese notations, shows rhythm by the use of dots and beams borrowed from Western 8th and 16th notes. Percussion accompaniments also can be found in a similar style, as can larger ensemble scores, but both are more characteristic of 20th-century China.

PERIOD OF THE REPUBLIC OF CHINA AND THE SINO-JAPANESE WAR

Under the influence of missionary and modernization movements, many musical experimentations occurred in the last dynasty, but these were greatly increased by the rise of the first republic in 1911 and the establishment of communist rule in 1949. During the period of the republic and of the Japanese war, a plethora of new songs were created in "modern" style, the most famous being shown in notation XI.

The piece, *March of the Volunteers,* was written in 1934 by Nie Er to text by the modern Chinese playwright Tian Han as a patriotic march and was adopted as the national anthem in 1949. It is an excellent example of a mixture of new and traditional Chinese music. The first phrase implies a major mode with its use of F#. However, after that point the entire piece is Chinese pentatonic. The first phrase also leads one to expect symmetrical four-bar phrases, but the tune quickly takes a more flexible Chinese course. Chinese and Western composers continued to try out bits of each other's traditions with only occasional success, and individual Chinese artists have become famous for their performance on Western instruments. Chinese instruments in turn have been subjected to many modernizations, such as the building of a family of *erhu* fiddles by the creation of bass and alto versions. In conjunction with this movement there was the appearance of concerti for such instruments accompanied by a mixed Western and Chinese orchestra.

COMMUNIST PERIOD

As was noted earlier, many completely traditional forms continued, particularly in foreign Chinese communities. The special point of interest since 1949, however, is the application of Marxist doctrine to the musical scene of China. The first obvious area of change was in the ever popular forms of regional and *jingxi*. Although the appeal of traditional tales of emperors, princesses, or mythological characters could not be suppressed, the emphasis of all new operas was on workers, peasants, soldiers, and socialism. Thus, *Sanguo zhi yanyi* ("Romance of the Three Kingdoms") or *Kongcheng ji* ("The Ruse of an Empty City") tend to be replaced by *Qixi Baihutuan* ("Raid on the White Tiger Regiment") or *Honghu chiwei dui* ("Red Guards of Hong Lake"). Aria topics also vary, such as "Looking Forward to the Liberation of the Working People of the World" or "Socialism Is Good."

As part of the encouragement of people's music, the national government emphasized regional folk music. Provincial and national research institutes were created to collect and study such music, and folk songs were incorporated into primary as well as advanced and Western music education. In general, folk music was "reconstructed" away from its former individualistic nature into collectives of choruses or folk orchestras. The topics of such regional songs also were reconstructed so that they reflected the new socialist life. The most famous new folk song from Shaanxi province is "Red Is the East," while the Miao people (called Hmong in Southeast Asia) were credited with "Sing in Praise of Chairman Mao." During the Maoist period, more than 50 minority groups and provincial Chinese ensembles had at least one song directly in praise of Chairman Mao, while other songs dealt with local industries and accomplishments. Such songs are sometimes performed in regional style with traditional accompaniments, although they may often be found arranged Western-style for use in the public schools of the nation. This effort, in addition to the number of recordings

In 1967, these members of the China Popular Liberation Army's choir performed songs under a portrait of Chairman Mao Zedong. AFP/Getty Images

available, made it possible for a Chinese citizen to become aware, perhaps for the first time in history, of the great variety of local music traditions, even though such music appeared in Marxist reconstructions. Marxist defense of this changed folk music was that music of a given period must reflect the views and aspirations of the masses (as understood by the government) and must be based on idioms of the people. Composers of concert music produced many folk orchestra compositions along with symphony, piano, and military band music based on the basic Marxist principle of Socialist Realism. When dealing with traditional instruments and vocal styles, the composers sometimes created extremely original and interesting pieces despite the general conservatism of government aesthetics policies. Vocal and choral music were preferred because of their ability to communicate specific national goals more efficiently than, for example, *The Sacred War Symphony*.

It must be remembered that music exists in a cultural context and that it has never remained static since the world began. In the early 21st century, music of all periods from every society was available to those with sufficient mass communication sources. Exchanges were made between Western and Chinese ensembles and musicians, and audiocassettes and radio broadcasts were not easily silenced. Euro-American music is part of China's urban culture, and new socialist messages can be heard in Western-style popular music settings. At the same time, tentative efforts have been made to use contemporary Western idioms in Chinese concert music. It does seem unlikely that the tuning of the *lü* pipes for rulers will ever be a major concern of Chinese musicians again, but the ability of China to preserve so many historical facts, materials, and idioms along with modern changes is sufficient to keep the musical world in awe for some centuries to come.

CHAPTER 9

CHINESE PERFORMING ARTS

The dance and theatre arts of China are tied from the earliest records to religious beliefs and customs. These date to 1000 BCE, and they describe magnificently costumed male and female shamans who sang and danced to musical accompaniment, drawing the heavenly spirits down to earth through their performance.

In China, as elsewhere in East Asia, the descendants of magico-religious performances can be seen in a variety of guises. Whether designed to pray for longevity or for a rich harvest or to ward off disease and evil, the rituals of impersonation of supernatural beings through masks and costumes and the repetition of rhythmic music and patterns of movement perform the function of linking humans to the spiritual world beyond. Hence, dance, music, and dramatic mimesis have been naturally fused through their religious function.

FORMATIVE PERIOD

Singing and dancing were performed at the Chinese court as early as the Zhou dynasty (1046–256 BCE). An anecdote describes a case of realistic acting in 402 BCE, when the chief jester of the court impersonated mannerisms of a recently deceased prime minister so faithfully that the emperor was convinced the prime minister had been restored to life. Drama was not yet developed, but large-scale masques (a short allegorical performance with masked players) in which dancing maidens and young boys dressed as gods and as various animals were popular. Sword-swallowing, fire-eating, juggling, acrobatics, ropewalking, tumbling, and similar stage tricks had come from the nomads of Central Asia by the 2nd century BCE and were called the "hundred entertainments." During the Han dynasty (206 BCE–220 CE) palace singers acted out warriors' stories, the forerunners of military plays in later Chinese opera, and by the time of the Three Kingdoms (220–280 CE) clay puppets were used to enact plays. These evolved into glove-and-stick puppets in later years.

TANG PERIOD

The emperor Xuanzong showed an interest in the performing arts, stimulating many advances in stage arts during the Tang dynasty (618–907). More than a thousand pupils were enrolled in music, dance, and acting schools. Spectacular masked court dances and masked Buddhist dance processions that soon were learned by Korean and Japanese performers were part of court life. Three types of play are recorded as having been popular. *Daimian* ("Mask") was about Prince Lan Ling, who covered his gentle face with a horrifying mask to frighten his enemies when he went into battle. Some suggest the colourful painted faces of warriors in contemporary Chinese opera derive from this play. *Tayaoniang* ("Stepping and Swaying Woman") was a farcical domestic play in which a sobbing wife bitterly complained about her brutal husband, who then appeared and, singing and dancing, abused his wife even more. The embezzling rascal hero of *Canqun* ("The Military Counselor") became a stock character in later plays. Thus, by Tang times, three basic types of drama were known: military play, domestic play, and satire of officialdom; and the establishment of role types had begun.

SONG PERIOD

The variety play (*zaqu*) was created by writers and performers in North China during the Bei (Northern) Song dynasty (960–1127). None of the scripts has survived, but something of their nature can be deduced from the 280 titles that remain and from court records. A play consisted of three parts: a low-comedy prologue, the main play in one or two scenes (consisting of extended sequences of songs, dancing, and perhaps dialogue), and a musical epilogue. Two, three, or four variety plays would be included in a program along with a sampling from the "hundred entertainments." In the following Nan (Southern) Song dynasty (1127–1279), northern writers continued composing plays of this general type under the name professional scripts (*yuanben*). None of the 691 professional scripts of which the titles are known has survived. Concurrently a new form of drama, southern drama (*nanxi*), emerged in the area around Hangzhou in southern China. Originally the creation of folk authors, it soon became an appealing and polished dramatic form. A southern drama tells a sustained story in colloquial language; flexible verses (*qu*) were set to popular music, making both music and poetry accessible to the ordinary spectator. Professional playwrights belonging to Hangzhou's writing societies (*shuhui*) wrote large numbers of southern dramas for local troupes. Of these, 113 titles and 3 play texts remain, preserved in an imperial collection of the 15th century. *Zhang Xie zhuangyuan* ("Top Graduate Zhang Xie") is probably the oldest of the three texts. It dramatizes the story of a young student who aspires to success, earns a degree and position, but callously turns his back on the girl who faithfully loves him.

Professional theatre districts became established during the Song dynasty. Major cities contained several districts (17 or more in Hangzhou), with as many as 50 playhouses in a district. Plays performed by puppets and mechanical dolls were extremely popular.

A legend attributes the origin of shadow theatre in China to an incident said to have occurred about 100 BCE: a priest, claiming to have brought to life the emperor's deceased wife, cast a woman's shadow on a white screen with a lamp. Others suggest the shadow play dates only from the Song period. In any case it was widely performed in Song times in the theatre districts. Puppets were made of translucent leather and coloured with transparent dye so they cast (like some Indian puppets) coloured shadows on the screen. In this respect they were unlike Javanese shadow puppets, which, though brilliantly coloured, are opaque and cast a largely colourless shadow. Shadow plays are still performed in China. Singers, dancers, actors, acrobats, and other performers were all employed at the professional theatres of the districts. Troupes were as small as possible for economic reasons, containing as few as five or six performers. They would tour the countryside if they had no work in the large cities, thus spreading urban styles of performing arts throughout the vast region of China.

YUAN PERIOD

Scholars turned to writing drama in the Yuan period (1206–1368) when they were removed from their positions in the government by China's new Mongol rulers, descendants of Genghis Khan. They developed the earlier northern style of *zaju* into a four-act dramatic form, in which songs (in the same mode in one act) alternated with dialogue. Singing was restricted to a single character in each play. Melodies were those of the Beijing region. The beauty of poetic lyrics was highly valued, while plot incidents were of lesser importance. About 200 plays survive, from the thousands of romances, religious plays, histories, and domestic, bandit, and lawsuit plays that were composed. *Xixiang ji* ("The Romance of the Western Chamber"), by Wang Shifu, is a 13th-century adaptation of an epic romance of the 12th century. The student Zhang and his beautiful sweetheart Ying Ying are models of the tender and melancholy young lovers who figure prominently in Chinese drama. Loyalty is the theme of the history play *Zhaoshi guer* ("The Orphan of Zhao"), written in the second half of the 13th century. In it the hero sacrifices his son to save the life of young Zhao so that Zhao can later avenge the death of his family (a situation developed into a major dramatic type in 18th-century popular Japanese drama). *Huilan ji* ("The Chalk Circle"), demonstrating the cleverness of a famous judge, Bao, is known in the West, having been adapted (1948) by the German playwright Bertolt Brecht in *The Caucasian Chalk Circle*. The class of bandit dramas are mostly based on the novel *Shuihu zhuan* ("The Water Margin") and its 108 bandit heroes, who live by their wits doing constant battle against corrupt and avaricious officials. The life of the common man is portrayed with considerable reality in Yuan drama, though within a highly formalized artistic frame. The lasting worth of Yuan plays is attested to by their constant adaptation to new musical styles over the years so that Yuan masterpieces make up a large part of the traditional opera repertory.

MING PERIOD

Plays of the Yuan period were widely popular with the people. When under the native Chinese Ming rulers (1368–1644) Mongol influence was eradicated, drama was, for a time, forbidden. Revived in the south, it increasingly became a literary form for a scholarly elite. A renowned

Ming play is *Pipa ji* ("Pipa [Lute] Song"), written in 42 affecting scenes, by the scholar Gao Ming in the 14th century. Its heroine, Zhao Wuniang, sets a perfect example of Confucian filial piety and marital fidelity, caring for her husband's parents until their tragic death and then playing the *pipa* to eke out a living as she patiently searches for her husband.

In the mid-16th century, a musician, Wei Liangfu, of Suzhou, devoted 10 years to creating the *kunqu* style of music, based on southern folk and popular melodies. At first it was used in short plays. Liang Chenyu, poet of the 16th century, adapted it to full-length opera in time, and it quickly spread to all parts of China, where it held the stage until the advent of *jingxi* (Peking [Beijing] opera), two centuries later. Important *kunqu* dramatists were Tang Xianzu (died 1616), famed for the delicate sensitivity of his poetry; Shen Jing (died 1610), who excelled in versification; and the creator of effective theatrical pieces, Li Yu (1611–85). A large-scale performance of *kunqu* for the Qing emperor Qianlong in 1784 marked its high point in Chinese culture. *Kunqu* had begun as a genuinely popular opera form; it was welcomed by audiences in Beijing in the 1600s, but within decades it had become a theatre of the literati, its poetic forms too esoteric and its music too refined for the common audience. In 1853 Suzhou was captured by the Taiping rebels, and thereafter *kunqu* was without a strong base of support and declined rapidly.

QING (MANCHU) PERIOD

Jingxi, or *jingju*, came into being over a period of several decades at the end of the 18th century, during the Qing dynasty (1644–1911/12). In the wake of the Taiping Rebellion, *kunqu* troupes resident in Beijing returned to their homes in the south. Their places in Beijing's theatres were quickly taken by opera troupes from the surrounding provinces, especially Anhui, Hubei, Gansu, and Shanxi. Anhui opera had been performed on the occasion of the emperor Qianlong's birthday in 1790. *Jingxi* was born of an amalgamation of elements from several sources: rhythmic beating of clappers to mark time for movements (from Shanxi and Gansu), singing in the two modes of *xipi* and *erhuang* (from Anhui), and increased use of acrobatics in fighting scenes. Undoubtedly, court support for *jingxi* from Cixi (1835–1908), the Empress Dowager, contributed to its rise, but it was also very widely patronized by local audiences. It became the custom to rehearse in public

A jingxi *troupe performing a scene from* Baishezhuan *("The White Snake"). © Wu Gang/ Liaison International*

teahouses, and in time these became regular performances providing troupes with much of their financial support.

Essentially, *jingxi* was a continuation of northern-style drama, while *kunqu* marked the culmination of southern-style drama. Musically they are very different: the former uses loud clappers and cymbals for scenes of action and the penetrating sound of fiddles accompanies singing; in the latter the flute is the major instrument, and strings and cymbals are absent. A limited number of melodies are repeated many times in *jingxi* (set to different lyrics), while in *kunqu* the melodic range is much wider. *Jingxi* lyrics are in colloquial language (they are often criticized as lacking in literary merit). Overall, the newer opera form is highly theatrical and vigorous, while the older form is restrained, gentle, and elegant. Some *jingxi* are Yuan plays or *kunqu* operas adapted to the new northern musical system. Many plays first staged as *jingxi* are dramatizations of the war novel *Sanguo zhi yanyi* ("Romance of the Three Kingdoms"), written in the 14th century by Lo Guanzhong. Mei Lanfang, the most famous performer of *jingxi* female roles in the 20th century, introduced a number of these highly active military plays into the repertoire. *Kunqu* dramas told a long and involved story in great detail, often in 40 or 50 consecutive scenes. It became the custom in *jingxi* to perform a bill of a number of acts or scenes from several plays, like a Western concert program.

Concurrent with the national forms of drama mentioned before, local opera is found in every area of China (the different forms have been estimated at 300). These operas are performed according to local musical styles and in regional languages. General characteristics of most forms of Chinese opera are similar, however. Action occurs on a stage bare of scenery except for a backdrop and sidepieces. A table and several chairs indicate a throne, wall, mountain, or other location. (More elaborate scenery is used in Guangzhou [Canton] and Shanghai, influenced by Western drama and motion pictures.) Actors enter through a door right and exit through a door left. Costumes, headgear, and makeup identify standard character types. Actors play a single role type as a rule: male (*sheng*), female (*dan*), painted-face warrior (*jing*), or clown (*chou*). Each role type can be subdivided into several role subtypes. Actors undergo seven years of training as children, during which time their appropriate role type is determined. Singing is essential for *sheng* and *dan* roles; minor actors and actors of clown roles must be skilled in acrobatics that enliven battle scenes. Singing is accompanied by a large number of conventionalized movements and gestures. For example, the long "flowing water" sleeves that are attached to the costumes of dignified characters can be manipulated in 107 movements. Pantomime is highly developed, and several scenes have become famous for being enacted without dialogue: in *Baishe zhuan* ("The White Snake") a boatman rows his lovely daughter across a swirling river; in *San zha gou* ("Where

Three Roads Meet") two men duel in the dark; in *Shi yu chuo* ("Picking Up the Jade Bracelet") a maiden threads an imaginary needle and sews. Symbolism is highly developed. Walking in a circle indicates a journey. Circling the stage while holding a horizontal whip suggests riding a horse. Riding in a carriage is represented by a stage assistant holding flags painted with a wheel design on either side of the actor. Four banners indicate an army. A black flag whisked across the stage means a storm, a light blue one a breeze or the ocean. Chinese opera is one of the most conventionalized forms of theatre in the world. It has been suggested that the poverty of troupes and the need to travel with few properties and little scenery led to the development of many of these conventions.

Confucian morality underlies traditional Chinese drama. Duty to parents and husband and loyalty to one's master and elder brother or sister were virtues inculcated in play after play. Spiritualism and magic powers, derived from Daoism, are themes of some dramas, but by and large Chinese drama is ethical rather than religious in direction. Plays were intended to uphold virtuous conduct and to point out the dire consequences of evil. The Western tragic view, which holds that the individual cannot understand or control the unseen forces of the universe, has no place in Chinese drama; the typical play concludes on a note of poetic justice with virtue rewarded and evil punished, thus showing the proper way of human conduct in a social world.

TWENTIETH AND 21ST CENTURIES

With the establishment of the Republic of China in 1912, court support for *jingxi* by the Manchu dynasty ended. Troupes, however, continued to perform for private patrons and in public at teahouses and in theatres. Following the liberal ideals of the time, attempts were made to write in colloquial language (rather than in classical Chinese, as previously), and old plays considered undemocratic were dropped from the repertoire. A school for *jingxi* acting, modeled on Western pedagogical methods, was established in 1930, women being admitted for the first time in three centuries. The basic style of opera remained unchanged, however.

Western spoken drama (*huaju*) was first introduced by Chinese students who had studied in Japan and there learned of Western plays. In 1907 a Chinese adaptation of *Uncle Tom's Cabin* was successfully staged in Shanghai by students, marking the beginning of a proliferation of amateur study groups devoted to reading and staging Western plays. Originally aimed at only a small group of Western-educated intelligentsia, spoken drama's appeal was broadened to the middle class by the China Traveling Dramatic Troupe, which toured many cities from its home in Shanghai. In 1936 it performed *Leiyu* ("Thunderstorm"), a four-act tragedy by Cao Yu. An extremely successful playwright in the Western style, by 1941 Cao had written six important plays, including *Beijingren* (1940; "Beijing Man"); heavily influenced by Eugene O'Neill and Henrik Ibsen, he portrayed dissolute members of the old gentry class and new rising entrepreneur class.

Nationalism, the upheaval of World War II, and changes of government in China between 1945 and 1949 are reflected in contemporary China's theatre and dance. An estimated 60,000 performers were mobilized into some 2,500 propaganda troupes during the Sino-Japanese War beginning in 1937 under the direction of the well-known playwright Tian Han. Hundreds of thousands of ordinary Chinese in the army were exposed to modern forms of drama for the first time, and, equally significant, artists discovered regional folk legends, songs, and dances, which they then incorporated into their work. For example, *Baimao nü* ("The White-Haired Girl") was developed from northern Chinese *yangge* folk dances into both a ballet and an opera. The heroine, an escaped concubine of a cruel landlord, symbolized all victims of feudal governments and oppressive social systems.

At Yan'an in 1942 Mao Zedong enunciated one of the basic principles of communist art: art should have the dual function of serving the masses and of being artistically superior. In the years since the establishment of the People's Republic of China in 1949, theatre activities have swung between these goals, depending on the current ideological line of the government. Initially, the traditional opera repertoire was purged of feudal, superstitious, or otherwise ideologically

incorrect material. Government policy encouraged realistic spoken drama (*huaju*); but, in spite of successes such as Lao She's naturalistic *Chaguan* (1957; "Teahouse"), audiences have not responded to this "foreign" form of drama. From 1964, when Jiang Qing, Mao's third wife, guided the composition of the first modern revolutionary operas, in which contemporary soldiers and workers were the heroes, until 1977, traditional operas were completely banned. During the Great Proletarian Cultural Revolution (1966–76), many traditional theatre artists were denounced or imprisoned. Famous modern drama figures such as Wu Han, author of *Hai Rui baguan* (1960; "Hai Rui Dismissed from Office"), were persecuted and their plays banned. With the fall of the Gang of Four in 1976, the traditional repertoire was reinstated once more and Jiang's "model" revolutionary operas no longer staged. During the decade-long open-door policy (1979–89), theatre contacts with the West were tentatively resumed after 40 years abeyance: Arthur Miller was invited to direct *Death of a Salesman* in 1983, and the Shanghai Kunqu Opera Company toured in Europe with its opera version of *Macbeth* in 1987. The influence of Western plays is seen in the social satire *Jiaru wo shi zhendi* (1979; "If I Were Real") by Sha Yexin and Gao Xingian's Artaudian *Ye ren* ("Wild Man"), initially banned, then produced in 1985.

Government policies strongly affect the economics of Chinese theatre as well as dramatic themes and forms. After the establishment of the People's Republic, professional theatre troupes received full government subsidy. Following economic liberalization policies of 1986–87, however, troupes were required to earn increasing revenues from box-office income. At the same time, urban audience attendance declined (in part because of competition from films and television), with the result that some troupes disbanded and others were reduced in size. Government-supported theatre academies in Beijing, Shanghai, Hong Kong, and regional capitals play an essential role in training young theatre artists in traditional as well as modern genres. Foreign theatre exchanges of the 1980s were welcomed by many theatre artists who wished to bring new ideas into Chinese theatre, in particular to appeal to youthful audiences who were abandoning theatre for film and television; these exchanges again were halted in 1989 in the wake of the government's suppression of the Chinese student democracy movement at Tiananmen Square.

The Nationalist government has supported *jingxi* on Taiwan since establishing the headquarters of the Republic of China on that island. Troupes of the air force and the army are active, and the Foo Hsing Opera School receives government support. Local opera (*kotsai-hsi*), sung in the Taiwanese dialect, is extremely popular in commercial theatres, and many itinerant Taiwanese troupes tour glove-puppet plays (*po-the-hi*) to towns and villages.

CHAPTER 10

CHINESE ARCHITECTURE

The first communities that can be identified culturally as Chinese were settled chiefly in the basin of the Huang He (Yellow River). Gradually they spread out, influencing other tribal cultures until, by the Han dynasty (206 BCE–220 CE), most of China was dominated by the culture that had been formed in the cradle of northern Chinese civilization. Over this area there slowly spread a common written language, a common belief in the power of heaven and the ancestral spirits to influence the living, and a common emphasis on the importance of ceremony and sacrifice to achieve harmony among heaven, nature, and humankind. These beliefs were to have a great influence on the character of Chinese art and architecture.

ELEMENTS OF TRADITIONAL CHINESE ARCHITECTURE

Because the Chinese built chiefly in timber, which is vulnerable to moisture, fire, insects, and the ravages of time, very little ancient architecture has survived. The oldest datable timber building is the small main hall of the Nanchan Temple, on Mount Wutai in Shanxi province, built sometime before 782 CE and restored in that year. Brick and stone are used for defensive walls, the arch for gates and bridges, and the vault for tombs. Only rarely has the corbeled dome (in which each successive course projects inward from the

Temple at Yungang near Datong, Shanxi province, China. Jorgen Bitsch—Black Star

beams); the roof-supporting brackets and truss; and the tiled roof itself. The walls between the posts, or columns, are not load-bearing, and the intercolumnar bays (odd-numbered along the front of the building) may be filled by doors (usually doubled in larger, institutional buildings) or by brick or material such as bamboo wattle faced with plaster, or the outermost bays may be left open to create peristyles. Typically, the intercolumnar filler of bricks or plaster leaves the structural wood exposed in a half-timber manner, turning function into visible geometry. The flexible triangular truss is placed transverse to the front side of the building and defines a gable-type roof by means of a stepped-up series of elevated tie beams (*tailiang,* "terraced beams," for which this entire system of architecture is named; also known as *liangzhu,* or "beams-and-columns"); the gable-end beams are sequentially shortened and alternate with vertical struts that bear the roof purlins (horizontal timbers) and the main roof beam. The flexible proportions of the gable-end framework of struts and beams, vertical rise and horizontal span, permits the roof to take any profile desired, typically a low and rather straight silhouette in northern China before the Song dynasty (960–1279) and increasingly elevated and concave in the Song, Yuan (1206–1368), Ming (1368–1644), and Qing (1644–1911/12). The gable-end framework is typically moved inward in a prominent building and partially masked in a hip-and-gable (or half-hip) roof and completely masked

course below it) been used for temples and tombs. Single-story architecture predominates throughout northern and much of eastern China, although multistory buildings constructed around a central earthen mound (*qiu*) date to the late Zhou dynasty (1046–256 BCE).

The basic elements in a Chinese timber building are the platform of pounded earth faced with stone or tile on which the building stands; the post-and-lintel frame (vertical posts topped by horizontal tie

in a full-hipped roof. The timber building is limited in depth by the span of the truss, with the weight of the roof growing three times with every doubling of depth; structurally, however, the building might be of any length along the front, although in theory it ought not to exceed 13 bays and may never actually have exceeded 11 bays in the more recent dynasties.

A distinctively different engineering system for supporting the roof appears today mostly in the southwestern region of China, using tall, thin roof purlin-to-ground columns along the full length of the gable end and horizontal tie beams that penetrate these timber columns. Known as *chuandou*, this system allows for endless possibilities in the geometrical design upon the gable wall, unlike the more standardized *tailiang* system. In place of column-top bracketing, slanting wooden struts extend support for the eaves purlin diagonally downward to the columns. It is possible that *chuandou* architecture was once standard throughout much of China before the Han dynasty and that it retreated to that region with the disappearance of tall timber in the north and with the arrival of the timber-saving bracketing system that gradually came to characterize most traditional Chinese architecture.

The origin of the distinctive curve of the roof, which first appeared in China about the 6th century CE, is not fully understood, although a number of theories have been put forward. The most likely is that it was borrowed, for purely aesthetic reasons, from China's

Southeast Asian neighbours, who cover their houses with *atap* (leaves of the nipa palm [*Nypa*]) or split bamboo, which tend to sag naturally, presenting a picturesque effect. The upswept eaves at the corners of the Chinese roof, however, do have a structural function in reducing what would otherwise be an excessive overhang at that point.

In the "pavilion concept," whereby each building is conceived of as a free-standing rectilinear unit, flexibility in the overall design is achieved by increasing the number of such units, which are arranged together with open, connecting galleries skirting around rectilinear courtyards; diversity is achieved through design variations that individualize these courtyard complexes. In the private house or mansion, the grouping of halls and courtyards is informal, apart from the axial arrangement of the entrance court with its main hall facing the gateway; but in a palace, such as the gigantic Forbidden City in Beijing, the formal halls are ranged with their courtyards behind one another on a south-to-north axis, the state halls building up to a ceremonial climax and then receding toward more private courts and buildings to the north. Ancestral halls and temples follow the palatial arrangement. The scale of a building, the number of bays, the unit of measure used for the timbers, whether bracketing is included or not, and the type of roof (gabled, half- or full-hipped, with or without decorative pent roof and with or without prominent decorative ridge tiling and prominent overhang) all accord with the placement and significance of the building within a courtyard arrangement, with the relative importance of that courtyard within a larger compound, and with the absolute status of the whole building complex. The entire system, therefore, is modular and highly standardized.

The domination of the roof allows little variation in the form of the individual building; thus, aesthetic subtlety is concentrated in pleasing proportions and in details such as the roof brackets or the plinths supporting the columns. Unused to any major variation, the Chinese became unusually sensitive to subtle architectural differentiation. Tang architecture achieved a "classic" standard, with massive proportions yet simple designs in which function and form were fully harmonized. Architects in the Song dynasty were much more adventurous in designing interlocking roofs and different roof levels than were their successors in later centuries. The beauty of the architecture of the Ming and Qing dynasties lies rather in the lightweight effect and the richness of painted decoration.

The radical standardization of Chinese architecture was best expressed in its system of measurement, which by the Song dynasty had developed eight different grades of measure, depending upon the status of the buildings and of individual buildings within a given compound. The unit of measure (a given inch) was larger for a more important building; the buildings flanking and facing it would use a slightly smaller unit, and

so forth. By that measure, as a building expanded in status and scale, each part of it expanded accordingly; the structure of a larger building was better supportive of the weight it had to carry, while visually and aesthetically, consistent proportions were maintained from one building to the next. Modular in the extreme, buildings were designed to persist through the repeated replacement of parts, so that any given building has not only an original construction date but may belong to many different periods in between.

This entire system of regularity produced an architecture that changed but little and therefore could be "read" with great clarity by all. It defined, with little ambiguity, who could go where and shaped a world that told everyone their place in it. On the one hand, its restrictiveness may account for why the names of so few traditional Chinese architects are known. On the other hand, a system so neatly integrated in all of its features from a very early time, from the Han period on, seems to have needed little improvement and never underwent periods of radical redefinition like that which left Europeans with Romanesque and Gothic, Renaissance and Baroque. The Chinese architectural system was not considered to have been man-made at all but essentially to have been revealed by heaven. With so little change being possible, and only slow, nearly invisible evolution taking place, with no one to take credit for it, it is understandable that until the late 1920s, with the research of Liang Sicheng (1901–72), Liang's wife, Lin Huiyin

(1904–55), and Liu Dunzhen (1896–1968), no one even knew which buildings were truly old and which were new.

STYLISTIC AND HISTORICAL DEVELOPMENT

The best evidence for early architecture in northern China comes from Neolithic villages such as Banpo, near present-day Xi'an, discovered in 1953 and datable to the 5th–4th millennia BCE, revealing building systems not yet traditionally Chinese. Two types of buildings predominated within a village surrounded by a deeply dug moat: circular buildings with conical roofs that were built aboveground and square buildings with pyramidal roofs, which were semi-subterranean. Already, however, the thatched roofs were suspended by means of columns, beams, and raftering, while the wattle-and-daub walls were not weight-bearing, just as would be the case in later times. And, as at the Banshan Neolithic village in the 3rd millennium BCE, cemeteries were already located in south-facing foothills to the north of the village, as was the ideal throughout much of later Chinese history.

SHANG DYNASTY (c. 1600–1046 BCE)

Excavations of the Shang era at Luoyang, Zhengzhou, and Anyang have revealed an architecture that begins to take on traditional Chinese form: massive earthen walls surrounding emergent urban centres, rectilinear buildings set up on rammed-earth foundations (layers of earth pounded to stonelike hardness and durability), and postholes of timber buildings with wattle-and-daub walls (woven rods and twigs covered and plastered with clay) and thatched roofs. The largest building yet traced at Anyang is a timber hall about 90 feet (30 m) long, the wooden pillars of which were set on stone socles, or bases, on a raised platform. Ordinary dwellings were partly sunk beneath ground level, as in Neolithic times, with deeper storage pits inside them. There is no sign of the structural use of brick or stone or of tile roofs in any of the Anyang sites. Along the banks of the Huan River to the northwest of modern Anyang, royal tombs consisted of huge, square, rammed-earth pits approached by two or four sloping ramps. Lined and roofed with timber, the tombs were sunk in the floor of the pit. Tomb walls and coloured impressions left on the earth by carved and painted timbers include zoomorphic motifs very similar to those on ritual bronze vessels. Traces of a painted clay wall found elsewhere at Anyang, in a royal stone- and jade-carving workshop, demonstrate that aboveground buildings were decorated with similar designs and indicate a uniformity of design principles and themes in virtually all media at that time, including ritual bronze decor.

ZHOU DYNASTY (1046–256 BCE)

Remains of a number of Zhou cities have been discovered, among them capitals of the feudal states. They were irregular in shape and surrounded by walls of rammed earth. Some long defensive walls also have been located, the largest being one that protected the state of Qi from Lu to the south, stretching for more than 300 miles (500 km) from the Huang He to the sea. Chu had a similar wall along its northern frontier.

Foundations of a number of palace buildings have been found in the cities, including Fengchu and, at Huixian, the remains of a hall 85 feet (26 m) square, which was used for ancestral rites in connection with an adjacent tomb—an arrangement that became common in the Han dynasty. An important late Zhou structure used for a number of functions in the conduct of state rituals and incorporating a complex range of symbolic numerical systems was the Spirit Hall (Mingtang), discussed in a variety of Zhou literature but not yet known for that period through excavations. Late Zhou texts also describe platforms or towers, *tai*, made of rammed earth and timber and used as watchtowers, as treasuries, or for ritual sacrifices and feasts, while pictures engraved or inlaid on late Zhou bronze vessels show two-story buildings used for this type of ritual activity. Some of these multistory buildings are now understood, through modern excavations of two- and three-story Qin and Han palaces and of state ritual halls at Xianyang, Xi'an, and Luoyang, to have been constructed around a large, raised, pounded-earth core that structurally supported upper building levels and galleries and into

which surrounding lower-level chambers were inserted.

The origins of the Chinese bracketing system also are found on pictorial bronzes, showing a spreading block (*dou*) placed upon a column to support the beam above more broadly, and in depictions of curved arms (*gong*) attached near the top of the columns, parallel to the building wall, extending outward and up to help support the beam; however, the block and arms were not yet combined to create traditional Chinese brackets (*dougong*) or to achieve extension forward from the wall. Roof tiles replaced thatch before the end of the Western Zhou (771 BCE), and bricks have been found from early in the Eastern Zhou.

QIN (221–207 BCE) AND HAN (206 BCE–220 CE) DYNASTIES

In 221 Qin Shihuangdi ("the First Sovereign Emperor of Qin") put in place the elements that provided the foundation for the succeeding Han dynasty: he centralized the Chinese state and its legal system and standardized the systems of weights and measures and the Chinese writing system. Further, he consolidated many of the walls of northern China into an architectural network of barriers and beacon towers for rapid communication. From these towers, watchmen could identify suspicious military movement and relay the information across the entire length of the wall across north China in a single day.

While little except walls and tombs remains of the architecture of either the Qin or Han dynasties, much can be learned about Han architecture from historical writings and long descriptive poems, known as *fu*. Clearly this was an era of great palace building. Shihuangdi undertook the building of a vast palace, the Efang Gong or Ebang Gong, whose main hall was intended to accommodate 10,000 guests in its upper story. He also copied, probably at reduced scale, the palaces and pavilions of each of the feudal lords he had defeated; these buildings displayed an encyclopaedia of regional architectural styles, stretched more than 7 miles (11 km) along the Wei River, and were filled with local lords and ladies captured from the different states.

The first emperor's tomb was part of a city of the dead that covered nearly 0.75 square mile (2 square km) and was surrounded by double walls, with numerous gates, corner towers, and a ceremonial palace. The mausoleum itself was surmounted by an artificial mound, or tumulus, a feature not known in the Shang or early Zhou and first found among the tombs of the 4th-3rd centuries BCE near Jiangling in Hubei province. About 141 feet (43 m) high, this tumulus was shaped like a triple-layered truncated pyramid symbolizing heaven, man, and earth. The tomb, which has not yet been excavated, reportedly featured a large chart of the heavens painted on its domed vault and a three-dimensional representation of the earth below, with rivers of liquid mercury driven by mechanical contrivances. Excavations around the tomb have uncovered a large protective terra-cotta

"spirit army" of some 8,000 life-size warrior figures along with 400 horses and 100 chariots placed in battle formation in a series of pits beneath the nearby fields. Molded in separate sections, assembled, then fully painted, these warrior figures were executed in minute and realistic detail and provide evidence of an early naturalistic sculptural tradition that was scarcely imagined by scholars before their discovery in 1974. For the heads, some 30 different models were used, and each was hand-finished to give further variety. In 1982 a pair of precisely engineered bronze replicas (40 inches [104 cm] high) of the imperial chariot, with considerable gold and silver inlay, was excavated, each with a charioteer and four horses.

The main audience hall of the Western Han Weiyang palace was said to have been about 390 feet (120 m) long by 115 feet (35 m) deep, possibly smaller than its largest Qin predecessor yet much larger than its equivalents in the Beijing palace today. From the Zhou dynasty (1046–255 BCE) through the Yuan (1206–1368 CE), no architectural structure called forth more intense consideration than the Spirit Hall, or Mingtang, which was the predecessor of Beijing's Temple of Heaven. The site of the Han ritual hall, in the southern suburbs of Han dynasty Chang'an, was excavated in 1956–57. Translating traditional ritual values into symbolic architecture, the Mingtang was surrounded by an outer circular moat and set on a circular foundation (the two circles together forming a disk, or *bi*, symbolic of heaven) that was further enclosed within an intermediate rectilinear colonnade (symbolic of earth). The three-story hall itself (the number three signifying heaven, man, and earth) was built around a raised earthen core. It is thought to have been a composite ritual structure that included a royal academy on the first floor; a second floor divided into nine zones, corresponding to the four seasons and the "five phases" theory of change, with five inner shrines and with outer spaces for monthly ritual offerings; and a third-floor central hall surrounded by a terrace (*lingtai*, or "spirit platform") for observation of the heavens and regulation of the calendar.

The Han palaces were set about with tall timber towers (*lou*) and brick or stone towers (*tai*) used for a variety of purposes, including the display and storage of works of art. Ceramic representations of Han architecture provide the first direct evidence of true bracketing, with simple brackets projecting a single step forward from the wall (and sometimes several steps upward from the wall) in order to support the roof projection.

Han tombs are among the most elaborate ever constructed in China. In some localities they are of timber, but more often they are of brick or stone, divided into several chambers, and covered with a corbeled vault or, more rarely, a true arched vault. The tombs of the Han emperors were enclosed in gigantic earthen mounds that are still visible today, but some royal tombs began the later practice of burial in hollowed-out natural hills. Many Han tombs were decorated with wall paintings, with more permanent and expensive stone reliefs, or with stamped or molded bricks.

The most remarkable excavated tomb of the period belonged to the wife of a mid-level aristocrat, one of three family tombs of the governor of Changsha found in a suburb of that southern city, Mawangdui, and dating from 168 BCE or shortly after. Small in scale but richly equipped and perfectly preserved, the wooden tomb consists of several outer compartments for grave goods tightly arranged around a set of four nested lacquered coffins. An outer layer of sticky white kaolin clay prevented moisture from penetrating the tomb, and an inner layer of charcoal fixed all the available oxygen within a day of burial, so the deceased (Xin Zhui, or Lady Dai, the governor's wife) was found in a near-perfect state of preservation. Included among the grave goods, which came with a written inventory providing contemporaneous terminology, are the finest caches yet discovered of early Chinese silks (gauzes and damasks, twills and embroideries, including many whole garments) and lacquerware (including wood-, bamboo-, and cloth-cored examples), together with a remarkable painted banner that might have been carried by the shaman in the funerary procession.

THREE KINGDOMS (220–280) AND SIX DYNASTIES (220–589)

After the fall of Luoyang (311) and Chang'an (316) to the invading Xiongnu, the building of great cities and palaces ceased until the Northern Wei moved their capital to Luoyang in 495. There they constructed a city of great magnificence (which was eventually sacked in 535). The main monuments of the 4th and 5th centuries were Buddhist temples and monasteries. By the mid-6th century there were some 500 religious establishments in and around Luoyang alone and about 30,000 in the whole of the northern realm.

Each Buddhist temple had a pagoda erected as a reliquary or memorial, and other pagodas dotted the city and the surrounding landscape. They have mostly disappeared, but one can get some idea of their form from reliefs at Yungang and from the earliest surviving pagodas at Nara in Japan. Based on an enlargement and refinement of the Han timber tower, or *lou*, they had up to 12 stories, with a projecting mast at the top ringed with metal disks. This mast was the only feature preserved from the Indian Buddhist burial or reliquary mound, the stupa, a hemispherical form that the Chinese rarely seem to have copied. The brick and stone pagodas, which were originally more Indian in form and were gradually Sinicized, are tiered structures with the stories marked by projecting string courses (horizontal bands) and architectural features borrowed from timberwork indicated in relief. The oldest surviving example is the Songyue Temple, a 12-sided stone pagoda on Mount Song (c. 520–525) that is Indian in its shape and detail.

SUI (581–618) AND TANG (618–907) DYNASTIES

The founding of the Sui dynasty reunited China after more than 300 years of fragmentation. The second Sui emperor engaged in unsuccessful wars and vast public works, such as the Grand Canal linking the north and south of China physically and economically. Work on these grand schemes exhausted the people and led them to revolt. The succeeding Tang dynasty built a more enduring state on the foundations the Sui rulers had laid, and the first 130 years of the Tang was one of the most prosperous and brilliant periods in the history of Chinese civilization. During this time, the empire was extended so far across Central Asia that for a while Bukhara and Samarkand (both now in Uzbekistan) were under Chinese control, the Central Asian kingdoms paid tribute to China, and Chinese cultural influence reached Korea and Japan. Chang'an became the greatest city in the world at that time; its streets were filled with foreigners, and foreign religions—including Zoroastrianism, Buddhism, Manichaeism, Nestorianism, Christianity, Judaism, and Islam—flourished. This confident cosmopolitanism is reflected in all the arts of the period.

The splendour of the dynasty reached its peak between 712 and 756 under the emperor Xuanzong (Minghuang), but before the end of his reign a disastrous defeat caused Central Asia to enter the control of the advancing Arabs, and the rebellion of General An Lushan in

755 almost brought down the dynasty. Although the Tang survived for another 150 years, its government and people largely turned against foreigners and foreign religions. In 845 all foreign religions were briefly but disastrously proscribed; temples and monasteries were destroyed or turned to secular use, and Buddhist bronze images were melted down.

Only the descriptions in literature and poetry, no doubt exaggerated, remain of the architecture of southern China from the Sui period. The great palaces, temples, and pagodas of 6th-century Nanjing have all disappeared. Evidence of wall paintings and reliefs suggests, however, that the curved roof was already beginning to make its appearance in the south, although it did not reach northern China until well into the Tang dynasty.

The Sui capital, Daxing (now Xi'an), was designed in 583 on imperial order by the great architect Yuwen Kai; renamed Chang'an, it was further developed by the Tang after 618. This vast city, six times the size of present-day Xi'an, was laid out in nine months on a grid plan, with eastern and western markets and the Imperial City placed in the north-central section, a plan later followed in the Ming dynasty rebuilding of Beijing. In 634 Tang Taizong built a new palace, the Daming Palace, on higher ground just outside the city to the northeast. The site of the Daming Palace, which became the centre of court life during the glittering reigns of Gaozong (649–683) and Xuanzong (712–756), was partly excavated. Remains were found of two great halls, Hanyuan Hall (reconstruction of

the foundation completed in 2003, now a UNESCO World Heritage site), with its elevated corridors extended like huge arms toward overlapping triple towers (foreshadowing the later Japanese Phoenix Hall at Uji and the Wu Gate at Beijing), and the Linde Hall; marble flagstones and bases of 164 columns of the latter give some indication of its splendour. Lost marvels of Sui Tang palace architecture include Yuwen Kai's rotating pavilion in the Sui palace, which could hold 200 guests, and the 295-foot-high (90 m) state Spirit Hall built for China's only reigning empress, the usurper Wuhou (or Wu Zetian, who changed the name of the dynasty from Tang to Zhou during her reign from 690 to 705). Surviving murals from Buddhist caves at Dunhuang and excavated royal tombs near Chang'an provide a graphic record of Tang architecture, its taste for multistory elevation, tall towers, and elaborate elevated walkways, its uncharacteristic use of brightly coloured tiles on the building surfaces, and its integration of architecture with gardens, ponds, and bridges.

The Sui-Tang period saw some of China's most lavish royal tomb building, before the onset of a relative modesty in the Song (960–1279) and a decline of qualitative standards in later periods. Excavated royal tombs at Changling, north of the capital, include three built for close relatives of Wuhou who were degraded or executed by her on her way to the throne; they were reburied amid much pomp and splendour in 706 after the restoration of the Tang royal lineage. In each, the subterranean sepulchre is surmounted by a truncated pyramidal tumulus and is approached through a sculpture-lined "spirit way" (*lingdao*). Inside, painted corridors and incised stone sarcophagi provide a lingering record of Tang splendour, with colourful renderings of palatial settings, foreign diplomats, servants-in-waiting, and recreation at polo and the hunt. Along the corridor, niches that had served temporarily as ventilating shafts are stuffed with ceramic figurines—riders, entertainers, Tang horses, and other fabulous animals—mostly done in bold tricolour glazes. The corridor leads to two domed vaults serving as an antechamber and burial hall. The tombs of some Tang rulers were so grand that artificial tomb mounds no longer sufficed, and funerary caverns were carved out beneath large mountains. The huge tomb of Emperor Gaozong and his empress, who later reigned as Wu Zetian (China's only joint burial of rulers), at Changling, has yet to be excavated but appears to be intact.

The Sui and the first half of the Tang were great periods of temple building. The first Sui emperor distributed relics

The Chinese-inspired Great Buddha Hall (Daibutsu-den) of the Tōdai Temple, Nara, Japan. The original Late Nara building was completed in 752; the present hall is an 18th-century reconstruction. Orion Press—Scala/Art Resource, New York

throughout the country and ordered that pagodas and temples be built to house them, and the early Tang monarchs were equally lavish in their foundations. Apart from masonry pagodas, however, very few Tang temple buildings have survived. The oldest yet identified is the main hall of Nanchan Temple at Wutai in northern Shanxi (before 782); the largest is the main hall of nearby Foguang Temple (857). However, they are both small compared with the lost Tang temple halls of Luoyang and Chang'an.

Tang and later pagodas show little of the Indian influence that so marked the Songyue Temple pagoda. Tang wooden pagodas have all been destroyed, but graceful examples survive at Nara, Japan, notably at Hōryū Temple, Yakushi Temple, and Daigō Temple. Masonry pagodas include the seven-story, 190-foot-high (58 m) Dayan Ta, or Great Wild Goose Pagoda, of the Ci'en Temple in Chang'an, on which the successive stories are marked by corbeled cornices, and timber features are simulated in stone by flat columns, or pilasters, struts, and capitals.

Tang cave temples at Dunhuang were increasingly Sinicized, abandoning the Indianesque central pillar, the circumambulated focus of worship which in Six Dynasties caves was sculpted and painted on all four sides with Buddhist paradises. In the Tang, major Buddhist icons and paradise murals were moved to the rear of an open chamber and given elevated seating, much like an emperor enthroned in his palace or like any Chinese host.

FIVE DYNASTIES (907–960) AND TEN KINGDOMS (902–978)

By the end of the Tang, the traditional Chinese techniques of architectural siting had been synthesized into geomantic systems known as *fengshui* or *kanyu* (both designating the interactive forces of heaven and earth). These had origins reaching back at least to earliest Zhou times (1046–256 BCE) and were undertaken seriously by architects in all periods. Practiced by Daoist specialists, northern Chinese traditions emphasized the use of a magnetic compass and were especially concerned with the conjoining of astral and earthly principles according to months and seasons, stars and planets, the hexagrams of the *Yijing* divinatory text, and a "five phases" theory of fire, water, wood, metal, and earth that was first propagated in the Han dynasty (206 BCE–220 CE). In the south, where landscape features were more irregular, a "Form school" emphasized the proper relationship of protective mountains (the northern direction representing dark forces and requiring barriers, the south being benign and requiring openness) and a suitable flow of water. In later periods, elements of both schools were used throughout China.

China's *fengshui* masters and carpenters shaped a practice distinctively different from that of architects in the West, characterized by their ability to grace a building with auspicious good fortune or to curse it with ill fate. And so for the Chinese, siting and the proper timing of events was a more critical feature than architectural engineering, the latter, after all, requiring good execution but allowing little innovation. Understanding the flow of the earth's vital energy (qi) and the relation of the stable earth to the ever-changing heavens, as known through astral charts and almanacs, provided these masters with an esoteric knowledge and authority that rivaled that of the emperor himself and brought it into the lives of every individual. Whether regarded, today, as superstition or as proto- or quasi-scientific knowledge, information about when to cut the first wood, how to position the building where the building materials would be stored, when to lay the threshold and build the hearth and marital bed or raise the main roof beam, were all matters of the utmost importance. Various charms, good or bad, might also be secreted away among the beams, and only certain numbers were used—all others avoided—in the measurement of parts, all of which made the *fengshui* masters and carpenters something like magicians or sorcerers, all-powerful in the lives of the people and as much to be feared as admired by their clientele.

SONG (960–1279), LIAO (907–1125), AND JIN (1115–1234) DYNASTIES

The Song capital, Bianliang or Bianjing (present-day Kaifeng), grew to be a great city, only to be burned by Juchen Tatars in 1127, just after the work was completed.

Nothing survives today, but some idea of the architecture of the city is suggested by a remarkably realistic hand scroll, *Going up the River at Qingming Festival Time*, painted by the 12th-century court artist Zhang Zeduan (whether painted before or after the sacking is uncertain). From contemporary accounts, Bianjing was a city of towers, the tallest being a pagoda 360 feet (110 m) high, built in 989 by the architect Yu Hao to house a relic of the Indian emperor Ashoka. Palaces and temples were at first designed in the Tang tradition, sturdy and relatively simple in detail though smaller in scale. The plan and grouping of the elements, however, became progressively more complex; temple halls were often built in two or three stories, and structural detail became more elaborate.

The style of the 10th century is exemplified in the Guanyin Hall of the Dule Temple at Jixian, Hebei province, built in 984 in Liao territory. A two-story structure with a mezzanine that projects to an outer balcony, the hall is effectively constructed of three tiers of supporting brackets. It houses a 52-foot-high (16 metre), 11-headed clay sculpture of the bodhisattva Guanyin, the largest of its kind in China, placed majestically beneath a central canopy. From the 11th century, the finest surviving buildings are the main hall and library of the Huayan Temple in the Liao capital at Datong (Shanxi), which was accorded the right to house images of the Liao emperors, installed in 1062. The library, perhaps the most intricate and perfectly preserved

Going up the River at Qingming Festival Time, *detail of an ink and colour on silk hand scroll by Zhang Zeduan, 12th century, Song dynasty; in the Palace Museum, Beijing. 24.8 cm × 528 cm.* Wan-go H.C. Weng Photo Collection, New York

example of the architecture of the period, was completed in 1038.

The new Song style is characterized by a number of distinct features. The line of the eaves, which in Tang architecture of northern China was still straight, now curves up at the corners, and the roof has a pronounced sagging silhouette. The bracket cluster (*dougong*) has become more complex: not only is it continuous between the columns, often including doubled, or even false, cantilever arms (or "tail-rafters," *xia'ang*), which slant down from the inner superstructure to the bracket, but also a great variety of bracket types may be used in the same building (56 different types are found in the five-story wooden pagoda built in 1056 at the Fogong Temple in Yingxian, Shanxi province). The tail-rafter, hitherto anchored at the inner end to a crossbeam, now is freely balanced on the bracket cluster, supporting purlins at each end, thus giving the whole system something of the dynamic functionalism of High Gothic architecture. The interior is also much more elaborate. Richly detailed rounded vaults, or cupolas, are set in the ceiling over the principal images; baldachins (ornamental structures resembling canopies) and pavilions to house images or relics reproduce in miniature the intricate carpentry of full-scale buildings; and extremely complex bookcases, some of which, as at the Huayan Temple, were made to revolve, also assume the form of miniature buildings.

Upwards of 60 Song, Liao, and Jin pagodas survive, the latter built by Chinese master craftsmen for their barbarian overlords. These pagodas are generally six- or eight-sided and made of brick or wood. A tall and very slender "iron-coloured" brick pagoda of the 11th century survives at Kaifeng, and, like the seven-story White Pagoda at Qingzhou, near Chengde, it reproduces in brick an elaborate bracketing system copied from timber construction. The 13-story Tianning Temple pagoda in Beijing (11th or early 12th century) shows a subordination of rich detail to a simple outline that is Song architecture at its most refined.

Practically nothing survives today of the Southern Song capital of Hangzhou, described as the greatest city in the world by the Venetian traveler Marco Polo, who spent much of the time from 1276 to 1292 in the city. The dense population and confined space of Hangzhou forced buildings upward, and many dwellings were in three to five stories. While palace buildings in the southern part of the city were probably crowded together, temples and high-platformed viewing pavilions overlooking West Lake were buildings of fairylike beauty. They survive today only in the work of such Southern Song landscape and architecture painters as Li Song.

The variety of form, structural technique, detail, and decoration in Song architecture reflects the sophistication of Song culture and a new intellectual interest in the art. Master builders such as Yu Hao and the state architect Li Jie were educated men. The latter is known today chiefly as the compiler of *Yingzao fashi* ("Building Standards"), which he presented to the throne in 1100. This illustrated work deals in encyclopaedic fashion with all branches of architecture: layout, construction, stonework, carpentry, bracketing, decoration, materials, and labour. The *Yingzao fashi* became a standard text, and, while it was influential in spreading the most advanced techniques of the time with its first publication in 1103, by codifying practice, it may also have inhibited further development and contributed to the conservatism of later techniques.

In contrast to the greater uniformity of later periods, Song architecture was experimental and increasingly diverse in nature. Two styles from the Southern Song period can be inferred from early Japanese buildings. One style is called by the Japanese name Tenjiku-yo, or "Indian style," but it actually originated on the southeastern coast of China, centred in Ningbo, where tall stands of evergreens stood. It sometimes employed timber columns rising to about 65 feet (20 m), directly into which were inserted vertical tiers of up to 10 transverse bracket-arms. This stern and simple style is exemplified by the Great South Gate at Tōdai Temple, built in Nara, Japan, about 1199. Another style, dubbed by the Japanese Kara-yo (Chinese: "Tang"—i.e., Chinese—"style"), was brought by Chan (Zen) Buddhist priests from the Hangzhou area and south to the new shogunal capital at Kamakura, where it can be seen in the 13th-century Reliquary Hall of the Engaku Temple. It features unpainted wood siding with multilevel paneled walls (no plaster wall or lacquered columns) and much attention to elaborative detail. The effect is rich and dynamic and displays none of the simplicity one might expect of Chan architecture, so it is thought by some to represent more a Chinese regional style than anything specifically Chan.

YUAN DYNASTY (1206–1368)

Little remains of Yuan architecture today. The great palace of Kublai Khan in the Yuan capital Dadu ("Great Capital"; now Beijing) was entirely rebuilt in the Ming dynasty (1368–1644). Excavations demonstrate that the Yuan city plan was largely retained in the plan of the Ming; originally conceived under the combined influence of Liu Bingzhong and non-Chinese Muslims such as Yeheidie'er, it appears to be thoroughly Chinese in concept. More detailed information survives only in first-generation Ming dynasty court records and in the somewhat exaggerated description of Marco Polo. This architecture was probably little advanced in point of building technique over those of the Liao and Jin palaces on which they were modeled. The ornate features of their roofs, their bracketing systems, the elevated terraces, and the tight juxtaposition of the buildings are reflected in architectural paintings of the period by such artists as Wang Zhenpeng, Xia Yong, and Li Rongjin. Perhaps the only original Yuan buildings in Beijing today are the Drum Tower to the north of the city and the White Pagoda built by Kublai in the stupa form most commonly seen today in the Tibetan chorten. The Mongols were ardent converts to Tibetan Buddhism and tolerant of the Daoists, but they seem to have found existing temples enough for their purposes, for they made few new foundations.

MING DYNASTY (1368–1644)

The first Ming emperor established his capital at Nanjing ("Southern Capital"), surrounding it with a wall more than 16 miles (30 km) in length, one of the longest in the world. The palace he constructed no longer exists. In 1402 a son of the founding Ming emperor enfeoffed at the old Yuan capital usurped the throne from his nephew, the second Ming ruler, and installed himself as the Yongle emperor. He rebuilt the destroyed Mongol palaces and moved the Ming capital there in 1421, renaming the city Beijing ("Northern Capital"). His central palace cluster, the Forbidden City, is the foremost surviving Chinese palace compound, maintained and successively rebuilt over the centuries. In a strict hierarchical sequence, the palaces lie centred within the bureaucratic auspices of the imperial city, which is surrounded by the metropolis that came to be called the "inner city," in contrast to the newer

(1556) walled southern suburbs, or "outer city." A series of eight major state temples lay on the periphery in balanced symmetry, including temples to the sun (east) and moon (west) and, to the far south of the city, the huge matched temple grounds of heaven (east) and agriculture (west). Close adherence to the traditional principles of north-south axiality, walled enclosures and restrictive gateways, systematic compounding of courtyard structures, regimentation of scale, and a hierarchy of roofing types were all intended to satisfy classical architectural norms, displaying visually the renewed might of native rulers and their restoration of traditional order.

Central to this entire arrangement are three great halls of state, situated on a high, triple-level marble platform (the number three, here and elsewhere,

The Hall of Supreme Harmony (centre), one of the former Imperial Palaces, now part of the Palace Museum complex in the Forbidden City, Beijing. Xinhua News Agency

symbolic of heaven and of the imperial role as chief communicant between heaven and earth). The southernmost of these is the largest wooden building in China (roughly 215 by 115 feet [65 by 35 m]), known as the Hall of Supreme Harmony. (The names and specific functions of many of the main halls were changed several times during the Ming and Qing [1644–1911/12] dynasties.) To their north lies a smaller-scale trio, the main halls of the inner court, in which the emperor and his ladies resided. The entire complex now comprises some 9,000 rooms (of an intended 9,999, representing a perfect yang number). The grandeur of this palatial scheme was matched by the layout of a vast imperial burial ground on the southern slopes of the mountain range to the north of Beijing, not far from the Great Wall, which eventually came to house 13 Ming royal mausoleums, with an elaborate "spirit way" and accompanying ritual temple complexes.

In its colossal scale, the monumental sweep of its golden-tiled roofs, and its axial symmetry, the heart of the Forbidden City is unsurpassed as a symbol of imperial power. In architectural technique, however, the buildings may be considered a decline from the adventurous planning and construction of the Song period. Here the unit is a simple square or rectangular pavilion with few projections or none, and the bracketing system is reduced to a decorative frieze with little or no structural function. Instead, emphasis is placed upon carved balustrades, rich colour, and painted architectural

detail. This same lack of progress shows in Ming temples also. Exceptional is the Hall of Prayer for Good Harvests (Qiniandian) at the Temple of Heaven, a descendant of the ancient Mingtang state temple. It took its present circular form about 1530. Its three concentric circles of columns, which range up to

Children sweeping the steps at the Hall of Prayer for Good Harvests, central building of the Temple of Heaven, in the Forbidden City, Beijing. Emil Schulthess/Black Star

59 feet (18 m) in height, symbolize the 4 seasons, the 12 months, and the 12 daily hours; in a remarkable feat of engineering, they support the three roof levels (a yang number) and, in succession, a huge square brace representing earth, a massive circular architrave denoting heaven, and a vast interior cupola decorated with golden dragons among clouds. (In its final rebuilding, in the 1890s, its tall timbers had to be imported from the U.S. state of Oregon.)

QING DYNASTY (1644–1911/12)

The Manchus began imitating Chinese ways even before their conquest of China, and the Qing rulers, particularly Kangxi (1661–1722) and Qianlong (1735–96), were well-educated men who were eager to enlist the support of Chinese scholars. They were extremely conservative in their political and cultural attitudes; in artistic taste, their native love of extravagance (which the Chinese viewed as barbarous) was tempered, ironically, by an equally strong conservatism. The art of the Qing dynasty, even the painting of many of its finest eccentrics and the design of its best gardens, is at once characterized by lavish decoration and ornate effects as well as by superb technique and conservative taste.

Qing dynasty work in the Forbidden City was confined chiefly to the restoration or reconstruction of major Ming buildings, although the results were typically more ornate in detail and brighter in colour than at any time since the Tang.

The Manchu rulers were most lavish in their summer palaces, created to escape the heat of the city. In 1703 the Kangxi emperor began the construction, near the old Manchu capital, Zhengde, of a series of palaces and pavilions set in a natural landscape. Engravings of these made by the Jesuit father Matteo Ripa in 1712–13 and taken by him to London in 1724 are thought to have influenced the revolution in garden design that began in Europe at about this time. Near the Zhengde palace were built several imposing Buddhist temples in a mixed Sino-Tibetan style that reflects the Tibetan Buddhist leanings of the Kangxi, Yongzheng, and Qianlong emperors.

About 1687 the Kangxi emperor had begun to create another garden park northwest of Beijing, which grew under his successors into the enormous Yuanmingyuan ("Garden of Pure Light"). Here were scattered a great number of official and palace buildings, to which the Qianlong emperor moved his court semipermanently. In the northern corners of the Yuanmingyuan, the Jesuit missionary and artist Giuseppe Castiglione (known in China as Lang Shining) designed for Qianlong a series of extraordinary Sino-Rococo buildings, set in Italianate gardens ornamented with mechanical fountains designed by the Jesuit priest Michel Benoist. Today the Yuanmingyuan has almost completely disappeared, as the foreign-style buildings were burned by the French and British in 1860. To replace it, the empress dowager Cixi greatly enlarged the new summer palace

(Yiheyuan) along the shore of Kunming Lake to the north of the city.

The finest architectural achievement of the period, however, occurred in private rather than institutional architecture—namely, in the scholars' gardens of southeastern China, in such towns as Suzhou, Yangzhou, and Wuxi. As these often involved renovations carried out on Yuan and Ming dynasty foundations, it remains difficult to discern the precise outlines of their innovations. With the aid of paintings and Ji Cheng's text *Yuanye* (1631–34; "Forging a Garden"), it becomes evident that, as in the worst of Qing architecture, these gardens became ever more ornate. The best examples, however, remain well within the bounds of good taste because of the scholars' cultivated sensibility, and they were distinguished by an inventive imagination lacking in Manchu court architecture. Such gardens were primarily Daoist in nature, intended as microcosms invested with the capacity to engender tranquillity and induce longevity in those who lodged there. The chief hallmark of these gardens was the combination of a central pond,

Garden of the Master of Nets (Wangshiyuan), Ming and Qing dynasties; at Suzhou, Jiangsu province, China. Caroline Courtauld

encompassing all the virtues of yin in the Chinese philosophical system, with the extensive use of rugged and convoluted rockery (yang), representing the Chinese adoration of great mountain systems that were thought to channel the vital energy of the earth. (The most precious rocks were harvested from the bottom of Lake Tai near Suzhou.) These rocks, which appear so natural, are actually composited and might be thought of as the leading products of the sculptor's craft in the last centuries of China's traditional period.

Throughout this urban garden tradition, where the scale was necessarily small and space was strictly confined, designers attempted to convey the sense of nature's vastness by breaking the limited available space into still smaller but ever-varied units. Among those gardens still preserved today, the Liu Garden in Suzhou offers the finest general design and the best examples of garden rockery and latticed windows, while the small and delicate Garden of the Master of Nets (Wangshi Yuan), also in Suzhou, provides knowledgeable viewers with a remarkable series of sophisticated visual surprises, typically only apparent on a third or fourth visit to the site.

INFLUENCE OF FOREIGN STYLES

Until the mid-1920s, official and commercial architectural commissions in China were chiefly designed in an eclectic European style popularized by such treaty ports as Guangzhou (Canton), Xiamen, Fuzhou, and Shanghai, much of it designed by foreign architects. However, about 1925 Lü Yanzhi designed the Sun Yat-sen Mausoleum located in Nanjing, one of the first important constructions designed entirely by a Chinese architect in modern history. The building's comprehensive plan drew on the style of emperors' tombs of the Ming and Qing dynasties, a notion of historical reference that greatly inspired young Chinese architects. In 1925 a group of foreign-trained Chinese architects, including Zhuang Jun and Fan Wenzhao (Robert Fan), launched a renaissance movement to study and revive traditional Chinese architecture and to find ways of adapting it to modern needs and techniques. In 1930 they founded Zhongguo Yingzao Xueshe ("The Society for the Study of Chinese Architecture"). The following year Liang Sicheng joined the group; he would be the dominant figure in the movement for the next 30 years. The fruits of these architects' work can be seen in new universities and in major government and municipal buildings built in Beijing, Nanjing, and Shanghai during the 1930s, where they contended with the rise of Western-designed architecture such as the old Shanghai concert hall (formerly known as the Nanjing Theatre) and the Customs House along Shanghai's Bund. The war with Japan (1937–45) put an end to further developments along these lines for a time; however, this tradition was revived in the 1950s with buildings such as the National Art Gallery of China (1959) in Beijing and is still practiced to this day.

After 1949, the urgent need in China for housing and industrial building led to many examples of purely utilitarian architecture and to major construction projects such as dams and bridges. Beijing and other big cities were transformed by spectacular planning projects, but an awareness of the traditional role of symbolism in architecture was often retained and adapted. Indeed, much of the architecture in the 1950s was built in the Soviet style of imposing edifices centered on grand squares and axes. During this period, large portions of the Forbidden City in Beijing were restored and established as a public museum. Lamentably, most of the city's great outer walls were taken down in the name of modernization and to facilitate vehicular circulation. A new primary thoroughfare (Chang'an Boulevard), now symbolically on an east-west axis rather than traditionally oriented north-south, was also established there. In 1959 a vast square for public political activity was completed in front of the Tiananmen (Gate of Heavenly Peace, the entryway to the Imperial City), flanked on one side by the complex containing the Museum of Chinese History and the Museum of Chinese Revolution and on the other side by the Great Hall of the People. These dignified structures, part of the "Ten Grand Buildings" built from 1958 to 1959, were modeled after the Soviet style, with a hint of the Chinese vernacular in details such as a slight turn of a cornice.

Over the course of the Cultural Revolution (1966–76), many magnificent older buildings and their exquisite decorations were seriously damaged or destroyed, as the new regime regarded them as emblems of decadence and moribundity. Most new commissions were monotonously imposing structures. The end of Cultural Revolution architecture was marked when the regime's founder, Mao Zedong, died in 1976 and was buried in a grand mausoleum, located at the south end of Tiananmen Square. Designed by a large team of architects that same year, the monument bears a resemblance to the Lincoln Memorial in Washington, D.C.

INTO THE 21ST CENTURY

After this rather fallow period in Chinese architecture, the Chinese building industry, beginning in the 1980s—with the implementation of China's new "opening up" economic and diplomatic policies—entered an unparalleled period of prosperity. This boom was in part a result of the new political structure, which provided sufficient funds for Chinese architects to explore different creative possibilities, and in part because China's economic development during this period created a need for an increased number of office towers, hotels, shopping spaces, and urban housing, accompanied by massive new roadway construction. All of this required the tearing down of older structures in the name of urban renewal, particularly of domestic urban housing, and the displacement and relocation of tens of millions of urban residents. Massive numbers of migrant construction workers flooded China's cities to carry out this labour, which has put the Chinese social and natural ecologies under extraordinary stress. Beijing, Shanghai, Guangzhou, Tianjing, and other provincial capitals in the eastern part of China became rapidly modernized within the space of a decade and similar to one another in appearance through unified urban planning and massive construction. These urban examples were followed afterward by inland cities such as Xi'an, Chongqing, and Chengdu in Sichuan, and Wuhan in Hubei. Among the largest commissions at the time were the Beijing Xiang Shan Hotel designed by Chinese-born American architect I.M. Pei in 1982; the Shanghai Grand Theater designed by French architect Jean-Marie Charpentier in 1994; and the Shanghai Jin-Mao Tower in 1998 (until 2008 the tallest skyscraper in China), designed by the American firm of Skidmore, Owings, and Merrill. The diverse nationalities of these architects and architectural firms reflect the determination of the government and Chinese architectural community to cooperate with other countries.

In the face of such rapid change, some worried that this massive expansion would come at the cost of tradition, beauty, and a sense of humanity. Critics pointed out that many of these tall new structures were characterless concrete or glass towers that made many Chinese cities virtually indistinguishable from each other. Moreover, the inclusion of the Chinese vernacular in these structures often took on the form of empty postmodern gestures, such as the inclusion of a pagoda on top of a glass skyscraper. Beyond issues involving the structures themselves, this rapid expansion posed serious problems in terms of congestion and pollution, a circumstance that became more problematic as the eyes of the world were turned toward Beijing, the site of the Summer Olympic Games in 2008. As a result of such concerns and as a result of the experiences and lessons of other industrial countries, architects and urban planners in China increasingly focused on issues such as preserving historical structures, controlling air pollution, creating public spaces, and creating "green" (energy-efficient, environmentally friendly) buildings.

At the turn of the 21st century, responding to the long-standing concern for preserving tradition as China entered deeper into the world economy and the accompanying effects of globalization, Chinese architects continued to search for a viable style of Chinese architecture for the new millennium. Some prominent architects as Zhang Bo, She Junnan, and Cheng Congzhou have continued to follow the pattern established earlier by Liang Sicheng. The large-scale Beijing Western Railway Station, designed by the Beijing Constructing and Designing Research Institute in 1995, reflects the continuation of this philosophy. The modern station, equipped with the newest forms of transportation technology, was executed with a combination of tradition and modernity that has continued to define much of Chinese architectural production in the early 21st century. Critics, however, have chastened this as "big roof architecture," traditional decoration on an essentially non-Chinese structure, and regard it as a dead-end hybrid product not likely to survive the forces of modernity.

With the Summer Olympic Games in 2008 came a group of internationally-renowned structures, together with a further demonstration of globalization in China's architectural sphere. The Olympic Green was designed by Albert Speer, Jr., son of Nazi Germany's leading architect; the genuinely original Olympic track and field stadium, the National Stadium popularly dubbed the "Bird's Nest," was designed by the Swiss firm of Herzog & de Meuron together with expatriate Chinese artistic consultant Ai Weiwei; the National Aquatics Centre, called the "Water Cube," was designed by an Australian-Chinese consortium. At the same time, the face of central Beijing's architecture was further altered by two massive and controversial constructions: the National Centre for the Performing Arts, called "The Egg" and contrasting with the rectilinear architecture of Tiananmen, which it adjoins, designed by French architect Paul Andreu; and the CCTV Headquarters, designed by Dutch architect Rem Koolhaas. As urban Chinese residents moved from small one- and two-story buildings into apartment blocks and condominiums more massive than any imagined by Maoist planners, some of the very wealthy were provided the opportunity to move into new

retro-style architectural gated communities being built in the outskirts of larger cities such as Beijing and Shanghai; avoiding the latest modernist trends, these protected communities mimicked Tudor-period English villages or German Bauhaus architectural schemes, designed by European firms such as that of Albert Speer, Jr., and providing city dwellers with free-standing single-family homes that feature all the amenities of the suburban European or American lifestyle.

While efforts have been made in cities such as Beijing to preserve something of China's architectural heritage, the prime result has been to facilitate further replacement of the old by the new. How this rapid expansion of urban architecture will be resolved in terms of the congestion and pollution it generates, both in the city and in the rural areas that produce the raw materials for this explosive growth, remains to be seen.

CONCLUSION

The people of China can be compared to a mosaic, united by a common writing system. Although there can be tension between the dominant Han and non-Han minority groups, the non-Han groups are increasingly adding their unique contributions to the great body of Chinese culture.

One of the most accessible ways to approach a foreign culture is through its foods. Cuisine encompasses not only what people cultivate and raise as food, but how those products are cooked and when and how they are eaten. The special preparation of food in China has deep and ancient roots. Much of Chinese history and ritual can be learned from the crispy skin of a Peking duck, the burn of a roasted Sichuan green bean, the comfort of a steamed pork dumpling, and a simple bowl of rice.

Perhaps second only to the appreciation of Chinese food is the appreciation of China's art. Whether it be the life-size terra-cotta warriors in Xi'an, the ritual bronze vessels of an early era, or the scroll paintings of emperors, Chinese art has been available to Western museumgoers for centuries. Though it may require some extra effort on the part of the Western viewer to understand the principles of artists who approach life and the world in a different manner, the effort is always rewarded many times over by expanded artistic horizons and by cultural growth.

In China and the countries most influenced by Chinese culture—Korea and Japan—calligraphy by long and exacting tradition is considered a major art, equal to sculpture or painting. It was said that Cangjie, the legendary inventor of Chinese writing, got his ideas from observing animals' footprints and birds' claw marks on the sand as well as from other natural phenomena. He then started to work out simple images from what he conceived as representing different

objects. The tools for Chinese calligraphy are few: an ink stick, an ink stone, a brush, and paper or silk. The calligrapher, using a combination of technical skill and imagination, must provide interesting shapes to the strokes and must compose beautiful structures from them without any retouching or shading and, most important of all, with well-balanced spaces between the strokes. This balance needs years of practice and training.

The music and performing arts of China, like the written language, are ancient. The archaeological resources go back to 3000 BCE, and extensive written documents refer to endless different forms of music in connection with folk festivals and religious events as well as in the courts of hundreds of emperors and princes in dozens of different provinces, dynasties, and periods. If a survey is carried forward from 3000 BCE, it becomes clear that the last brief segment of material, from the Song dynasty (960–1279 CE) to today, is equivalent to the entire major history of European music.

This volume gives ample evidence of the richness and depth of Chinese culture. While contemporary news relates the vitality of China's economic engine, it tends to minimize the incredible vibrancy of the country's ancient culture—its invention of paper, silk, movable type, and even fireworks.

analect A collection of teachings.

Animism A belief that not only do humans and animals, have souls, but that inanimate objects such as stones, rivers, and weather events (such as storms) also have souls and life as well.

apotheosis Deification, or raising to a godlike status.

architectonic Relating to architecture.

bodhisattva In Buddhist thought, an enlightened being; someone who doesn't enter nirvana so that he or she can help others attain enlightenment.

celadon A glaze for ceramics which is typically green with a yellowish-gray cast.

cenobitic Referring to a religious group such as monks who live in community following shared rules and strict discipline.

colloquy A high-level, serious conversation.

colophon Identifying information such as an inscription, a mark, or an emblem that is used by a printer or a publisher.

dao In Chinese philosophy, a concept signifying "the proper way," or "heaven's way."

de Virtue.

dharma In Hinduism the moral law guiding individual conduct; in Buddhism, the universal truth.

eremitic Being like a hermit in values or actions.

ewer A jug in the shape of a vase.

excrescence Something that projects outward in an abnormal way, especially something ugly or undesirable.

florescence Flowering.

hegemony Dominance of one group over another.

laity Common followers of a faith who are not members of its clergy.

nirvana The state of ultimate enlightenment in Buddhism that transcends suffering and which is an ultimate goal to be sought and cherished.

putonghua "Common language"; the dialect of Mandarin spoken in Beijing that is considered a national language.

qi Vital energy, breath.

quietism A religious philosophy that emphasizes the idea that passive contemplation and suppression of the will can provide spiritual peace.

repoussé A jewelry-making technique of pressing shapes into metal.

sericulture The raising of caterpillars for the production of raw silk.

shaman A religious figure who uses magic to intercede between the natural and supernatural spheres.

soteriological A theological belief concerning salvation by a heroic or godlike figure.

stratum Layer.

sumptuary laws Laws that control extravagances such as food and dress, or personal behaviours that offend a community.

supramundane Beyond or above the earth; heavenly; celestial.

suprasegmental Related to vocal features such as pitch or length that take place at the same time as consonants and vowels in spoken language.

volutes Scroll-shaped or spiral patterns.

wuwei The philosophical principle of non-action.

ziran Spontaneity.

Berthrong, John H., and E. Nagai-Berthrong *Confucianism: A Short Introduction*. Oxford: Oneworld, 2000.

Bo, Shi. *Between Heaven and Earth: A History of Chinese Writing*. Boston, MA: Shambala Publications, Inc., 2003.

Clunas, Craig. *Art in China* (Oxford History of Art). Oxford: Oxford University of Press, 2009.

James H. Ford (ed.) and James Legge (trans.). *The Teachings of Confucius*. El Paso, TX: El Paso Norte Press, 2009.

Gao Xingian. *Return to Painting*. New York, NY: HarperCollins Publisher, 2002.

Gifford, Rob. *China Road: A Journey into the Future of a Rising Power*. New York, NY: Random House, 2007.

Gudnadson, Jessica, and Gong Li. *Chinese Opera*. New York, NY: Abbeville Press, 2001.

Hearn, Maxwell K. *How to Read Chinese Paintings* (Metropolitan Museum of Art). New York, NY: Metropolitan Museum of Art, 2008.

Kohn, Livia. *Daoism Handbook*. Leiden and Boston: Brill, 2000.

Kohn, Livia. *Daoism and Chinese Culture*. Cambridge: Three Pines Press, 2001.

Kurian, George Thomas (ed.). *Encyclopedia of the World's Nations and Cultures*. New York, NY: Facts On File, Inc., 2007.

Li, He. *Chinese Ceramics: The New Standard*. San Francisco: Asian Art Museum of San Francisco, 1996, reissued 2006.

Liu, Jee Loo. *An Introduction to Chinese Philosophy: From Ancient Philosophy to Chinese Buddhism*. Malden, MA: Blackwell Publishing, 2006.

Miller, James. *Daoism: A Beginner's Guide* (Beginner's Guide). Oxford: Oneworld Publications, 2008.

Morton, Scott W., Charlton M. Lewis. *China: Its History and Culture*, 4th edition. New York, NY: McGraw-Hill edition, 2005.

Rees, Helen (ed.). *Lives in Chinese Music*. Champaign, IL: University of Illinois Press, 2009.

Sullivan, Michael. *The Arts of China*, 5th edition. Berkeley: University of California Press, 2009.

Vainker, Shelagh. *China Silk: A Cultural History*. London: British Museum Press, 2004.

Vainker, Shelagh. *Chinese Pottery and Porcelain*, 2nd ed. London: British Museum Press, 2005.

Watson, Burton (trans.). *Zhuangzi: Basic Writings*. New York, NY: Columbia University Press, 2003.

Welch, Patricia Bjaaland. *Chinese Art: A Guide to Motifs and Visual Imagery*. North Clarendon, VT: Periplus Editions (HK) Ltd., 2008.

Whitfield, Susan. *Life Along the Silk Road*. Berkeley, CA: University of California Press, 2001.

INDEX

Z